Gen

General Washington's Commando

Benjamin Tallmadge in the Revolutionary War

RICHARD F. WELCH

McFarland & Company, Inc., Publishers
Jefferson, North Carolina

Library of Congress Cataloguing-in-Publication Data

Welch, Richard F.
    General Washington's commando : Benjamin Tallmadge in
the Revolutionary War / Richard F. Welch.
        p.   cm.
    Includes bibliographical references and index.

    ISBN 978-0-7864-7963-4 (softcover : acid free paper)
    ISBN 978-1-4766-1536-3 (ebook)

    1. Tallmadge, Benjamin, 1754–1835.   2. United States—
History—Revolution, 1775–1783—Biography.   3. United
States—History—Revolution, 1775–1783—Secret service.
4. United States—History—Revolution, 1775–1783—Military
intelligence.   I. Title.
E302.6.T2W45 2014
973.3'85092—dc23
[B]   2014006899

British Library cataloguing data are available

On the cover: Benjamin Tallmadge as a Dragoon Officer,
1783, miniature by John Ramage (Litchfield Historical Society.
Benjamin Tallmadge Collections)

Manufactured in the United States of America

McFarland & Company, Inc., Publishers
  Box 611, Jefferson, North Carolina 28640
  www.mcfarlandpub.com

For John Richard "Dick" Welch (1920–2013),
who was always there.

Acknowledgments

Historical works typically have one author, but none are possible without the support and aid of the many individuals who generously offer their time and expertise to make the project successful. This book is no exception. The research was carried out over several years and in many places, with the assistance of many people. I invariably found the curators and staffers at libraries, universities, and historical societies to be welcoming, knowledgeable, and helpful.

Thanks are due the staffs of the Long Island Collection, East Hampton Library, the Westchester County Historical Society, and the Manuscripts and Archives Division of the New York Public Library. Thanks, also, to Emilie Hardman of the Houghton Library, Harvard University, who provided me with important Tallmadge correspondence. I am indebted to Diane McCain of the Connecticut Historical Society, which made its voluminous archive available, and to Rich Malley, Head of Research and Collections at CHS, for permission to quote from the material for publication. Linda Hocking at the Litchfield Historical Society and Charles E. Greene and Don C. Schemer of Princeton University's Rare Books and Special Collections Department provided ready access to their extensive Tallmadge material, and approved its use in book form. I'd like to give an additional nod to Jessica Jenkins, collections curator at the Litchfield Historical Society, for furnishing copies of key paintings for this publication, and to Robin Benson of Frazzled Graphics, who redid the map at the beginning of the book.

Several people read all or part of the manuscript at various stages of its progress and offered constructive criticism and suggestions. Sara Gronim of the History Department of Long Island University, C.W. Post campus, was particularly helpful in this regard.

A special note of appreciation is also due Harriet Gerard Clark, director of the Raynham Hall Museum, Oyster Bay, New York, who enlisted me as guest curator for the "Spymaster" exhibition in 2008. The preparations and research for the exhibitions ignited my interest in Tallmadge, which ultimately resulted in the book you are now holding.

Suffice it to say, any flaws or shortcomings which may appear are the sole responsibility of the author.

Table of Contents

Preface

My earliest introduction to the Revolutionary War on Long Island came from a great-uncle who enjoyed collecting local historical lore. When I was still a boy he'd sometimes take me on drives around the North Shore of Long Island and point out hills and woods where rebel raiders shot up Tories and British troops, and vice-versa. Years later, when I began on a career path in history, I sometimes found myself thinking about these early sojourns and tried to incorporate them into what I had learned about of Long Island's experience during the War of Independence—defeat for the Revolutionaries in Brooklyn, occupation for the bulk of the war, and amphibious warfare carried out across Long Island Sound, with rebels attacking the supporters of the crown and the British retaliating.

While my college courses and readings took me in several directions, my interest in the Revolutionary era never waned. Through one source or another, I first became acquainted with the name Benjamin Tallmadge. A native of Setauket, Long Island, Tallmadge joined the Continental Army in 1776 and fought in the ensuing New York campaign, and the 1777 struggle for Philadelphia. His conduct won him respect, appreciation, and promotion, and he was soon to play a key role in the relentless fighting which ravaged the Lower Hudson Valley for the remainder of the war. I marked him as an interesting character, but did not delve deeply into his life.

Regional history became one of my specialties in the 1980s and 1990s, leading to a dissertation, three books, and a stint as editor of a local history magazine. These pursuits frequently brought me back to the Revolutionary period, and I kept running into Tallmadge, who always seemed active on several fronts at once. Most of what was in print about him emphasized his role as Washington's major spy runner on Long Island and New York City, but it was clear that there was much more to his military career than just espionage. And, of course, there was the additional question of what a warrior does after his war.

In 2008, the Raynham Hall Museum in Oyster Bay, home of one of Tallmadge's key agents, Robert Townsend, organized an exhibition on Washington's Long Island Spy Ring, and I signed on as guest curator. The exhibition included artifacts from the Townsend family, military antiquities, a Washington letter owned by Raynham Hall, and a letter from General Washington to Tallmadge on loan from the Special Collections Department of Stony Brook University. Museum director Harriet Gerard Clark named the exhibition "Spymaster," and both of us initially expected that the exhibition would focus on Washington's role in Long Island–Manhattan espionage. But we quickly realized there were two spymasters, Washington *and* Tallmadge, and that while Washington was the overall master of American military intelligence, Tallmadge ran the network on a day-to-day, operation-to-operation level.

Work on the exhibition stoked my interest in Tallmadge, and I began a five-year project to investigate, uncover, analyze, and present the military career of a remarkably dynamic and significant figure. In the years since Charles Swain Hall wrote the first biography of Tallmadge in 1943, new documents have come to light, and archives have become better organized and more accessible, particularly now, with the explosion of online material. For example, the George Washington Papers, easily accessed on the Library of Congress site, are a gold mine of Tallmadge material. Additionally, several historical societies and universities have major holdings of Tallmadge-related documents. But pertinent material is found in many other venues—personal collections, auction houses, colleges, and local historical societies, each of which may have only one or two revealing documents.

The Benjamin Tallmadge who emerged from my research was a man of intelligence, energy, steadfastness and versatility—attributes which served him well in both his Revolutionary and postwar endeavors. His later activities as businessman, financier, land speculator, and banker are fascinating in themselves, and provide a personal dimension to the evolution of the socio-political milieu in the New England during the first decades of the nation's independence. The same can be said about his service as a Federalist member of the House of Representatives. Holding fast to the long-revered values of the Whig tradition and Federalist world view, Tallmadge and his party fought a rear-guard action against the populist ideology of the Jeffersonian Republicans. Yet, when assessing Tallmadge's lengthy life and varied interests, it is his youthful experiences in the Revolution that command the most attention.

This is not simply because they were more dramatic and colorful, though they were. Rather, Tallmadge's wartime service is a testament to the importance of keen, effective officers in crucial commands at critical junctures. His presence and performance materially aided in the survival of the Revolutionary cause, especially in the war-weary days between Saratoga and Yorktown, and again in the drawn-out transition to peace, between Yorktown and the Treaty of Paris. For these reasons, Benjamin Tallmadge's operations in the War of Independence comprise the lion's share of the book.

Tallmadge's assignments and responsibilities were many. By 1778 he was a key intelligence officer in charge of the most continuously operational intelligence network in New York and on Long Island. He also commanded his own dragoon troop, and was later entrusted by Washington with an autonomous legion. Tallmadge played a pivotal role in protecting patriot families and territories on the east side of the Hudson. This entailed repelling raids by the British and Tories, launching counter-strikes against British strongholds close to New York, and bolstering the morale of a pro-revolutionary population caught between the two armies. Determined to shake the British stranglehold on his native island, he launched audacious cross-sound attacks which smashed British positions, threw them on the defensive, and encouraged the rebel population to persevere.

Nor was that all. Tallmadge busied himself in the never-ending quest to supply food and remuneration for his men, activities which brought him into contact with state and Continental officials. Tallmadge also cultivated key financial figures, and began to master the mysteries of securities, paper money, and currency manipulation. Indeed, he had begun to lay a foundation for a successful peacetime career in business, finance, and politics, even before the guns fell silent.

Current understanding and interest in the Revolution has also expanded and sometimes shifted from the approaches and interests of previous generations of scholars. Interest in the internecine nature of

3

the war, formerly viewed mostly as a Southern phenomenon, has grown, and Tallmadge's operations in Westchester County and on Long Island reveal much about the bitter, ruthless struggle between rebels and Tories in these areas. The nature and extent of patriot support for the war, the culture of the Continental officer corps (especially the cult of the gentleman), are now seen as important areas of study. Again, Tallmadge's activities, observations, and reactions shed much light on these aspects of the struggle.

Tallmadge had a knack for appearing at crucial moments during the conflict. His quick thinking led to the arrest of the British spy Major John André, and foiled Benedict Arnold's scheme to betray the American stronghold at West Point. Shortly before the British evacuated New York City, Tallmadge became the first American officer to visit the still-occupied city under a flag of truce, and subsequently accompanied Washington on the latter's triumphal return to Manhattan. He was present when General Washington bade farewell to his officers at Fraunces Tavern, and left the only account of that poignant leave-taking.

In short, Tallmadge's importance—and fascination—derives not just from one role he performed successfully, but from the fact that—from beginning to end—he did so many so well. His achievements exceeded his rank, and his resolute commitment to the cause of independence, and the intelligence and courage he brought to his patriotism, significantly contributed to the ability of the Continental Army to stay the course of the war in New York.

1

The Young Whig

While the course and outcome of the American Revolution was largely decided by set piece battles between the Continental and British armies, it was also a civil war, fought by Americans with conflicting loyalties. Those armies despoiled and bloodied each other with relentless abandon in combat whose level of viciousness was intensified by the belief that their opponents were traitors. Although the most celebrated practitioners of this style of warfare hailed from the South, one of the American masters of commando-style warfare was a regular Continental Army officer who conducted some of his most successful operations within British lines in southern Westchester and Long Island. This was Benjamin Tallmadge, whose exploits have led some historians to dub him the "Francis Marion of the North."

Benjamin Tallmadge was born and raised in Setauket on the north shore of Suffolk County, Long Island, New York. Suffolk, the easternmost of Long Island's then-three counties, was settled primarily by colonists from New England, and the inhabitants maintained close ties with New England well into the 19th century. The New England orientation manifested itself both politically and religiously. Suffolk's population was heavily Calvinist—Puritan (Congregationalist) and Presbyterian— denominations which were strongly Whiggish in outlook. The American Whigs, reflecting their roots in the 17th century struggles with the Crown, were steeped in a tradition which made them reflexibly suspicious of governmental power, with a concomitant devotion to individual liberties and local self-government. The British army certainly saw a connection between revolution and religion. During their occupation of Long Island following the Battle of Brooklyn, British and Tory troops frequently desecrated, vandalized, or destroyed Presbyterian churches, and sometimes forbade its congregations from meeting.[1]

The Tallmadge family fit the Suffolk archetype perfectly. The first Tallmadges appeared in America in the late 17th century with different branches rooting themselves in East Hampton, Long Island, and Branford, Connecticut, near New Haven. Benjamin's father, also named Benjamin Tallmadge, sprang from the Connecticut line. The elder Tallmadge graduated from Yale in 1747 and was ordained at Setauket six years later. He became minister of the Setauket Presbyterian Church and spent the remainder of his life in the village. He married Susannah Smith, daughter of another Presbyterian minister, in 1750. The couple had five sons, of whom Benjamin, born February 25, 1754, was the second oldest.

Being the son of a minister conferred several advantages upon young Benjamin, not the least of which was a first-rate education. He was precocious enough that the president of Yale pronounced him ready for college in 1767. Concerned that his 13-year-old son was too young for college, the Reverend Tallmadge tutored him at home for two more years before allowing him to enroll in New Haven. His father's academic preparations had been so thorough that Benjamin had an easy time of it in his first two years, though a bout of measles slowed him in his junior and senior years. For his 12-shilling tuition, plus four pence for contingency fees and thruppence for glass, the young scholar received his education, meals, and quarters in Connecticut Hall, a Georgian-style structure built about 20 years earlier.

The class of 1773, to which Tallmadge belonged, was the largest in Yale's total student body of 100. Benjamin was intelligent, personable, and made friends readily. Several of those he befriended at Yale, and later in Wethersfield, remained close confidants for life. He became especially close with the two Hale brothers, Nathan and Enoch. When Benjamin and Nathan joined a Yale literary society, the "Brothers in Unity," they took to referring to each other as Damon and Pythias. The three undergraduates found time for less than intellectual pursuits and were all fined for smashing glass on campus. Tallmadge explained his minor vandalism as a case of too much time (and possibly too much wine?) resulting from the thorough preparation his minister father had given him. "Being so well versed in the Latin and Greek Languages," he later wrote, "I had not much occasion to study during the first two years of college life, which I have always thought had a tendency to make me idle."[2] As Tallmadge approached graduation, he secured a position to "superintend" the high school in Wethersfield, a thriving Connecticut river town a little south of the capital at Hartford. One of his last formal acts at Yale was to participate in a debate with Nathan Hale on the subject of whether "the Education of Daughters be not, without any just reason, more neglected than that of sons."[3]

Tallmadge adjusted to his new environment quickly. He roomed at the town's late Presbyterian minister's home, which stood near a dwelling called "Hospitality Hall," the site of many social events. Tallmadge's interests in women extended far beyond the issue of their education. Affable, good-looking and flirtatious, he had a keen eye for female beauty, and was attractive to and attracted by many young women, whose names, or descriptions, appear frequently in his letters. Writing to his friend Nathan Hale, who had taken a school teacher's job in Coventry, Connecticut, he described a dance at the Hall, where he flirted "with the attractive daughters of the town's best families. The female part of the place, you have often heard, is very agreeable."[4] Just as importantly, he made the acquaintance of many prominent members of the merchant community in both Wethersfield and nearby Hartford. Among these were Silas Deane, soon to play a significant role in American diplomacy during the Revolution, and Jeremiah Wadsworth, a promising young businessman, who would parlay his skills into a position as a commissary officer for both the Continental Army and the French during the War for Independence. Tallmadge would enjoy both their friendship and the monetary advantages of their connection in the years to come.

But the novice teacher's enjoyable life, like that of virtually all Americans, was soon roiled by the agitation against British policy. These tensions had been brewing for nearly a decade and finally spilled over in the Boston Tea Party of 1773. The imposition of the Coercive Acts by the British, which closed the port of Boston, suspended the Massachusetts Assembly, and sped British military reinforcements to New England, presented the colonists with the immediate prospect of armed conflict with the mother country. Tallmadge was visiting his parents in Setauket when the Wethersfield minutemen marched off to join the insurgent forces besieging Boston, but when he returned he found the atmosphere electric with anticipation and resolve. In May 1775, he penned a letter to Hale, who was then in New London, in which he revealed apprehension and uncertainty while leaving no doubt which course he would take when the choice came.

> America, my friend, at the present period, sees such times as She never saw before ... the great wheels of the State and Constitution seem to have grown old and crazy; Everything bids fair for a change.... How soon a great, flourishing, and powerful State may arise from that now stigmatized by the Name of Rebels, God only knows. The prospect however for the same seems to be great; but that we ought at present to desire it is far from being clear. We ought by all means to prepare for the worst, and then we may encounter Danger with more firmness and with better prospects of success.[5]

Tallmadge and some Wethersfield friends sped off to Boston shortly after the Battle of Bunker Hill, during which the British won a pyrrhic victory over the local militiamen. While investigating the military deployments around Boston, he met with Captain John Chester, whom he had known at Wethersfield, and who first urged him to put aside his books and take up the sword. A "True Whig" from nature and nurture, Tallmadge was already convinced that the argument between the colonies and Britain was a struggle between tyranny and liberty. Chester's exhortations, combined with what he had witnessed of the bloodshed around Boston, convinced him to put his ideology into action. As he later described his political evolution:

> While I was at Cambridge with my military friends, I was continually importuned to think of the oppression which was so abundantly exhibited by the British government towards the Colonies, until I finally became entirely devoted to the cause in which my country was compelled to engage. I finally began to think seriously of putting on the uniform, and returned to Wethersfield full of zeal in the cause of my country.[6]

Tallmadge's friend Chester, newly elevated to the rank of colonel in one of Connecticut's six-month regiments, offered him a lieutenancy, and position of regimental adjutant. Tallmadge accepted and received his first commission, signed by Governor John Trumbull, on June 26, 1776.[7] But an educated young man from a ministerial family could not march off to war without a proper uniform. While back at Wethersfield, Tallmadge obtained the support of the "respectable female inhabitants of the Town of Wethersfield, in the County of Hartford in the Colony of Connecticut in New England" in calling upon William Lockwood to answer Tallmadge's "grievance" that the lack of a proper uniform might prevent his service to his country.[8] The warrior-in-waiting and his lady supporters informed Lockwood, who was apparently a merchant, that it was known that he had on hand sufficient linen for a uniform, and it had been resolved that the cloth should be handed over to Tallmadge. Should Lockwood fail to do so, Tallmadge was authorized to seize it, and Lockwood would be branded a Tory.[9] The letter to Lockwood, couched in the form of resolves, was clearly intended in jest, and Lockwood was a friend, or at least a friendly acquaintance. Nevertheless, it testifies to Tallmadge's popularity among the young women of the town and his familiarity with them. While the result of the missive is unknown, Tallmadge joined the army, and he was properly uniformed when he did so.

Tallmadge embarked on his military career as General George Washington was in the process of moving his army from Boston to New York. The commander of the Continental Army correctly divined that the British would attempt to seize the city, secure the Hudson River and Champlain Valley, and sever New England, which they considered the epicenter of sedition, from the remainder of the colonies. The troops that Washington began deploying around New York were largely untrained, possessing enthusiasm, but little discipline. Chester's regiment, now attached to Brigadier James Wadsworth's brigade, was as green as most of the American units, and Tallmadge and his fellows would work diligently to prepare themselves and their men to face the British onslaught. They hadn't much time.

2

First Blood

Tallmadge took advantage of the army's movement to New York to visit his father in Setauket. The Reverend Tallmadge was taken aback at seeing his son in full uniform and armed with a sword. "Although he was a firm and decided Whig of the revolution," Tallmadge recalled afterwards, "yet he seemed very reluctant to have me enter the army. However, the die was cast and I soon left the paternal abode and entered the tented field."[1]

Benjamin was the third of the Reverend Tallmadge's sons to enlist in the patriot cause, a fact that may have triggered the emotional response his son remembered. His brother Samuel served throughout the entire war in New York regiments, rising to the rank of lieutenant. Tallmadge's eldest brother, William, fought at the Battle of Long Island, where he was captured and confined to a British prison ship from whose fetid hold he did not emerge alive.[2]

Initially, Tallmadge, appointed regimental adjutant on July 22, was stationed at Wall Street, where he attempted to drill and train his recruits. Exactly where Tallmadge acquired his military knowledge is unknown, though he probably received guidance from more experienced officers, and, perhaps like Henry Knox, read up on the subject. Of course, the greater part of the American army was at the beginning of the learning curve, and Tallmadge was no exception. Like most of his compatriots, he was long on enthusiasm and short on experience. That would change shortly. But, in the meantime, General Washington struggled to instill a military discipline and expertise among his largely untested militia levies, a process which was far from complete when the moment of truth arrived.

The struggle for New York began in earnest with the arrival of the British fleet off Sandy Hook, on June 29, 1776. (The British invasion force, comprised of over 25,000 troops that landed on Staten Island, was the largest invasion force ever assembled until the Normandy invasion of 1944.) As they awaited the inevitable British attack, the Continental forces were caught up in the mounting expectation that Congress would announce the colonies' independence, and their transformation into a sovereign state. On July 2, 1776, as Congress was voting a resolution declaring the birth of the United States, army headquarters issued orders anticipating the measure. "The time is now at hand," it began,

> which must probably determine whether Americans are to be free men or Slaves—whether they are to have any property they can call their own; whether their houses or farms are to be pillaged and destroyed, and consigned to a state of wretchedness from which no human efforts will, probably, deliver them. The fate of unborn Millions, will now depend under God, on the Courage and Conduct of this Army; our cruel and unrelenting Enemy, leaves us no choice but a Brave resistance or the most abject Submission. This is all we can expect. We have, therefore, to resolve to *Conquer or Die!*[3]

However inspiring Tallmadge thought the exhortations of the army's headquarters is not known, but the young officer did record that, upon the reading of the Declaration of Independence to the troops, everyone was "filled with enthusiastic zeal, as the point was now forever settled, and there was no further hope of reconciliation and dependence on the mother country."[4] Resistance had finally given way to revolution.

Defending New York was a daunting undertaking. Three islands, Staten Island, Long Island and Manhattan—the city itself—met in New York Harbor, and British naval superiority opened the possibility that the Revolutionary forces could be cut off and destroyed on any one of them. Nevertheless, conceding the city without a fight was politically and psychologically unthinkable, and Congress directed the Continental Army to repel the British. Washington was well aware that the assignment was difficult, if not impossible. Writing to his cousin after being forced to withdraw from the city, the commander-in-chief declared:

> Had I been left to the dictates of my own judgment, New York should have been laid in Ashes before I quitted it.... It was obvious to me (covered as it may be from their [British] ships) that it will be next to impossible for us to dispossess them of it again as all their Supplies come by water, whilst ours are derived by Land.... By leaving it standing, the Enemy are furnished with warm and comfortable Barracks, in which their whole force may be concentrated—the place secured by a small garrison (if they chuse it) having their

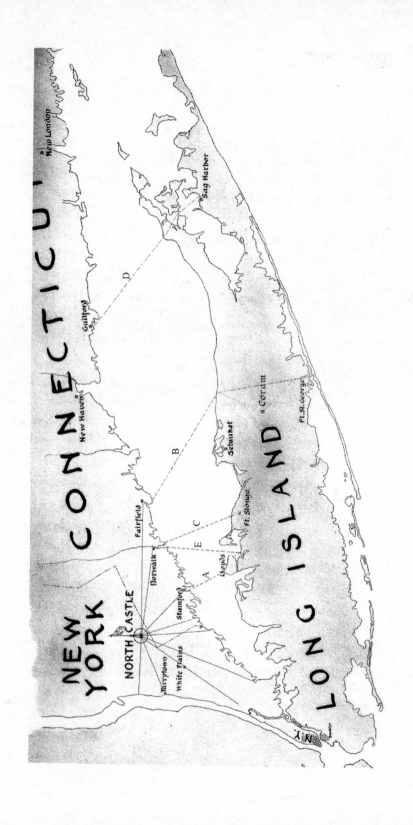

Ships round it & only a narrow Neck of Land to defend—and their principal force left at large to act against us. This in my judgment may be set down am[on]g one of the capitol errors of Congress.[5]

Washington deferred to Congress, hoping that he could bloody the British in a manner similar to the Battle of Bunker Hill the year before, the effect of which might sap their aggressive instinct and demoralize the ranks. Though he realized preventing the British from seizing the city was unlikely, the Continental Army's commander hoped to make them "wade thro' much blood and slaughter," rendering their success "a melancholy and mournful victory." Perhaps such a pyrrhic triumph would induce the British to quit the struggle. Indeed, General William Howe, the British commander, intended to prevent another Bunker Hill, a determination that led him to assume a cautious and desultory campaign which cost him the best opportunity for crushing the Revolutionary army the British would have in the war.

In preparation to meet the British invasion, Washington ordered his subordinates to erect a series of forts north of the city, which was then limited to the southern tip of Manhattan, as well as the shores of New Jersey and on Brooklyn Heights, which overlooked the island. Unfortunately, the Revolutionary command failed to fortify the Narrows, the choke point between the Long Island and Staten Island shores. Guns, trained on the waterway, might have blocked British ships from approaching the city, but the step was not taken.

British movements indicated that Howe intended to strike at Washington's army from Long Island, seizing Brooklyn Heights and forcing the Americans to evacuate Manhattan or face a bombardment. Washington countered by moving 10,000 men to Kings County, where they took up positions on a series of forts which had been prepared along the high ground. Additionally, General John Sullivan, who commanded the Revolutionary forces before the arrival of General Israel Putnam, positioned troops at the gaps in the passes piercing the moraine behind which lay the American defensive positions. Unfortunately, the Jamaica Pass on the northernmost or left flank of the Continental line was only

Opposite: **Tallmadge's Area of Operations. (A) 1779, Tallmadge's Lloyd's Neck Raid; (B) 1780, Tallmadge's Mastic-Coram Raid; (C) 1781, Ft. Slongo Raid; (D) 1777, Meigs Sag Harbor Raid; (E) 1776, Nathan Hale lands on Long Island at Huntington.** *Sons of the Revolution in the State of New York, 1904.*

protected by a few pickets who were ordered to report if the British attacked on that point instead of on the south, or right flank, of the American position, as Washington expected. Wadsworth's Brigade, including Tallmadge and the rest of Chester's men, were part of the forces placed in the forward positions outside the forts.

Howe landed his massive force of 24,000 men at Gravesend Bay and deployed his regiments parallel to the American defenses. On August 27, the British and Hessians surged forward, with the key assault bursting through the virtually undefended Jamaica Pass, throwing the Patriot forces into confused retreat. Tallmadge was engaged in action for the first time at Bedford Pass, experiencing bloody fighting as the entire American line became unzipped by the breakthrough at Jamaica Pass on their left flank.

By the end of the day, the Continental Army was badly mauled with the surviving troops flooding back into the forts ringing the village of Brooklyn. The Battle of Long Island, or Brooklyn, the largest of the war in terms of numbers, cost the Americans 200 soldiers' lives and 900 taken prisoner. British losses amounted to under 400.[6] Though the destruction of Washington's army was in his grasp, Howe suspended his assault to give his brother, Admiral Sir Richard Howe, who carried an additional assignment as a peace commissioner, the opportunity to confer with American delegates. Predictably, the negotiations collapsed over the American refusal to drop their claim of independence. But the respite gave Washington the chance to reorganize, and when the British again began to threaten to overrun the precarious Brooklyn position, Washington began ferrying his men across the East River, from Brooklyn to Manhattan. Fortunately for the Continentals, a thick fog prevented the Royal Navy from sweeping up the river and trapping the American army in Brooklyn. Tallmadge remembered that it was "so dense an atmosphere that I could scarcely discern a man at six yards distance."[7]

Assigned to the Continental Army's rear guard, Chester's regiment covered the American withdrawal from Brooklyn, and Tallmadge "stepped into one of the last boats" pushing off from the Brooklyn ferry slip for Manhattan. Upon reaching the safety of the New York shore, he began to regret leaving his favorite horse behind in Brooklyn, and received permission to raise some volunteers to accompany him back to Brooklyn to retrieve it. It was a gutsy (if foolhardy) decision, but it worked. Tallmadge successfully retrieved his mount and was halfway back across the East River when the British reached the Brooklyn shore and commenced firing at him. By then, the distance was too great for the British muskets, and no one was wounded.[8]

Howe finally recommenced his offensive and prepared to land his forces at Kips Bay in Manhattan. Tallmadge was deployed with an artillery battery which was dug in at Turtle Bay along the East River. As the British began their opening maneuvers, the Revolutionaries opened fire on a British frigate with a few eighteen pounders, but the warship returned "so heavy a fire upon our redoubt, that in less than thirty minutes she entirely dismounted our guns, and we were glad to leave so uncomfortable a place."[9] Tallmadge and the cannoneers were ordered northward up Manhattan island and wheeled their guns into an American redoubt near Hell Gate. There, directly across the East River, was a battery of British heavy cannon. It was no contest. The British artillery fire blew a hole in the earthen walls of the rebel position, and once again disabled the American fieldpieces.[10] When the British began landing their troops in force, Washington ordered a retreat to the hilly ground at Harlem Heights, guarding the key crossings over the Harlem River into Westchester. In the sporadic fighting that ensued during the withdrawal, Major Willis of Wadsworth's brigade was captured, and Tallmadge was immediately appointed to his position.[11]

Declining to assault the American lines head-on, Howe pulled most of his men back across the East River to Long Island and then ferried them across the East River, where they landed at Throgs Neck on the mainland. Howe intended to get behind Washington and trap him in northern Manhattan. The strategy was sound, but Howe's laggard pace and flawed preparations again prevented the operation from achieving conclusive success. Seeing the danger, Washington pulled his forces out of Manhattan and took up a defensive position near White Plains, in Westchester County.

Before Howe began to execute his Throg's Neck gambit, while Continental and British forces were still blazing away at each other in inconclusive skirmishing, Tallmadge's Yale friend, Nathan Hale, met his famous death. After the Battle of Long Island as the British took hold of the city, Hale volunteered to enter behind British lines to gather information about their intentions. He crossed Long Island Sound on September 12 and landed near Huntington, from which he made his way westward towards the city. He was captured by the British and kept a prisoner near Howe's headquarters. While his espionage mission was clear to the British, they may also have believed he was involved in the outbreak of the great fire which broke out on September 21, destroying a considerable part of the city. In any event, he was hanged on September 22, 1776. How long it took for word of his execution to reach Tallmadge in the lines along the Harlem River is impossible to calculate, but probably not longer than a week. Tallmadge left no account of his feelings at the time, though they must have been deep—and bitter.[12] Certainly, Hale's hanging, and the death of his brother at British hands a little later, deepened his commitment to the cause of American independence, and hardened his determination to see the struggle through to the end. The personal and ideological melded in his mind and heart, fostering an implacable resolve which sustained him through the dark days of defeat, frustration at incompetent state and Continental governments, and disgust with the tepid or apathetic support among supposedly patriotic civilians.

Once more, Howe's leisurely pursuit into Westchester gave the Americans the chance to dig themselves in strong positions on a series of hills girding the village. The key to the American defense was Chatterton's Hill, a large wooded ridge situated behind the 14-foot-wide Bronx River, which anchored the American right. Should the hill fall, the British would be able to flank the entire Revolutionary army. Chatterton's was defended by seven American units, including Lord Stirling's Brigade of General Joseph Spencer's division, in whose command Tallmadge (recently promoted to brigade major) was serving. Spencer's 1,500 men were placed on the low ground in front of the Bronx River, where it was hoped they could slow—if not stop—any enemy attack. Tallmadge later recollected that many of the men were issued long poles tipped with iron pikes to offset a lack of bayonets.[13]

Finally, on October 28, Howe ordered his army forward against the American lines, placing the German regiments of Leib, Knyphausen, and Rahl in the vanguard against the Continental right, with his British regiments deployed against the American left. Tallmadge quickly found himself in the heat of the action as the Hessians launched their attack. Though initially slowed by a volley from the American line, the Germans, under Colonel Johann Gottlieb Rahl, began working around the

American flanks, finally forcing the defenders back across the narrow waterway.[14]

Like most officers, Tallmadge was mounted when the fighting began; a practice intended to allow for better command and control, but which also provided attractive targets for enemy riflemen. When the pressure of the German assault finally made it necessary for the American defenders to fall back across the Bronx River, Tallmadge was nearly taken prisoner when the regimental chaplain leapt up behind him on his horse, which bucked and bolted, hurling them both into the water. Scrambling up the bank to the American lines, Tallmadge and the clergyman were saved from capture by a volley from troops under General Alexander MacDougall, which temporarily staggered the Hessian attack. Tallmadge managed to regain his mount, and galloped to Washington's headquarters on Miller Hill on the American left to give him a full report about the fighting on Chatterton's.[15] This was Tallmadge's first recorded meeting with the commander-in-chief, with whom he would develop a close personal and professional relationship.

Washington's Headquarters, White Plains. *Author's Collection.*

The situation at Chatterton's grew increasingly grave as combined Hessian-British regiments charged the American lines from the southeast. As the Americans were concentrating on blunting this threat, Rahl's troops, who had moved into a concealed position on a rise slightly south of Chatterton's, sprung into action, striking the rebel's extreme right.[16] The weight of the combined assaults proved too much, and the Anglo-Germans "drove the [rebels] from hill to hill and through the woods."[17] By three pm, Chatterton's Hill was in Howe's possession. Tallmadge's exact role in the final defense of the hill is not clear, but he probably rejoined his regiment after reporting to Washington, and saw further action as the American units executed a fighting withdrawal from the doomed position. Fortunately for the retreating Americans, Howe, repeating his performance at Brooklyn, declined to go in for the kill. When he finally decided to attack again on October 31, he discovered that Washington had pulled his men back to another strong position, near North Castle.

The British commander then changed direction and turned south and west, intending to capture Fort Washington and Fort Lee, two bastions Washington had left on opposite sides of the Hudson to block the British navy from sailing up the river. Fort Washington, on the northern tip of Manhattan, was the most vulnerable and isolated. The fort and its 3,000 defenders, including Col. Daniel Morgan and his Southern riflemen, fell to determined Hessian attack as Washington and the bulk of the army, which had crossed into New Jersey after Howe marched south, watched impotently from Fort Lee. With another British force closing in from the north, Washington abandoned Fort Lee and fell back across New Jersey, ultimately crossing the Delaware River into Pennsylvania.

When he crossed into New Jersey, Washington left about three thousand men under Major General Heath to guard the passes through the Hudson Highlands, above Peekskill. This force, which soon rose to 7,000, consisted mostly of New England regiments, including Tallmadge's.[18] On November 10, General Charles Lee assumed command of the troops east of the Hudson with the task of harrying the British in hopes of forcing them to detach troops from their pursuit of Washington's main army. Lee was to join Washington if it became clear the British were concentrating in Jersey. Camped with Lee's forces around North Castle, Tallmadge missed Washington's bold winter counterstrokes at Trenton and Princeton, which kept the cause of independence alive.

During the dismaying fall campaign, Congress recognized that its military forces had to be both professionalized and enlisted for longer terms of service. In the reorganization that followed, Washington authorized the raising of four light dragoon regiments. The Second Continental Dragoons, recruited primarily from Connecticut but containing patriot refugees from Long Island, was commanded by Colonel Elisha Sheldon, who had experience as an officer in the prewar Connecticut Light Horse, and whose father was a Connecticut legislator. Though Sheldon's regiment was designated the Second, it was actually the first to be commissioned and raised, making it, as historian Burt Garfield Loescher pointed out, the first regular cavalry unit in the Continental Army.[19] The regiment was comprised of six troops (companies) consisting of 44 rank and file plus officers, giving it an authorized strength of 228 men. None of the dragoon regiments ever reached that goal at any one time, although some 700 men passed through the ranks of the Second during the course of the war.[20]

Like all the early six-month regiments, Chester's command was dissolved in the new reorganization. Most of the men, Tallmadge included, immediately enlisted in the new Continental units. His performances at Brooklyn, Manhattan, and Westchester had already attracted favorable notices from his superiors. Even before the Battle of White Plains, Chester had marked him as worthy of promotion. In a letter to his family in Wethersfield, Chester remarked, "For my part I think it is of the last importance to the future well-being of America that good men should now be appointed. No tongue can tell the difficulties this army has labored under for want of them. I wish Major Tallmadge might be provided for. I have recommended him … all allow him fit for any post."[21] With such support, Tallmadge was offered command of the first troop (company) of the Second Continental Dragoons (Connecticut), his appointment having been approved by Washington. There was apparently no break in his service, the dragoons being organized as the six-month regiments ended. The young officer recruited his men from the infantrymen he had commanded in Chester's regiment, receiving a bonus of two and two-thirds dollars for his services in that regard.[22] He then proceeded to Philadelphia, the Continental capital, for instructions regarding raising and equipping the new regiment. There he received his captain's commission, signed by John Hancock, president of the Continental Congress, on December 14, 1776.[23]

While Washington and the bulk of the army settled into winter quarters at Morristown, New Jersey, the Second Dragoons spent the winter organizing near Wethersfield, Connecticut. The regiment's commander, Colonel Sheldon, was busy trying to procure accouterments for the horses and men, leaving Tallmadge as officer in charge of the dragoon's encampment. Fighting generally slowed during the winter months when it was more difficult for both horses and men to move, and the gunpowder necessary to fire flintlock muskets easily became wet and useless. Sheldon took advantage of the season to begin acquiring gray mounts for the troop, a measure which had Washington's approval and which cost between five and six thousand dollars.[24] Using an archaic term for a horse-training compound, Tallmadge remembered that as mounts streamed in, he "erected a large, circular *Manage* for the purpose of training and breaking our horses."[25] Preparing the mounts was critical work since the steeds obtained were primarily trotters, purchased from local farmers for $100 in Continental currency. As the Congress operated a printing press rather than a treasury, the value of its money quickly depreciated, which greatly hindered the acquisition of fresh horses as the war went on. Indeed, the inability to purchase the requisite number of mounts would ultimately lead to a major reorganization of the dragoons.

Hoping to spur enlistments, the Continental Army instituted a bounty system for those joining the colors. In the dragoons, each private was to receive twenty dollars on signing up, with a "regular pay monthly" of £2, 10s.[26] Sheldon, as commandant-commander, drew £22, 10s, while Tallmadge, who held the rank of major through most of the conflict, was allotted £18 per month. The remainder of the officers and non-commissioned officers received between £15 and £3 per month.[27] Interestingly, the fledgling government was utilizing both the British monetary system as well as the dollar-denominated method which was would eventually take its place. Additionally, each non-commissioned officer and private was to be furnished with a good horse, saddle, bridle, sword, carbine, and pistol at government expense. Officers were expected to supply their own equipment.[28] Many of these necessities were in short supply, and replacing lost or broken down equipment occupied much of Tallmadge's time and energy. This was especially the case as the currency steadily lost value, finally reaching the point when the phrase "not worth a Continental" was commonly used to describe anything considered worthless.

During the first winter of the war, Tallmadge also began implementing Washington's orders to inoculate the Continental Army against smallpox.[29] A growing epidemic of the dreaded disease posed a major problem for the Revolutionary Army as most British troops had been exposed to the pox in Europe and had some resistance to the disease, whereas most Americans had not. Consequently, the outbreak threatened to wreak far greater havoc on the Continental Army than on its foes. Indeed, the remnant of the Arnold-Montgomery Expedition, which had been engaged in a failed attempt to capture Quebec, was ravaged by the disease as it attempted to reorganize its decimated ranks on the north shore of Lake Champlain. Perceiving the dangers the deadly pathogen posed to the Revolutionary cause, Washington ordered the inoculation of the entire army over the winter of 1776–1777. Tallmadge's anti-pox measures were part of the overall, and successful, project.[30]

Tallmadge's correspondence with Washington dates from his service in the Second Dragoons. From the beginning to the end, his letters were couched in the highly formalized and diffident language common to the time. Tallmadge's reports and correspondence served the dual purposes of duty and ambition. It was his duty as an officer to keep Washington informed of his operations, activities, difficulties, and requirements. Additionally, Tallmadge was ambitious as well as enthusiastic and committed, and he clearly intended to impress his commander with his diligence, intelligence, and initiative. Events would show how successful he was.

3

Philadelphia and New York

In June 1777, as the contending armies girded themselves for the renewed campaign, Washington called in trained troops from New England. Tallmadge's troop was the only one in the Second Dragoons which was properly mounted, equipped, and manned, a likely result of his diligence and increasing professionalism. Upon receipt of Washington's orders, he and his men rode quickly towards the American encampment at Morristown with the remainder of the regiment expected to follow when ready. Tallmadge's troop was mounted entirely on dapple gray horses, and accoutered with black saddle straps and black bearskin holsters which, Tallmadge boasted, "looked superb."[1] As soon as the dragoons reached Morristown, the freshly minted captain reported directly to Washington, who reviewed his detachment the next day and complimented him on the appearance and demeanor of his men. Official recognition soon followed approbations and Tallmadge was promoted to major on April 7, 1777.[2]

The Second Dragoons did not have long to wait to prove they were as good as they looked. Ranging out from their camp near Morristown, they found themselves repeatedly engaged in skirmishes with British troops. "Since my arrival at Camp," Tallmadge wrote to friends in Hartford, "I have had as large an allowance of fighting as I could in a serious mood wish for. I have had here and there a horse & rider or two wounded, but have lost none from my Troop as yet, though several Horsemen have been killed in the same skirmishes with me from other Regiments."[3]

The fighting shortly grew more "serious" when Howe and Washington began to maneuver for advantage in a series of feints and counterfeints, leading up to the Battle of Short Hills. The short, abortive campaign began when Howe moved his army from Staten Island to Perth Amboy, and then marched on towards New Brunswick. His objective was to draw Washington from his defensive positions in the Watchtung Mountains and defeat him in the open terrain. Washington refused to take the bait. With the Continental Army remaining in place, Howe concluded that his gambit had failed; he then reversed his route, arriving back at Perth Amboy across the Kill van Kull from Staten Island by June 22. Washington decided to shadow the British, and moved out of the mountains. Tallmadge and his men were part of a strong detachment of 2,500 men under General William Alexander, a.k.a. Lord Stirling, who were ordered to Scotch Plains, north of New Brunswick.[4]

On June 25, 1777, Tallmadge's squadron, joined by Moylan's Fourth Dragoons, Blanding's Continentals, and supported by Daniel Morgan's riflemen, was dispatched to demonstrate in front of the British, near Perth Amboy. While they were so engaged, Colonel Theodrick Bland, of the First Dragoons, who apparently had seniority or field command of the advance party, spontaneously decided to attempt a frontal assault on the waiting British. Tallmadge considered the action foolhardy to the point of stupidity. With withering sarcasm, he described to his friend and mentor Jeremiah Wadsworth how Bland attempted to attack 10,000 British regulars with a force of 260 Dragoons, supported by 300 of Morgan's riflemen. The assault was to be carried out a distance of nine miles from the rest of the Continental Army, increasing the chances of utter disaster.[5]

"Notwithstanding these trifles," Tallmadge facetiously explained, "the Heroe [Bland] determined to gain some laurels, & so we moved on till we came within long musket shot & then drew up practically at that Distance where the Kings arms could do execution & and our Carbines do none." The British musketry apparently brought home the reality of the situation to the impetuous colonel. "After we had tarried here long enough to loose [sic] a few men & horses," Tallmadge wrote, "it was wisely resolved that it was best to take ourselves away as soon as possible, inasmuch as we had to pass through thickets, which by this time were filled with the Enemies advanced Parties, which gauled us in our retiring."[6] Continuing to vent his disgust with Bland, whom he believed endangered the mounted troops through incompetence and vainglory, Tallmadge sarcastically concluded that the dragoons' "losses & trouble" were compensated by the capture of "one Hessian & [we] brought off the poor dog with shouts of Joy, for Victory was now ours."[7] As for Bland, Tallmadge wished "so deserving an Officer of the Horse in the Army, that Col. B. was safely landed in heaven for so noble an Exploit."[8]

After Bland's ill-considered foray against the British, the dragoons fell back towards the American lines where they camped for the night, still three miles from the actual lines. The dragoons had barely saddled their horses the following morning when they detected a column of British infantry closing in on them. Howe had discovered that the rebels had left their mountain bastion and launched a sudden attack with the hopes of destroying Stirling's detached command. They had also cut off any retreat by Washington, who would then be forced to battle in open terrain. "We scampered like lusty fellows," Tallmadge informed Wadsworth, "and carried tidings to Camp."[9] The dragoons' warning gave Stirling just enough time to prepare for the attack, resulting in the Battle of Short Hills. The British and Germans, 11,000 strong, were able to use their artillery and numbers to press the Americans back towards Middlebrook. However, Stirling accomplished the fighting retreat in good order, and Washington, on learning of Howe's attack, pulled the army back to a strong position in hilly country. After reconnoitering the American lines, Howe concluded they were too strong for an assault and he withdrew back to Perth Amboy and then into New York. Howe's hopes of inflicting a debilitating defeat on the rebels were dashed. Casualties from the battle were light. The British counted among their casualties five killed and 30 wounded. They claimed that 100 Americans had been either killed or wounded, though the Continental Army reported no such loss. They did agree with the British that Stirling lost three field pieces and that 70 of his men were captured.[10]

"The Enemy ... have now left the Jerseys," Tallmadge noted on July 9,[11] "& Gen'l Washington waits Sir Howe's movement to direct his own."[12] Howe had already determined his next course of action. He would leave a garrison in New York, and embark the bulk of the army for the Delaware Bay, land them on the northern end of the water body, and seize the Revolutionary capital at Philadelphia. Rough seas worked against the British: it took Howe 32 days to complete the voyage and land his men at the Head of the Elk, near Elkton, Maryland, on August 24. Howe's drawn-out journey allowed Washington to discern his intentions and gave him plenty of time to move south with 18,000 men to block the British advance on the struggling republic's capital. Indeed, the slow transit of the British allowed Washington to hold a grand review of the Continental Army near Germantown, which Tallmadge later recalled as "the grandest military parade I ever beheld."[13] As events would prove, grand parades did not necessarily translate into grand victories.

Tallmadge represented the only part of the Second Dragoons to serve in the ensuing Philadelphia campaign. As would happen throughout most of the war, the regiment was scattered among different commands, with one troop assigned to General Horatio Gates, who led the American forces opposing General John Burgoyne's British army, pressing southwards towards Albany from Lake Champlain. Two other troops under Sheldon were serving with Israel Putnam in the Hudson Highlands. Despite their position as the only mounted command with Washington, the dragoons were absent at the first collision in the Philadelphia campaign, being detached for the mundane, but necessary, duty of escorting supply wagons from the army depots to the field.

Determined to strike the British before they reached Philadelphia, Washington deployed his men on the banks of a narrow river called the Brandywine, where a full-scale battle opened on September 11, 1777. Though the battle was stubbornly fought, Howe succeeded in repeating the flank attack he had unleashed at Brooklyn, and the Americans were again forced to yield the field, having suffered 1,100 casualties to the British army's 500. Yet, most importantly, the Continental Army had fought well and remained intact. Concluding that Philadelphia could not be defended, Washington abandoned the capital and fell back towards Germantown while the Congress scurried off to York, Pennsylvania. But the Continental commander was not prepared to surrender the capital without another fight and prepared to launch a counter strike against the British at Germantown. This time, Tallmadge and his men would be in the thick of the fighting.

Washington planned to destroy a separated British force at Germantown before reinforcements could arrive from nearby Philadelphia. Local militia were to attack the British on the flanks while the divisions of John Sullivan and Nathaniel Greene were to assault the right and left of the British positions. When the attack began on October 3, Washington's plan began to break down immediately with only Sullivan's men jumping off at the appointed time. Tallmadge was posted with Sullivan's force, and their attack came close to turning the British flank. Unfortunately for the Revolutionaries, the arriving militia became confused and, more fatally, General Henry Knox halted his advance and ordered his regiments to drive the British from a large stone house. Anticipating this, the British soldiers poured a murderous fire from an upper-story window onto the advancing Continentals. The slackening of the American attack gave the British the chance to regroup, and their subsequent counterattack threw the American army into confusion. Retreat became a rout. Washington sent Tallmadge to place his dragoons across the road to stem the retreat and rally the soldiers. Tallmadge and his men did the best they could, but nothing could stop the panicked men from fleeing the field. Fortunately, Howe remained true to form, and followed his pattern of cautious pursuit, which allowed the Continentals to regroup near Shippack.

Following the events at Germantown, the Philadelphia campaign slowly flickered out. The British turned their attention to the American forts which guarded each side of the Delaware, effectively impeding naval access to the city. Though they succeeded in taking the forts, they paid dearly for victory; the Hessians in particular suffered severely in the fighting at Fort Mercer on the New Jersey side of the river.

Though the heavy fighting had ended, the Continental Army was still on full alert in case the British sallied out of their lines, looking for a battle. On November 18, 1777, Tallmadge took time from the incessant picket duty to write an old friend, Lieutenant Colonel Samuel B. Webb, who had been captured during a failed raid at Setauket on September 10, 1777. Following the military customs of the times, after giving their word that they would not attempt to escape or return to the war unless officially exchanged, officers like Webb were paroled and allowed their freedom within certain parameters of the British lines. The word of an officer was a point of honor and few prisoners seem to have violated their parole. Webb spent the bulk of his parole in Manhattan and Flatbush, Kings County, until exchanged in 1781. Military convention also permitted correspondence across the lines of war, and Webb, like most officer prisoners, was in frequent contact with American officers who, in turn, wrote back to him. Such privileges applied only to the fraternity of commissioned officers. Enlisted men and non-commissioned officers were penned up in prisons or on prison ships, where conditions were generally atrocious.

Although he must have known Webb's correspondence was read by the British, Tallmadge's letter to his old friend was remarkably candid about the struggle for the Delaware River forts and he even described the deployments of the American army. Possibly, Tallmadge assumed that the British were already well informed about Washington's deployments. It was also an age before military censors and the understanding that prisoners were required to provide only name, rank, and serial number to their captors. Tallmadge described his own duties as daily "piquet," and responding to the "constant firing."[14]

In early December, both armies maneuvered for advantage at Chestnut Hill, near Philadelphia. Tallmadge, who was posted with Morgan's riflemen again, believed a major battle would ensue, but neither general chose to attack. Howe pulled back into the relative comforts of Philadelphia, while Washington went into winter quarters at Valley Forge. The campaign, which Tallmadge deemed "the most sanguinary of any that took place during the war," had closed.[15] The Continentals had been bested on the field, but Howe again failed to destroy them and bring the contest to a close. The British soon discovered that Philadelphia, however comfortable, gave them no strategic advantage. Indeed, Howe's Philadelphia campaign left General John Burgoyne's expedition in the Champlain-Hudson Valley unsupported, which resulted in his catastrophic—for the British—defeat and surrender at Saratoga.

As the Continentals settled into their miserable camp at Valley Forge, Washington assigned Tallmadge and his dragoons to picket duty between the Delaware and Schuylkill Rivers. His task was to report on British movements and prevent "the disaffected from carrying supplies to Philadelphia."[16] British light horse continuously challenged the dragoons and Tallmadge and his men stood on constant alert, and seldom tarried in one place for very long lest they be caught unawares by their adversaries. Indeed, the dragoons' most serious action occurred on December 14 when Lord Rawdon, leading about 90 British horsemen, caught Tallmadge on a scout with a small squad. The Americans initially tried to resist, but were forced to flee towards their lines when Rawdon's men got around their flanks. The affair resulted in the deaths of four rebels, and four were wounded.[17] Tallmadge was incensed by the skirmish, not so much for the number of the casualties, but the manner in which the men suffered. Writing to Jeremiah Wadsworth, he reported that three of his men were ordered killed by British officers after they had surrendered and been disarmed. He continued to describe the grisly account:

> Notwithstanding the Entreaties and Prayers of the prisoners for mercy, the soldiers fell upon them with their swords, and after *hacking, cutting,* and *stabbing* them till they supposed they were dead, they then left them there (one excepted whom they shot) setting fire to the barn to consume any who might be in it. They also coolly murdered an old man of the house, first cutting and most inhumanly mangling him with their Swords and then shooting him.[18]

On December 30, Tallmadge sent off another missive to "Dear Wadsworth," reporting that he and his men were ten miles in front of the army, and he had "not pulled off my boots or clothing for eighteen days," a testament to the constant round of raids, skirmishing, and scouting.[19] Still seething at the British butchering of his men, he had the satisfaction of getting some payback. The British, Tallmadge wrote, had returned to Philadelphia after a foraging raid, which he described as "plundering." The Second Dragoons had "several pretty severe brushes" with the British which were "much to their loss. 13 Lt Horsemen were taken by about 16 of ours."[20] The British prisoners were from Preston's regiment and Tallmadge admired their "fine" black horses. He did not admire the riders' black hearts. "These were the Devils that murdered those Lads of my Troop, wish to God I could take some of them to show them that we dare and will retaliate such unprecedented barbarities."[21] What stayed his hand—scruple, orders, or uncertainty as to which of the individual prisoners had perpetrated the massacre—Tallmadge did not say.

When not dueling with his British counterparts, Tallmadge had to deal with the problems of desertion and diminishing supplies. The two were linked, and it was going to be a difficult winter. The army had received no provisions for three days after they reached their positions following Germantown. The lack of adequate supplies was "enough to have made an honest man desert and I am told it was the Cause of a great many leaving us."[22] Tallmadge noted that "the General was in great anxiety about it [the lack of supplies], and I believe most heartily cursed the Commissary."[23] He was convinced that the Commissary Department, responsible for supplying the army, had deteriorated since Joseph Trumbull resigned. Trumbull (1737–1778) was the son of Connecticut governor John Trumbull, and had, on Washington's recommendation, been appointed to the post in July 1775. He later came under criticism by some members of Congress, who succeeded in taking some of his duties away. Feeling slighted, Trumbull resigned from the post.[24] Tallmadge, who probably was personally acquainted with Trumbull—he had succeeded in forging personal contacts with most people of importance in the Hartford area—believed the growing problem of supplies for the Continental Army began with Trumbull's departure. "I have many apprehensions and fears from that Qr," Tallmadge confided to Wadsworth, "& should any fatal Consequences arise from the new destructive Establishment, Congress may have the full satisfaction and honour of taking the whole Credit of it to themselves."[25]

Shortages of food and supplies, as well as a lack of funds to secure them, were a major source of anxiety for Tallmadge (and, indeed, the rest of the Continental Army) throughout the war. Tallmadge often looked to Wadsworth for relief in that regard. Wadsworth held the position of commissary for the Northeastern States, and was later in charge of providing provender to the French when they arrived after 1778. In addition to acting as a major purveyor of food and equipment to the Revolutionary cause, he was an adept financier and speculator, a combination which was neither illegal nor uncommon in the era, although individuals lacking the means or the opportunity to participate in such arrangements saw it differently. Almost continuously on his horse, scouting, fighting, likely sleep deprived, and probably wearing the same stinking uniform, Tallmadge viewed the supply situation as a looming catastrophe. "I pray to God you may not let us starve," he begged Wadsworth, "just when our prospects just begin to be promising."[26] But the dark nights of the soul passed for the young officer, whose youth, enthusiasm, and resolve always served to buoy him even in the most desperate periods of the war. But the deficiency of money and support, not to mention dissatisfaction with Congress, remained.

The rebels were often bitter about the number of inhabitants who traded happily with the British. But not all the local civilians doing so were Tories. While on the picket line near Philadelphia, Tallmadge received orders to provide an escort for a "country girl" who had volunteered to enter the city to gather information about British dispositions. Tallmadge led his men a few miles beyond Germantown to a tavern called the Rising Sun, where he was met by a young woman coming from the British-occupied city. Tallmadge introduced himself and was debriefing the girl when a troop of British light horses galloped towards the tavern. The dragoon major sprang to his mount, and, in a scene out of a cowboy movie, the young woman climbed up on the horse behind him and the two sped off. The woman's composure clearly impressed Tallmadge, who recalled that "during the whole ride, although there was considerable firing of pistols, and not a little wheeling and charging, she remained unmoved, and never once complained of fear after she mounted my horse. I was delighted with this transaction, and received many compliments from those who became acquainted with it."[27] Little did he suspect at the time that his encounter with the girl spy was but a portent of more significant espionage activity to come.

Tallmadge spent most of the early months of 1778 in winter quarters at Chatham, New Jersey. When not dealing with British cavalry forays, the young major busied himself with supplying his men with mounts, equipment, and new recruits. He sent reports of his activities to Washington and General Casmir Pulaski, who had briefly been placed in command of all Continental mounted troops.[28] The dragoon leader was able to inform his superiors that he had received new issues of leather breeches for his men, and had submitted a requisition for boots. He also acknowledged receipt of a key item of dragoon gear which were part of the spoils of the Saratoga campaign—sabers. "I have just received 149 [German] Horseman's swords, taken with General Burgoyne, which are all that we may expect in that Q[uarter]—They are very strong and heavy having steel scabbards."[29]

Supplies, mounts, and new recruits required money, a key ingredient of war always in short supply among the Revolutionaries. Both states and the Continental Congress had resorted to paper currency, and the soundness of this issue fluctuated, generally declining in value as states and Congress printed more and more, ultimately leading to major inflation by the end of 1778. Money was a constant concern to Tallmadge as it was to most Continental Army officers, the commanding general not excepted. Tallmadge wrote Washington of his attempts to recruit fresh volunteers, complaining that Pulaski had approved his enlistment efforts, but had provided no funds for them. Tallmadge reached into regimental coffers and dug into his own pockets to pay the expenses of the non-commissioned officers he dispatched to purchase mounts and grease recruiting. Nevertheless, he feared the money available wouldn't be enough for the job.[30] A few months later he was still lamenting that supplies of all kinds were "much retarded for want of money."[31]

In May 1778, Tallmadge suffered his only disagreeable exchange with Washington. Col. Stephen Moylan of the Fourth Dragoons sent a report to Washington in which he painted a poor picture of the Second Dragoons' performance in the previous year's campaign, which he blamed on the shortcomings of the officers entrusted with procuring necessary supplies and equipment. Washington responded with a blistering letter to Sheldon and Tallmadge, accusing them of allowing their men to wear out their horses by "galloping about the country" on personal matters.[32] Stung by this unwarranted criticism, Tallmadge defended his efforts, concluding, "My own honour as well as the honour and Services of all my Brother officers seem to have so depreciated in your Excellency's opinion that unless a Change of Sentiments is experienced, I am well convinced we can serve with but little credit, and no Satisfaction thereafter."[33] Perhaps recognizing that further criticism might undermine the morale of diligent officers who were struggling to cope with difficult circumstances, Washington let the matter drop, and a "Change of Sentiments" soon manifested itself.

As the weather turned warmer and the spring campaign opened, the Americans faced a new adversary, General Henry Clinton, who had replaced Howe. Clinton's position was rendered more difficult as rumors of a French alliance with the United States turned the Revolution into a world war. The new commanding general decided to evacuate Philadelphia, the occupation of which had brought few benefits to the British war effort, and reconcentrate in New York, from which he could dispatch reinforcements against French islands in the Caribbean or open a new front in the Carolinas. Such a dispersal of forces would make it more difficult for the normally aggressive Clinton to take the war to Washington, but the measures were dictated by the changed nature of the conflict. Tallmadge foresaw the British move as early as May, an assessment which might have been gleaned from scouting or information brought in by spies.[34] In any event, Clinton was not ready to begin his change of base until July. As the British marched towards New York, Washington attacked them near Monmouth, New Jersey.

As harsh as the winter at Valley Forge had been, the army used their time there to good advantage. Reflecting the positive effects of Prussian General Baron von Steuben's training, the Continental force which took the field in 1778 was significantly improved from the year before. The American army fought well at Monmouth, and many thought they might have done better had it not been for the performance of General Charles Lee, whom Washington removed from command while the fighting was still raging. Clinton was content to break off the engagement and hasten to New York, fearing a descent by the French fleet on the city. Indeed, Admiral D'Estaing's failure to arrive in time to trap Clinton's army on Sandy Hook and destroy British admiral Richard Howe's scattered and inferior fleet cost the new Franco-American alliance its best chance to bring the war to a swift and victorious conclusion. The lost opportunity doomed the belligerents to a long war with an uncertain outcome.

Neither Tallmadge nor anyone else in the Second Dragoons fought at Monmouth. In May, Tallmadge's troop was sent to the Hudson Highlands, which was then commanded by Horatio Gates, still basking in the triumph at Saratoga. While Gates's role in the American victory was overestimated, he knew how to celebrate the Fourth of July. On the second anniversary of the Declaration of Independence, he invited all general and field officers under his command to join him in a holiday feast. Tallmadge, whose love of a good party had been a matter of record since his Yale days, was one of the attendees. As he described the festivities in a letter to his friend Barnabas Deane:

> We had 13 as Catholick [varied] toasts given us by General Gates as Men ever drank. I presume I need hardly inform you that we were very merry on the occasion, wine at any time being such a Rarity, the effluvia and Influence of which, joined to the noble occasion, You may depend on it made us as sociable as any Sons of Bacchus in any Quarter of the World.[35]

The return to New York gave Tallmadge the opportunity to savor one other pleasant event. On September 9, he traveled to New Haven, where, after paying a twelve-dollar "gratuity" to the college president, he received his Master of Arts degree from Yale.[36] The degree must have been honorary, perhaps a testimonial to his growing military reputation, as he had been far too busy with military affairs to consistently pursue any academic or scholastic interest.

While Gates's Fourth of July party was a welcome respite from the duties and dangers of the war, the officers were soon back with their commands, resuming military operations. Tallmadge's troop was soon joined by those of Sheldon and Seymour, providing one of the rare instances in the war when all of the Second Dragoons were together as a regiment. Following the fighting at Monmouth, Washington shadowed Clinton as he made his way back to New York. Washington stationed his units in an arc around the British stronghold. His arrangements allowed him to counter a British offensive from almost any quarter while simultaneously permitting him to launch attacks on a variety of fronts. The Revolutionary forces were posted at Middlebrook, Elizabeth, and Ramapo, New Jersey, West Point and Fishkill in New York, and Danbury in Connecticut. The Second Dragoons were attached to General Scott's Light Corps, which faced off against Lt. Col. John Simcoe's Queens Rangers, Delancey's Tories, and Emmerick's horsemen in Westchester County on the New York mainland. Making their camps in the Greenburg Hills, the dragoons sometimes probed as close to the enemy as Valentine's Hill below Yonkers.[37] Tallmadge was now back in the coastal areas of New York and Connecticut that he knew so well. He would spend the bulk of his military career in the region, and it was here that he would win a reputation as one of Washington's most daring junior officers.

4

Spymaster

From 1778 to the end of the war, the lower Hudson valley and adjacent Connecticut coastal area became the base of operations for Tallmadge and his men. The dragoons were in almost constant service, performing a variety of duties which presented little opportunity for "downtime." When not otherwise deployed, they patrolled the no-man's-land in central Westchester. This entailed scouting, suppression of "cowboys"—nominally Tory bandits who often preyed on civilians without regard to political loyalty—parrying British incursions and raids, participating in major army offensives, and, increasingly, engaging in special operations.

Washington kept a sharp eye out for talented and resourceful young officers, whom he would then appoint to his staff, or place in key positions.[1] The relatively small size of the Continental Army gave the commander-in-chief abundant opportunity for close personal observation which allowed him to form his own judgments about the abilities of his officer corps. Tallmadge had first attracted Washington's notice in the battles around New York and Philadelphia. He had first met the young major during the fighting at White Plains, and called upon him to try to stem the rout at Germantown. Tallmadge's constant skirmishing and scouting outside of Philadelphia in the winter of 1777–1778, and the after battle and reconnaissance reports that he sent in to his superiors, probably caught the commanding general's attention as well. Impressed with the young major's performance and potential, in 1778 Washington gave him an assignment of immense importance, and one which brought the two in constant contact and communication, a relationship which led to mutual affection and, on Tallmadge's part, deep devotion.

From his days as a young militia officer in the French and Indian War, Washington recognized the critical importance of solid, reliable intelligence. As the two armies maneuvered and feinted against each other in and around New York, Washington became especially anxious to garner accurate information concerning British intentions, dispositions, and operations in their New York nerve center. Long Island, occupied by the redcoats following the Battle of Long Island, was an integral part of the British command structure, furnishing supplies of wood and provisions, as well as locales for quartering troops. Long Island patriots, primarily Suffolk County Presbyterians and Congregationalists, especially those with good reasons to travel into the city, were prime candidates for the role of intelligence agents. With his Setauket-Presbyterian roots, and his tested dedication to the cause of independence, Tallmadge was the obvious candidate to organize and run an espionage network in Manhattan and Long Island. Tallmadge readily accepted the assignment, and devoted a considerable amount of his military career to obtaining, evaluating, and forwarding reports from the British-occupied islands. Naturally, he revealed little about his activities during the war. More surprisingly, he said little about it after independence was secured in 1783. In his memoirs he remarked opaquely that, in 1778, "I opened a private correspondence in New York (for Gen. Washington) which lasted throughout the war. How beneficial it was to the Commander-in-Chief is evidenced by his continuing the same to the close of the war."[2]

The idea for using Long Island as the hub and conduit for intelligence in New York City may have first been suggested by Caleb Brewster. Brewster, another resident of Setauket, was part of the exodus of Whigs fleeing Long Island to Connecticut following the Continental Amy's defeat at Brooklyn. Although a member of a Continental regiment, Brewster was most often on detached duty, crossing Long Island Sound to raid the British occupying his native shores. This combination of raid and counter-raid became known as the "Whaleboat War" after the long, double-bowed watercraft in which the raids were carried out. Equipped with a sail, and usually a swivel gun, whaleboats were large enough to hold up to 12 men, and maneuverable enough to put into the myriad coves and harbors that characterized the North Shore of Long Island— and Brewster knew most of them well. He also perceived that he could use his forays on the island to gather information about British troop dispositions, fortifications, supplies, numbers, and, possibly, plans. Some of this might even shed light on what the redcoats were plotting in their

Manhattan base. Brewster contacted Washington directly, suggesting that he engage in precisely such activities. Washington was agreeable, but he envisioned something far more ambitious. What he wanted was a network, focused on agents in Manhattan, who could pass their reports back to him by way of Long Island and the whaleboat couriers. Originally, he placed command of the nascent network with Captain Charles Scott. Scott was astute enough to leave the actual business of intelligence gathering to someone who knew the territory and its inhabitants far better than he—Benjamin Tallmadge, who quickly replaced Scott as the official as well as de facto leader of the operation. Though the overall conception of the intelligence system was Washington's, he left the running of the network to Tallmadge.

Tallmadge carefully recruited agents he knew and trusted for his network, relying on Setauket friends, neighbors, and members of his father's congregation. In addition to Brewster, a boyhood friend, Tallmadge tapped Abraham Woodhull, a local farmer, whom he had also known since childhood. Woodhull's political leanings were certainly shaped by his Presbyterian faith, but he was also the cousin of patriot General Nathaniel Woodhull. Nathaniel Woodhull had been captured after the Battle of Long Island and died of wounds which many Revolutionaries believed were inflicted after he had surrendered. No doubt, the death of his cousin provided further motivation for Woodhull. The Setauket farmer made frequent trips to Manhattan to sell his produce, and Tallmadge set him to collect information on his visits. The intelligence-gathering duties were highly dangerous since Woodhull had to pass various British checkpoints at which he might be detected or robbed. Additionally, the war and British occupation of Long Island had unleashed a wave of brigandage in which criminal gangs looted from Patriot and Tory sympathizers alike. Indeed, in April 1779, Tallmadge reported that Woodhull was "robbed of all his money & was glad to escape with his life."[3] Not surprising, the Setauket spy, who had heretofore lived the quiet life of a farmer, grew increasingly stressed and anxiety ridden as he made his putative marketing excursions across Long Island and into the hub of British power in Manhattan. As Tallmadge explained to Washington, the Setauket agent evinced "extreme Cautiousness & even timidity" and if his real identity was ever revealed he "should leave [Long Island] immediately."[4]

Setauket men also served as couriers, taking information collected by Woodhull in Manhattan and carrying it back to Setauket when Woodhull himself was unable to leave. Austin Roe and Josiah Hawkins, more friends and fellow Presbyterians, were the most frequently employed riders. Once intelligence was collected in Setauket, usually with Woodhull serving as the clearinghouse, it was necessary to wait for Brewster to make one of his frequent trips across Long Island Sound. Local legend has it that Anna Strong, wife of Selah Strong, a patriot refugee in Connecticut, would signal Brewster that intelligence was ready and in which cove to land his boat to avoid detection. Supposedly, she used a code based on the color and placement of the laundry drying on her clothesline for signaling Brewster. Though the story is unverifiable, the British learned that a woman was involved in "disloyal" activities in Setauket, and Anna fits the bill.

Robert Townsend, who became the ring's key Manhattan operative, was the anomaly in the organization. Townsend, a member of a prominent family in Oyster Bay, Queens County, sprang from a Quaker-Anglican background. In contrast to Suffolk County on eastern Long Island, the western counties of Kings and Queens Counties were home to large numbers of Tories and neutrals. Townsend's father, Solomon, was one of the few well-known outspoken pro-independence leaders in Oyster Bay, but he had been forced to submit to the British after the American defeat in Brooklyn. Robert Townsend spent much of his time in New York City, where he operated a merchant business at Peck's Slip. Though he had acted as a commissary officer for the revolutionary army before August 1776, he, like his father, took the oath of loyalty to the crown after the British occupied Long Island, and may have even served briefly in a Tory militia unit. Though his business interests required him to overtly cooperate with the British, events would show that his personal experience propelled him to undertake an active role in the cause of independence.

In the fall of 1778, Oyster Bay was occupied by Colonel John Graves Simcoe's Queens Rangers, one of the most effective Tory units raised during the war. Simcoe's men constructed a bastion on Townsend land situated on the high ground just south of the family residence, destroying a family orchard in the process. Additionally, the occupiers "requisitioned" indiscriminately and frequently ruined property for policy or sport. Residential activity was constrained by a curfew. Moreover, Simcoe chose the Townsend residence, later dubbed Raynham Hall, for his personal quarters. Robert Townsend was forced to watch as the overbearing British officers used the family homestead as they saw fit, and treated the Townsends as servants. He was further offended by Simcoe's efforts to woo his attractive sister, Sally.

Back in Manhattan, Townsend made the acquaintance of Abraham Woodhull, who was scouting for someone with a legitimate reason to stay in the city to serve as the network's Manhattan agent. Exactly what was said remains a mystery, but Townsend joined the organization. On October 31, a delighted Woodhull reported that he was "successful in ingaging a faithful friend and one of the first characters in the City to

The only known image of Robert Townsend, drawn two decades after the close of the Revolutionary War. *Raynham Hall Museum, Oyster Bay, Long Island, New York.*

make [intelligence gathering] his business and keep his Eyes upon every movement and assist me in all requests and meet and consult weekly in or near the City. I have the most sanguine hopes of great advantage will accrue by his assistance."[5] A few months later, Woodhull expanded on his enthusiasm for Townsend by describing him to Tallmadge as "respectable [and] capable of acting the business well ... and signified that all the encouragement that I had received should be conferred on him."[6] The timing of Townsend's recruitment, coming just after Simcoe's occupation of Oyster Bay and Raynham Hall, suggests that for Townsend, like Tallmadge and Woodhull, the war was both ideological and personal.

As he undertook the organization of his espionage operation, Tallmadge also took pains to develop what later became known as "tradecraft." He devised a numerical code system, creating over 710 specially coded words. Long Island, for example was 728; Manhattan, 727. Agents were assigned both numbers and codes. Woodhull was both 722 and "Culper, Sr." while Townsend became "Culper, Jr." as well as 723. The use of the Culper pseudonyms later led historians to dub Tallmadge's network the "Culper Spy Ring." Tallmadge himself assumed the *nom de guerre* "John Bolton," or 721. Only Brewster, already famous—or infamous—as a whaleboat warfare captain, declined to adopt an alias or code, though in his secret reports Woodhull always referred to him as 725.

As a further precaution, Tallmadge and Washington secured a supply of a specially concocted invisible ink which they called the "sympathetic stain," or "white ink." The substance, which was developed by Sir James Jay, brother of John Jay, seems to have been difficult to procure in large quantities, and was apparently delivered directly to Washington, who doled it out as needed. Writing from his headquarters at West Point on July 25, 1779, Washington informed Tallmadge that "all the white ink I now have—indeed all that there is any prospect of getting soon—is sent in phial no. 1.... The liquid in no. 2 is the counterpart, and brings to light what is wrote by the first, by wetting the Paper with a fine hair brush—These you will send to C----- Jnr. As soon as possible, and I beg you that no mention ever be made of your having received such liquids from me or anyone else."[7] Reports from Townsend on New York to Woodhull in Setauket might utilize all three anti-detection devices—

code names, numbers, and the "stain"—or one or two depending on time and circumstances. But only Washington, Tallmadge, Woodhull, and Townsend seem to have had the "stain," and only Tallmadge knew the true identity of the Culpers. Washington never requested their identities from Tallmadge, and the information was not offered. Indeed, the nervous Woodhull made it clear that, if his identity became known by anyone other than Tallmadge and the other members of the ring, he would quit the operation.[8]

Townsend became the key agent in the espionage network. His merchant activities in Manhattan provided the perfect cover to spend lengthy periods in the British-occupied city, while his close friendship and partnership with James Rivington, an ostensible Tory who published the pro–British *Rivington's* (later *Royal*) *Gazette*, provided the perfect cover for gaining the confidence of the British officers who frequented the coffee shop adjoining Rivington's newspaper office.[9] In actuality, Rivington was a double agent, or at least willing to play both sides, and he, too, supplied Washington with information. Interestingly, there is no indication that either he or Townsend was aware of the other's activities.

Though Washington was content to let Tallmadge run the Culper network, he was always anxious for further intelligence from the anonymous sources, and his letters to Tallmadge frequently urge him to hasten the reports from the ring. At times, his keen interest in intelligence gathering led him to offer advice to Tallmadge as to how Townsend should operate. The commander-in-chief asked Tallmadge to pass on his suggestion that the man he knew only as "Culper, Jr." should write his reports on the blank pages of pamphlets which "he may forward without risqué [*sic*] of search or the scrutiny of the enemy as this is chiefly directed against paper made up in the form of letters."[10] Alternatively, Washington proposed that Townsend/Culper, Jr.

> may write a familiar letter … to his friend in Setauket or elsewhere, interlining with the stain, his secret intelligence or writing it on the opposite blank side of the letter. But that his friend may know how to distinguish these from letter addressed solely to himself, he may always leave such as contain secret information without date or place; (dating it with the stain) or fold them up in a particular manner, which may be concerted between the parties.[11]

Washington was also explicit in the intelligence he required. In another letter to Tallmadge he instructed him to inform Townsend that he wanted to know

> the quantity and quality of the provisions in New-York, comprehending their whole stock whether in magazines or on ship-board. He will be particular as to the kind and size of the works that are lately formed, or that may be erected. And at all times keep his attention on changes of situation, or the new positions which may be taken by the enemy. He will inform me what new works are erected on Long Island besides those at Brooklyn, and where, and of what nature. I wish also to know where their shipping lyes, and if they appear to be taking measures for their security in case of a french [sic] fleet's entering the harbor.[12]

Townsend did his best to comply. Acting as "Culper, Jr." the merchant-agent forwarded a steady stream of intelligence reports throughout 1778–80. The following is a decoded excerpt from a typical letter reporting on British deployments in New York and on Long Island from early 1779.

> [There is one] Hessian Regt near Jones and Delancy's land and the other near the Water Works. The number on Staten Island I do not know. On Long Island the number is as mentioned a Regt of Horse about Flushing, a guard of about 30 men of the 3rd Battalion of DeLancy's Brigade with a party of Militia Horse are at Jamaica as a guard for the General [DeLancey]. He might have been taken off with much ease sometime ago, but it would now be very difficult as the Queens Rangers are at Oyster Bay. Their number is about 120 men, 100 of whom are mounted. The 3rd Battalion of Delancy's Brigade are at Lloyd's Neck. From [near] the vicinity of the Queens Rangers who can be there by means of an alarm gun in two hours. I think it would by no means be advisable to attack them—They were alarmed on Thursday night last and was there [Lloyd's Neck] in one and a half hours after the alarm.[13]

None of the Culpers engaged in espionage for money. They expected reimbursement for their expenses, but never requested pay for their service. At least one of them, however, hoped that his wartime service would entitle him to some sort of position or reward in the United States government whose establishment they were so materially aiding. When Woodhull recruited Robert Townsend into the Culper network, he explained to Tallmadge that the new informant's "chief aim is to have such a recommendation at the close of this war as may intitle him to some imployment as a compensation for the disadvantage and risqué he plans."[14] A year into the game, Townsend sent an inquiry to

Washington, via Tallmadge, asking if he would receive any preferment from the new government should the war be successfully concluded. Washington replied in a September 16, 1780 letter to his spy runner: "It is impossible for me, circumstanced as matters are to give a positive answer to C----- Junior's request, as I cannot, without knowing his views, tell what his expectations are. Of this, both you and he may rest assured, that should he continue Serviceable and faithful, and should the issue of our affairs prove as favorable as we hope, I shall be ready to recommend him to the public, if public employ should be his aim, and if not, that I shall think myself bound to represent his conduct in the light it deserves, and procure him compensation of another kind. I shall take the first opportunity of sending you a further sum of money for contingencies."[15]

Whether or not Townsend brought up the matter again after receiving Washington's reply, money, or the lack of it, remained an ever-present problem. On April 25, 1781, Tallmadge reported to Washington that Townsend needed money for his agents. Woodhull was willing to advance 100 guineas, more if necessary, upon "receiving your Excellency's assurance that it shall be refunded by the Public, with reasonable Interest, after the War."[16] Washington's answer was affirmative, and both Culpers remained in service, but the scarcity of funding—for spying and military operations in general—remained a chronic concern.

The importance of Culper Ring activities to the Continental cause is difficult to assess. Intelligence regarding British dispositions, strength, order of battle, forage and supplies, morale, and even intentions no doubt played a significant role in Washington's calculations. Messages from Townsend clearly helped Washington forestall a British attack on the French during their initial landing at Newport, Rhode Island, before they had the chance to secure their positions. Warned of the British expedition, Washington deceived the British into believing he was planning a major attack to capture New York, which led the British to drop their plans to descend on Newport, and prepare for a non-existent offensive. The Culper Ring also revealed British intentions to counterfeit Continental currency. In August 1780, Woodhull informed Tallmadge that the "Refugees [Loyalists who fled from Patriot-held territory] keep up a constant communication with your coasts and carries over large sums of counterfeit currency of every [issue] and puts it in the hands of the Tories for to pay their taxes with."[17] By that point in the struggle, Continental currency was already so devalued that the actual effect of unleashing counterfeits is hard to ascertain, though any further decline in its value was damaging.[18]

Townsend certainly improved the overall quality of the Culper Ring's intelligence, which made the network's operation a genuine strategic asset. In June 1779, Washington complained that Culper, Sr.'s, Woodhull's, troop estimates were sometimes faulty, and cautioned his successor, Culper Jr., or Townsend, against "giving positive numbers by guess—this is deceptive."[19] Townsend, who had the advantage of familiarity with British officers at Rivington's, fulfilled Washington's hopes. "I rely upon his intelligence," Washington wrote Tallmadge about Culper, Jr. in 1780. "His accounts are intelligent, clear and satisfactory."[20]

The commanding general's only criticism related to the time lag between Townsend's preparation of intelligence reports and when they finally reached headquarters. This may have been the cause of a message from Washington to Woodhull, undoubtedly through Tallmadge, which clearly wounded the Setauket agent. In a letter to Tallmadge, Culper remarked, "I perceive that [Culper intelligence] estimates hath bene of little service. Sorry we have bene at so much cost and trouble for little or no purpose. He also mentions my backwardness to service. He certainly hath bene misinformed—you are sensible I have bene indefatigable and have done it for principal of duty rather than any mercenary end."[21] Washington's harsh letter likely derived from his anxiety to receive timely intelligence as well as the constant worry over money, which affected every aspect of the army's operations. Tallmadge likely endeavored to both satisfy Washington as to the Culpers' diligence, and assuage Woodhull's feelings. In any event, the incident passed, and Woodhull remained in service, supplying a constant stream of intelligence from his own and Townsend's observations, which satisfied the commanding general. Nevertheless, Washington's unhappiness about the costs of running the Culper Ring surfaced again as the war drew to a close.

Washington instructed Tallmadge to "press" Townsend to open up a more direct route of communication, and asked him to find some reliable couriers for the new arrangement.[22] Tallmadge and Townsend did their best to oblige. In August 1780, Tallmadge informed his commander that he was "endeavoring" to set up a route from Cow Neck (Port Washington), across the Sound to Westchester. Located to the west of Oyster Bay, the Cow Neck operation would cut the transmission time to "twelve hours in emergencies."[23] The agent selected for the proposed Cow Neck route was a "near relation" of Townsend's, which Tallmadge saw as bolstering Culper Jr.'s confidence, and encouraging him to stay active. Unfortunately, it is not known if this alternative route was ever put into action. While the lines of communication would indeed be shorter, Cow Neck would bring the network's communications closer to the centers of British land and naval strength. Townsend's relative might also have had second thoughts about becoming involved in the game. In any event, the New York-Setauket-Long Island Sound-Westchester system remained the Culper Ring's major conduit of intelligence until the end of the war.

Certainly the British and their Tory allies were aware of the effectiveness of the Culpers, even though they did not know their identities. As early as May 1778, the *Rivington Gazette* complained:

> The rebels have constant information by signals from many disloyal Islanders residing between Huntington and Setauket of every vessel passing up the Sound, as well as the situation of persons and things in several parts of Long Island; and they also convey all the information their emissaries daily procure of the several occurrences in New York City.[24]

Though the Culper Ring provided the most continual stream of reliable information, especially from Manhattan, it was not the sole source of Tallmadge's intelligence. In his correspondence he mentions, though seldom by name, other residents of the island and city who secured information or otherwise made themselves useful. Some of these seem to have worked with Woodhull, but others were run independently of the Culper network. On numerous occasions, Tallmadge risked capture by making the dangerous voyage across Long Island Sound to confer directly with Woodhull, and probably Townsend, as well as undertaking his own reconnaissances.[25] At other times he was met by informants and agents who were not part of the Culper Ring, but who supplied him with additional information or provided safe shelter from British and Tory patrols.

Establishing an effective intelligence operation was a considerable accomplishment—and Tallmadge could not point to any real accomplishments in his more conventional military duties. This could be said of the entire Second Dragoons. The efficacy of Sheldon's horse was chronically sapped by its dispersal to several areas and commands, and the difficulties in acquiring adequate mounts and accouterments. Worse, the summer and fall of 1778 witnessed a drop in morale which many ascribed to Sheldon's uninspiring leadership. Indeed, hostility to the regimental commander resulted in accusations that he had allowed the dragoons to degenerate into "a banditti of refugees from the justice of their country and the halter."[26] Tallmadge himself seems to have kept a higher opinion of his regimental leader, and supported him when he later faced court-martial hearings, in which he was cleared of all charges. Nevertheless, the problems facing the dragoons were real enough. In September, Tallmadge informed Washington that of the 204 non-commissioned officers and enlisted men, 50 had no horses, some had worn-out horses, and many others lacked such basic necessities as blankets.[27]

But neither political infighting, low morale, nor day-to-day exertions dampened Tallmadge's energy and commitment. In November, he and John Webb rode into British lines under a flag of truce so Webb could visit his brother, a prisoner of war in New York. While Webb continued into the city, Tallmadge remained at the British outpost, conversing with the soldiers stationed there. The royal troops expressed the hope that some sort of settlement might be reached between the rebels and the Crown and that they would combine forces against the French. Tallmadge shot down the fantasy that had been optimistically circulating through the British encampments.[28]

However satisfying it might be to declare open support for the Revolutionary cause in front of British troops, what Tallmadge craved was action. As the dragoons settled into their winter encampments around Durham, Connecticut, Tallmadge's thoughts kept returning to Long Island, which offered the best opportunity to disrupt and weaken the enemy, while giving hope and comfort to his friends and family living under a harsh and sometimes brutal occupation.

5

The Oppressed Island

The "Whaleboat War," which raged across Long Island Sound after 1776, was borne of misery and chaos. The misery arrived with the British occupation of Long Island following the patriot disaster at the Battle of Brooklyn. The British established forts, barracks, disposed residents, requisitioned supplies—which often meant confiscating them or paying the owners in notes which could not be redeemed, and oppressing presumed Whigs while allowing the Tories to torment their rebel neighbors. The chaos resulted from the uneven effectiveness of the British occupation—too few troops to control the entire population—a situation compounded by British disdain for provincials, and rife corruption in the occupation administration.

Moreover, the Island was essentially a borderland. The border was the Long Island Sound, whose alternative name, "The Devil's Belt," became all too appropriate in those turbulent times. Across the watery border lay rebel-held Connecticut, to which many pro–Revolutionary Long Islanders had fled after 1776. Among those who fled were Declaration of Independence signer William Floyd and his family, the Reverend Benjamin Tallmadge, and Caleb Brewster, the younger Benjamin's friend, agent, and subordinate.

Brewster (1747–1827) grew up on a farm in Setauket, but shipped out on a whaler at the age of 19. Maritime pursuits soon became his life's occupation. He joined the Brookhaven minutemen after Lexington and Concord, and rose to the rank of second lieutenant in the seventh company of Colonel Josiah Smith's Suffolk Minuteman Regiment. After the Revolutionary defeat at Brooklyn, the Suffolk regiment dispersed, and those who wished to continue the fight were told to regroup across the Sound in New Haven. Brewster was among the refugees and joined Colonel Livingston's Fourth Continental Line Regiment as a lieutenant.[1] A portent of things to come, on October 28, 1776, he took part in one of the first whaleboat raids on Long Island. The raiders marched across the Sound to William Floyd's home at Mastic to retrieve as much of his property as they could before the British despoiled the estate. On their return, the raiders captured two sloops loaded with wood for the British in New York.[2] Shortly after his return to Connecticut from the raid, Brewster transferred to Colonel John Lamb's artillery, but he was mostly on detached duty, fighting the British on the Sound, on Long Island, and playing a major role in transmitting intelligence from New York to Tallmadge and Washington. In his various roles, which made him feared and notorious among the British and Loyalists, he was frequently under overall command of his Setauket neighbor Benjamin Tallmadge.

A different type of raid was carried out shortly after by 150 Long Island refugees and Connecticut rebels. On November 5, 1776, they crossed the Sound from New Haven and landed at Setauket, where they ambushed a party of British soldiers, killing a few and taking 23 prisoners back to Connecticut.[3] They managed to contact Brigadier Oliver DeLancey, who was then in Oyster Bay, offering to trade their prisoners for some Americans held on the British prison ships in Wallabout Bay. After some hesitation, the British agreed to the transaction, and both sides resorted to raiding the opposite shore of the Sound to gain prisoners for exchange.[4] Tallmadge, always searching for ripe targets on Long Island, also considered abducting prominent British or Tory figures for exchange. In January 1779, Woodhull responded to his query about the possibility of quickly snatching a British officer. Woodhull was doubtful about undertaking such a mission at that time, writing, "I cannot give you any Incouragement about making any Incursion on Long Island with Small parties. I know not of any Officer so detached from his Corps that a small party might surprise him."[5] Tallmadge would bide his time, and opportunities would come.

But the acquisition of captives quickly became a minor motivation, as British and Tory raiders from the island launched their boats to attack and plunder the Whigs, and Revolutionaries from Connecticut, often including exiled Long Islanders, returned to Long Island, seeking plunder and payback. The governments of Connecticut and New York authorized seizing goods from pro-British residents, though goods taken in such a manner were supposed to be disposed of legally through court action. It took little time for many of the raiders to degenerate into pirates and robbers, lacking even the pretense of confining their plundering to their putative foes, robbing Revolutionary and Tory alike, and selling their booty wherever they could get the best price. Sporadic attempts by Washington and state authorities to curtail such abuses proved ineffectual.[6] The island's residents suffered grievously from the activity. Writing on September 22, 1776, when the occupation and raiding had only just begun, Samuel Buell, pastor of the East Hampton Presbyterian Church, observed, "The people are as a torch fired at both ends, which will be speedily consumed; for the Continental Whigs carry off their stock and produce, and the British punish them for allowing it to go. I hope the Whigs will not oppress the oppressed."[7] But they often did, using the excuse that Islanders were cooperating with the British as a dodge for their depredations.

Indeed, the situation only deteriorated as the war lengthened. By 1778, the government of New York attempted to curtail the practice, and asked the governor of Connecticut to reign in marauders operating from his state. The following year, the New York legislature passed a resolution forbidding confiscations in British-occupied territory and again calling upon Connecticut for cooperation. Other than jawboning, little was accomplished.[8] Indeed, the situation probably worsened after 1780 when the British contracted their permanent deployments on Long Island, leaving the inhabitants of Suffolk even more vulnerable to the pillaging and theft. Further petitions to Governor Trumbull of Connecticut were met with anodyne responses citing the legal instructions that supposedly constrained whaleboat raiders, and the equally lame argument that afflicted New Yorkers had recourse to law.[9] In the midst of a revolution which was also a civil war, Hartford's control over the freebooting whaleboat men was probably less complete than New Yorkers assumed. It is also likely that local officials in the coastal towns connived at the plundering expeditions, and shared in the profits as well.

The problem was that no one's law was permanently in control over much of the island, especially east of Huntington, and too many benefitted from the proceeds of the depredations. Even a Congressional request for Connecticut to repeal all commissions of privateering on Long Island had no effect. In August 1781, Abraham Davenport asked for protection from the supposedly patriot raiders. He estimated that

Artist's rendering of freebooting whaleboatmen demanding valuables from a Long Island home, 1881. The reality was far less formal. *Author's Collection.*

some 60 homes or residents had been robbed in recent months, with several wounded or killed.[10] In 1781, Long Islander William Floyd, signer of the Declaration of Independence and Tallmadge's future father-in-law, bitterly concluded, "If the enemy were to Quit our Country tomorrow, it is clear to me that the State of New York has suffered more damage from the State of Connecticut than from the Enemy, tho we have had war in our State for five years."[11] Only with the restoration of peace in 1783 would the pillaging cease.

Tallmadge's own network of agents was sometimes caught up on the wrong end of incessant raiding. In December 1778, Tallmadge wrote to Washington, complaining that Woodhull had been captured by "one of our armed sloops," probably a Connecticut raider with a state license, and had been brought to Connecticut as a prisoner suspected of Tory activity.[12] The Connecticut authorities released the spy on parole, but subsequently ordered him to return to Connecticut, an order that Woodhull could ignore only at his own peril.

The Whaleboat War was not solely a matter of partisan/brigand attacks, nor were the attacks the work of just one side. Officially authorized and planned attacks, carried out by regularly enlisted troops, began early in the conflict. The British launched the first large attack across the Sound on April 25, 1777, when 200 troops under General William Tryon landed in Connecticut and marched deep into the interior to destroy military stores accumulated at Danbury, defeating a Revolutionary force sent to block him, and killing American general David Wooster in the process. The American counterstroke occurred a month later. The British had been actively scouring eastern Long Island, accumulating agricultural supplies and using Sag Harbor on the South Fork as their base for transport and storage. On May 23, Lt. Colonel Return Jonathan Meigs embarked 170 men in two armed sloops at Guilford, Connecticut, and landed at Southold, on Long Island's North Fork. The raiders crossed the narrow northern fluke of the island's "fish-tail," relaunched their boats in the Peconic Bay, which separates the two Forks, landed outside Sag Harbor on the South Fork, and stormed into the village the next morning. Achieving total surprise, they captured the British fort and its garrison as well as a hospital, forage party, 12 brigs and sloops, and 120 tons of hay, corn, and oats. Ten hogsheads of rum were also taken. Six British soldiers were killed in the attack and 90 were taken prisoner. Meigs suffered no casualties and was safely back in Guilford by two in the afternoon.[13]

The next major action struck close to Tallmadge. Early in 1777, Colonel Richard Hewlett, commanding a battalion of General Oliver DeLancey's Tory Brigade, took up quarters at Setauket. As they did elsewhere on the island, and throughout the colonies, the British targeted the Presbyterian Church for desecration and destruction. The outspokenly Whiggish Reverend Tallmadge had fled to Connecticut following the Battle of Long Island, and was beyond the reach of the British, but his church was turned into a barracks around which Hewlett's men constructed a stockade, destroying part of the burial grounds in the process. In August, acting on orders from General Israel Putnam and General Parsons, Colonel Samuel B. Webb crossed the Sound to put an end to Hewlett's occupation. Caleb Brewster was part of the raiding party and probably acted as guide as well. The American force landed at Crane Neck on August 22 and marched quickly on Setauket, where Hewlett awaited them behind his fortified positions. Webb demanded that the Tories surrender, which they refused to do, leading to some ineffectual exchanges of musketry. Fearful of being cut off by British naval patrols, and seeing little prospect of successfully taking the church, Webb called off the attack and returned to Connecticut.[14]

At the end of the year, Parsons drew up an even more ambitious three-pronged raid designed to upset British dispositions and control on Long Island. One party was to strike east, near Southold, a second under Meigs was to land near Hempstead Harbor and march overland to attack the British at Hempstead and Jamaica. The third detachment, under Webb, was expected to beach their boats near Huntington and move in support of whichever of the other two enterprises seemed most promising. The entire plan unraveled when Meigs's departure was stymied by heavy seas, and Webb's force was spotted on the Sound by a British frigate which forced the American vessels aground near Old Man's (Mt. Sinai), resulting in the capture of Webb and 60 of his men.[15]

Tallmadge was well informed of the battle flaming up on his home island, and was no doubt especially pained by the events at Setauket. His concerns centered on both the British and Tory operations as well as the opportunistic whaleboat plunderers. In 1779, he reported that the whaleboat robbers had struck Setauket, and noted that they "never bring their goods before a Court for trial and condemnation, but to proceed to vend them at will."[16] So much for the legalities cited by Trumbull.

While lamenting that "these marauders from our shore [Connecticut] make no distinction between Whig & Tory," Tallmadge was further alarmed that the pirates continued to jeopardize his intelligence operations. In at least one instance, the boat ferrying Culper's dispatches across the Sound was pursued, not by the British, but by freelance plunderers.[17] The incident further frightened the ever-nervous Woodhull, and Tallmadge informed Washington that if steps were not taken to suppress the looters, both Culper and even the aggressive Brewster would suspend their operations.[18] Washington complied and wrote Governors Trumbull and Clinton, asking them to take steps to halt the marauding, but the Sound and bordering coastlines were too vast for either the civil or military authorities to adequately control. Tallmadge, who knew at least some of the perpetrators by name, sought Washington's approval to capture them and hand them over to New York authorities for trial. While successful on occasion, especially during the last year of the war when the decrease in fighting left him more time to patrol the Sound, the plundering and outlawed trading could not be satisfactorily suppressed.

Tallmadge understood that the war and the British occupation created the conditions which allowed the indiscriminate plundering, and he knew that the fastest way to bring the lawlessness to an end was to defeat the British and their Tory allies. Though his means were limited, Tallmadge concluded that one of the most effective ways of convincing the British that they could not subdue the rebellion was to shake their hold on their most convenient granary, lumberyard, fuel supply, and barracks—Long Island. At one point, Tallmadge envisioned a campaign to destroy the sawmills which the British used to cut wood and lumber, but dropped the plan when Woodhull argued against destroying private property "if it can be avoided."[19] In addition to the normal difficulties in launching a successful cross–Sound raid, Tallmadge was probably deterred by Woodhull's description of the sawmills as cheap to build and rebuild, meaning little long-term advantage would be gained for the risk involved. As for the sawmill owners whose facilities the British used, Woodhull said most were "friends to the country [Independence]," but "it is the Nature of the People here that they will do anything to get money." Tallmadge had already seen plenty of that.

From Woodhull and his other agents across the Sound, Tallmadge received a steady stream of reports providing him with a clear picture of British deployments—and depredations against the inhabitants. In the winter of 1778, his men were stationed at Durham, Connecticut, but Tallmadge himself was "from Choice stationed at Greenfield, from which I could easily cross to L. Island."[20] And he did.

British power on Long Island was strongest in Kings and Queens Counties. Although their garrisons sometimes shifted, they maintained a continual presence at Brooklyn Ferry, Flatbush, Bushwick, Newtown (Elmhurst), Flushing, Jamaica, and were frequently in camps at Jericho and Oyster Bay.[21] Further east, the Crown's forces were concentrated in the west-central areas of Suffolk. While the British continued to launch foraging—effectively punitive—expeditions east of the Carman's River, they did not establish another permanent outpost on the East End after Meigs Raid in 1777.[22] Indeed, in the spring of 1778, they repositioned their forces and destroyed their existing forts in Huntington village and Setauket, though they soon erected a new bastion in the Huntington area. Somewhat later they began constructing a stronghold on the estate of Revolutionary refugee Judge Benjamin Strong, at Mastic, which they christened Fort St. George. On the north shore, facing Long Island Sound, British Lieutenant John Graves Simcoe had established the Oyster Bay encampment to protect food and firewood collected for transport to New York. About 12 miles to the east Fort Slongo was established to house British woodcutters and foragers.

On May 15, 1778, the Third Battalion of Brigadier General Oliver DeLancey's Loyalists began work on what was arguably the Crown's most formidable fortification outside of Kings and western Queens. Named in honor of Benjamin Franklin's Tory son, Fort Franklin was situated on the western edge of Lloyd's Neck, a small peninsula jutting out from Huntington. DeLancey selected his ground well, for the fort was built on a bluff commanding the entrance into both Oyster Bay and Cold Spring Harbor.[23] Should any rebel foray succeed in getting through the chokepoint to those water bodies they would fall under the range of the fort's guns, and be hard pressed to escape. Additionally, the fort and its garrison—which reached near 500 men at times—provided protection to Tory whaleboat raiders who based themselves in the inlets and harbors of the area.[24] For Tallmadge, the British outposts in Suffolk County—home to friends, family and a pro–Revolutionary populace—were enticing targets. As he later recalled to his daughter, "I had long conceived the idea of capturing all these fortifications & driving the Enemy out of Suffolk County from which [they] drew such vast supplies of forage, grain, and fresh meat."[25]

Tallmadge identified Fort Franklin as the key to the British operations in central Long Island, and a staging area for British raiders. "I intended to kill or take the whole gang of Marauders & Plunderers ... which have for so long a time infested the coast on the sound," he wrote General Robert Howe.[26] The dragoon major no doubt savored the opportunity to inflict payback on the British for General William Tryon's July raid on Connecticut coastal towns. As usual, he was well prepared with intelligence about the British position and its troop strength, mostly through Woodhull, who received it from his sources near the fort. In addition to Ludlow's regiment, the Neck was occupied by a large number of Tory refugees and deserters from the Continental forces "that know they will be hanged [if captured] and ... will make a desperate resistance."[27]

If the Lloyd Neck position was formidable, Tallmadge was determined. At eight p.m. on September 5, 1779, he embarked a mixed force of dismounted dragoons, assorted Continental troops and 50 boatmen and volunteers from the Long Island refugees—about 130 in all—and crossed the Sound from Shippen Point, near Stamford.[28] His first objective was to clear out a camp of Tory whaleboat men just east of the fort, and then seize Ft. Franklin itself. The American force made landfall about ten and, after detailing 30 men to guard the boats, Tallmadge's men quickly fell upon the Tories, who were quartered in two houses and a number of nearby huts. The rebel raiders were divided into two sections, the first consisting of Captain Edgar and 50 troops who were given the task of capturing one of the houses, while Tallmadge and the second party took the other. Tallmadge had hoped that the entire camp could be overrun without gunfire, so as not to alert the British troops within Fort Franklin itself, on the western edge of the neck. At first all went as planned, with the two houses taken quickly and quietly. The Tories, sheltering in huts, quickly recovered from their surprise and opened fire on their attackers. The resistance was brief, however, as Tallmadge swept aside the defenders, secured the camp, and set about gathering up prisoners, supplies, and papers. But some of the Tories managed to escape and continued firing at the raiders from the woods and swampy areas. The sound of musketry gave the alarm to the redcoats stationed inside Fort Franklin and along the narrow sand spit which connected the Neck to the island. Tallmadge realized the element of surprise had been lost, and with it went any chance of taking the largest prize.

The dragoon leader and his men contented themselves with destroying and burning the Tories' boats and camp, and then rowed back to Connecticut with their prisoners, having suffered no casualties themselves. Among the prisoners was Captain Glover, a Tory refugee from Connecticut, who was captain in the Loyalist militia at Lloyd Neck. Tallmadge charged Glover with "having plundered property from the friendly Inhabitants to the AmoT of many thousands of dollars."[29] In addition, Tallmadge brought off a document issued by Lieutenant Colonel John Simcoe of the Queens Rangers which revealed Glover had been reconnoitering in Connecticut. "In fine," Tallmadge wrote in his report, "perhaps few men have been more active against us, & the capture of no one could have given more satisfaction to the people."[30] Tallmadge did regret that Glover's rank in British service prohibited his being executed, but consoled himself with the knowledge that "those so atrociously guilty can be exchanged for some of our friends" in British captivity.[31]

Interestingly, one of Tallmadge's prisoners was a slave, "a Negro who belongs to one John McAlpin," a captain in Ft. Franklin's garrison. He did not mention what befell the men when the expedition returned to Connecticut. As far as the booty taken from the Tory encampment, Tallmadge expected "the goods will be sold for the benefit of the captors," a common practice in eighteenth century warfare.[32] Though he had sufficient reason to be pleased with the expedition's outcome, his inability to take Fort Franklin rankled, and the British presence in the stronghold taunted him to the end of the war.

Typically major military activity slowed with the onset of colder weather. In the winter of 1779–80, Washington assigned his infantry to encampments in Danbury, West Point, and Middletown. The Continental horse was dispersed in an even wider arc from New England into the Shenandoah Valley.[33] The commanding general believed the deployments would prevent the British from launching an unexpected offensive, and it placed him in a position to reorganize his forces to meet a threat from any quarter. Tallmadge's troop of the Second Continental Dragoons spent the winter around his old haunts at Wethersfield. The decline in active campaigning gave Tallmadge little time for leisure. The Culper Ring required constant supervision, and the danger of British raids was ever present. As always, Tallmadge had his eye on the Sound coastline and the British-occupied island.

The condition of the men and their steeds was a constant source of anxiety. On February 22, 1780, Tallmadge reported that only seven men, a trumpeter, a farrier, and five privates were adequately housed. Additionally, the horses were worn down, and uniforms, boots, and other clothing unavailable or in short supply. As the winter ended, Tallmadge was able to rectify the situation at least in part by obtaining 386 uniforms in Boston, presumably using Continental currency or notes.[34] While Tallmadge fretted about equipment and horses for existing troops, Sheldon was off attempting to recruit the regiment.

The continual shortage of clothing, equipment, and pay inevitably depressed morale, leading to another headache for Tallmadge and his fellow officers: desertion. Three of his men deserted in October, though two were quickly apprehended. Tallmadge had them clapped in irons and wrote to Washington that he hoped they would receive "a Speedy trial, as I esteem them villains of the first magnitude."[35] The monetary situation did not improve as the new year advanced. On May 20, 1780, Tallmadge again called upon Wadsworth to help find money to pay so the regiment could "keep what few soldiers we have from leaving the Corps."[36] The situation was somewhat alleviated the following month due to resources gained from an additional "revenue stream" available to the Revolutionary forces—property confiscated from Tories. Writing to a contact in New London, Tallmadge explained that with "the little hard money arising from the sale of a confiscated estate at Hartford, I have been able to engage all the Saddlery, furniture, Swords, Boots, etc, etc for Col. Sheldon's Regt."[37]

Supplies and recruitment again raised the problem of money, and Tallmadge was among those delegated to once again meet with Connecticut State officials to argue for an increase in pay for Connecticut troops. The year 1780 was the nadir of the war in terms of depreciation of currency. It was also the year when the enlistments of most Continental troops expired. The two issues were interconnected: soldiers were unlikely to reenlist, and new men would be resistant to recruitment, unless they were adequately paid. Congress dodged the problem by handing the responsibility for soldiers' compensation to their respective states.[38] Most states, including Connecticut, reached an agreement with their troops, though negotiations were often tense and revealed considerable suspicion between the army and civilian authorities.[39] Tallmadge also took time at Hartford to provide testimony before Connecticut officials concerning what he termed the "Jesuitical" and "odious" officer he only named as "Gen'l W----- B."[40]

Not all was gloom and worry, however. Tallmadge's mood was brightened by the opportunity to socialize with the opposite sex. A young, handsome officer, attired in a dashing dragoon's uniform, renowned for his combat exploits, Tallmadge was highly popular with the young women of Patriot disposition, and he was certainly interested in them. References to young women are sprinkled throughout his letters, and his romantic—or at least flirtatious—encounters probably extended much further than the written record reveals. In early March

1780, for example, he attended "an agreeable hop at Mr. Lockwoods. A very agreeable collection of ladies attended." Indeed, Tallmadge remarked cryptically that "the number [of ladies] was rather to [sic] great."[41] At other times he asked to be remembered to various ladies, such as "little Sally Ab-----" or "Miss Chester."[42] In an entirely different (but no less satisfying) vein was his growing attachment to Jeremiah Wadsworth and his family at Wethersfield. Tallmadge was a frequent guest at their home, and became affectionately known by the Wadsworth children as "Uncle Tallmadge."[43] In his letters to the Hartford financial wizard, Tallmadge seldom failed to express his compliments to Wadsworth's "lady." The two men clearly developed a close friendship, but Tallmadge was fully aware of his influence and connections. Running the Continental Commissary in Connecticut with the rank of colonel, Wadsworth was at the center of the military-governmental complex in the northeastern states, and Tallmadge respected and valued his confidence, advice, and business and financial acumen.

Like most Revolutionaries, Tallmadge had rejoiced over the announcement of the alliance with France, which was the most positive result of the patriot victory at Saratoga. Indeed, he was initially convinced that the French participation in the struggle was certain to make "the independence of our country *absolutely sure*."[44] In this, the young major and his fellow rebels were being overly optimistic. More than two years of hard fighting, numerous trials and devastating setbacks lay before the Revolutionary forces. Indeed, the period from 1779 to 1781 would prove the most trying of the war.

The pro–Revolution inhabitants of Long Island were also buoyed by the word of the treaty with France, but their hopes that the alliance would soon result in liberation from British occupation were soon dashed. The highs and lows of morale among the patriots on Long Island can be traced in the letters Woodhull sent to his dragoon superior. In November, 1778 he was so upbeat about the consequences of Saratoga and the new alliance, and the British and Tories so pessimistic, that he thought that 10,000 men could take New York. Such an attack might not even be necessary, he opined, citing the widespread belief that American independence would soon be granted by Parliament.[45] But Woodhull's high hopes for imminent victory soon eroded as the conflict raged on without decisive allied action.

Indeed, 1779 proved an anxiety-ridden time for the vulnerable Woodhull. A Long Island Tory, released by Connecticut, went to Col. John Greaves Simcoe in Oyster Bay and told him Woodhull was involved in traitorous activities.[46] Simcoe rode out to Setauket with a party of Queens Rangers to seize the rebel agent, but Woodhull was in New York at the time. Venting his frustration, Simcoe "fell upon my father and Plundered him in a most shocking manner."[47] Hearing of the events at Setauket, Woodhull scrambled to prevent his arrest. Fortunately, a friend who had contacts at British headquarters convinced them that Woodhull was innocent of the allegations. "[A]nd only that saved me," he reported to Tallmadge, but added, "I am very obnoxious to them and think I am in continual danger."[48] The operations of British forage parties at Smithtown, a few miles southwest of Setauket, further unnerved Woodhull, who wrote Tallmadge that if they began to head for Setauket, "I shall most certainly retreat to your side as I think it will be impossible for me to be safe."[49] But the British remained where they were, seizing whatever provisions they needed for the winter and then withdrew. Greatly relieved, Woodhull admitted, "Their approach was like death to me [I] did not know wheather [sic] to stand or flee. Had they been the Queens Rangers [Simcoe] or the [British] Legion [Tarleton] I should have bene with you before now."[50]

Continually fearful of arrest, Woodhull looked to the French for salvation. Reflecting the apprehension of his fellow patriots, Woodhull wrote repeatedly to his contact across the Sound, inquiring as to when Admiral D'Estaing's fleet would appear. By the fall of 1779, he had grown pessimistic, saying he had "impatiently" awaited the arrival of the French, but feared the onset of colder weather meant they would not soon come.[51] In November, with British foraging parties operating about ten miles west of Setauket (near present-day Northport), Tallmadge's dejected agent wailed, "We shall see more distress this winter than ever since the war began. The inhabitants of this Island at Present live a miserable life, which you may readily judge when having the reafuse of three kingdoms and thirteen States amongst them Plundering and rapine at no small rate. I am tired of this business [.] It gives me a great deal of trouble especially when disappointment [may?] appear. I could not consent to be any longer an assistant if I was not almost an Enthusiast for our Success."[52] The "reafuse of three kingdoms" was Woodhull's characterization of soldiers and Crown supporters from England, Scotland, and Ireland, though he might have included Hessians from German principalities as well. Additionally, New York's population was swollen by Tory refugees from rebel-controlled states and territories which accounted for their inclusion in the list of "reafuse."

Shortly before New Year, the morose (if not distraught) spy sadly admitted that "the day of our deliverance is farther distant than we ever glanced."[53] The following March, Woodhull reported that there was "no prospect of peace. The Enemy [is] in high spirits." His mood was darkened by the visible effects of the British foraging parties seizing what they could from the "miserable inhabitants" who suffered from a lack of food for themselves and their own animals over the long, gray winter.[54] From the perspective of the Long Island Whigs, the prospects for victory and independence seemed bleak. "Methinks your situation is bad also your money is done," Woodhull warned Tallmadge. "You must have some substitute or you cannot support the war and will fall at last [.] At least 300 deserters [are] believed to have come to the Enemy."[55] For Tallmadge, secure in rebel-held territory, things probably did not seem so desperate. Nevertheless, the near-constant stream of gloomy and pessimistic letters from one of his key operatives must have troubled him. Between the hops and socializing, writing yet another letter to Washington explaining the need for funds to outfit the troops, he must have recognized that Woodhull's blunt appraisal was chillingly close to the truth.

On August 10, 1780, shortly before setting out to trounce DeLancey's Tories in Westchester, Tallmadge received information that a detachment of British horsemen were "scattered through Suffolk County ... living on the honest Whig Inhabitants."[56] The increased British activity eastward on Long Island was intended to provide better protection for the Crown's foraging parties, an ongoing operation which was buttressed by the erection of new fortifications. The eager dragoon contacted Washington, telling his commander that, if he approved, Tallmadge was prepared to lead a party of 50 or 60 dismounted dragoons across the Sound and "endeavor to take advantage of the enemy's situation."[57]

In addition to securing provisions and forage that which they badly needed, the British operations eastward on Long Island also served to provide bases and cover for those plying the "London Trade." The "London Trade "entailed the exchange of European (primarily British) imports from New York, for grain, fodder, food, and other forms of sustenance from Connecticut. The commerce was illegal for both British and Continental forces, but both sides—especially the British—tended to wink at it. The king's army was never able to live off the land as they had originally assumed, and their supplies from Cork, Ireland—the major source of provisions for the army in America—often ran low. Consequently, they needed the grains, vegetables, dairy products, and meat offered by American traders, while the Americans craved imported goods they could not acquire at home. The Revolutionary command, well aware of British vulnerabilities in terms of provender—the food supply in New York had become an increasing problem after 1778—were more actively committed to suppressing the trade. Moreover, many "London Traders" from Long Island were Tories who, when they weren't bartering contraband goods, robbed Americans and destroyed their property when the opportunities arose. Tallmadge saw attacks on British forts and camps as a way to unsettle their business and shake, if he could not break, the British hold on Long Island.

Throughout 1780, Tallmadge continued to press the issue of launching raids on Long Island "for beating up the enemy's quarters and disturbing their repose."[58] Washington thought the matter over and, in the summer of 1780, decided to give his aggressive young subordinate his chance, and placed him in command of a detachment perfectly suited for commando-style actions. As Tallmadge put it, the commander-in-chief "honored me with a separate command, consisting of the dismounted dragoons of our regiment and a body of horse. Our dismounted dragoons had been formed into two companies of light infantry, and were commanded by excellent officers, who, to a man, rejoiced at the idea of separate and active duty."[59] Effectively, Washington gave Tallmadge his own "legion," a mixed infantry/mounted unit, which he commanded semi-autonomously from the regular Second Dragoons organization.

This was more than a gesture of confidence in the young major. Having witnessed the myriad difficulties of keeping the light dragoons mounted, supplied, and at full strength, Washington was moving in the direction of converting all the light dragoons into legions—units of mixed cavalry and infantry. Tallmadge's new assignment seems to have been the commanding general's initial move in that direction, with Congress giving official approval to the reorganization the following October 21. The new legions were to consist of four mounted and two dismounted troops of 60 privates with the numbers of commissioned and non-commissioned officers to remain the same.[60] Tallmadge's unit, in addition to being first, was also distinctive in that it was a legion within a legion, conducting its own operations unless ordered elsewhere.[61]

Since the entire Second Continental Light Dragoons was to be converted to a legion, the exact arrangements governing Tallmadge's command are unclear. Tallmadge himself explicitly stated that he held an independent command, which suggests that the former regiment was somehow split. In any event, Tallmadge now had his own Ranger detachment, one which he intended to unleash as soon as the moment was ready. Shortly after receiving Washington's appointment, Tallmadge moved his newly reorganized troop to the Horse Neck–New Canaan–North Stamford area of the Connecticut coast. From this base he could parry British thrusts into the interior of Westchester if necessary, and launch his own assaults on their positions on Long Island when opportunities arose.

Fort Franklin again loomed as the obvious target. Indeed, on August 7, 1780, Woodhull sent a detailed map of the bastion.[62] Tallmadge enthusiastically agreed when General Samuel Parsons, commander of the Connecticut militia, approached him with a proposal to attack the fort using his own commandos augmented by 700 men from the Connecticut line. His interest cooled, however, after Parsons dispatched a presumed Long Island refugee back to Huntington to acquire fresh information about the British. Tallmadge had become a veteran intelligence handler by this point, and he kept his agents—and his networks—safe by relying only on those he knew he could trust. His professional instincts told him something was wrong about Parsons's supposed refugee. These misgivings led him to decline when Parsons suggested that he take personal command of the expedition, though he agreed to serve under Parsons in the proposed operation. Apparently, Parsons also began to have second thoughts about the loyalty of his refugee-spy, and declined the responsibility Tallmadge had handed back to him. The project fell apart. Sometime later, reliable sources informed Tallmadge that the British garrison had advance warning of the planned expedition—probably from the supposed refugee—and was waiting in ambush at the

Americans intended landing site which, as he put it with wry under-statement, "probably would have annoyed us greatly."[63]

All in all, the war seemed to have become stalemated, and the rush of optimism that followed Saratoga dissipated as the French alliance proved indecisive, and the British seemed to regain their balance and determination to pursue their goals to crush the rebellion. Tallmadge shared the anxieties of the patriots. While he could draw satisfaction from his attack on Lloyd's Neck and his successes in supplying intelli-gence to Washington, he had not been able to unleash the heavy blows he knew were necessary to weaken the British and bolster the sagging spirits of his oppressed family, friends, and supporters on Long Island. But if it was action he sought, he would quickly get his fill.

6

Slash and Parry in the Neutral Ground

Though Tallmadge sought opportunities to wreak havoc on the British on Long Island, events on the mainland consumed much of his energy and attention. The Culper network required constant supervision, while the seemingly never-ending combat against British and Tories in Westchester meant he was frequently in the saddle, leading his men in the swirling skirmishes which characterized this part of the war. And, of course, the more mundane but essential tasks connected with organizing, equipping, and paying his men.

In early spring 1779, before his descent on Fort Franklin, the dragoons altered their recruitment regulations. Henceforth, new enlistees signed up for the duration of the war. Bowing to the constant difficulties in obtaining horses, the new recruits were expected to serve as infantry until "it shall be thought proper or convenient to mount them."[1] Indeed, anticipating later army directives, the Second Continental Dragoons organized two troops entirely as infantry in preparation for the campaigning season, though that change was mostly due to necessity. Obtaining adequate mounts and equipage for the full regiment was never satisfactorily achieved.

The rebels' British counterparts were highly aggressive, and both sides laid plans to surprise the other. Even as the British were preparing to shift their major offensive to the Carolinas, Clinton unleashed a series of swift, punishing raids in Westchester and Connecticut. He hoped this would draw Washington into a decisive engagement which, in turn, might render the shift of the war southward unnecessary. Washington, for his part, had determined on a Fabian strategy, to parry the British, destroy their smaller detachments and outposts but, at all costs, keep the Continental Army intact, and await the arrival of French forces. The

Continental Army's main bases were at West Point, and New Windsor, with a major supply depot at Fishkill, all situated on or near the Hudson River, north of the British stronghold in New York City.

The dragoons, sometimes supported by small detached units of Continentals and local militia, were charged with reporting on British intentions in New York and Lower Westchester, as well as preventing British horsemen, raiders, and Tories from despoiling areas inhabited by pro–Revolutionary inhabitants. The American front line in Westchester was elastic. When the British were numerous and active, as they were from 1776 to 1778, the dragoons were positioned in the northern end of the county, above Mt. Kisco and Dobbs Ferry, often behind the Croton River. After 1780 many British units were sent south, and garrisons in and around New York reduced in number. The Continentals then sometimes camped farther south, near Bedford, Pound Ridge, or, later, Dobbs Ferry. The British operated from permanent fortifications located around northern Manhattan and adjacent Westchester across the Harlem River and Spuyten Duvil (the area now known as The Bronx). The main water crossing was at Kingsbridge, and, after the conquest of the city, the British established a series of forts and redoubts to protect the crossing and give them a defense perimeter on the mainland. However, when Clinton was required to dispatch many of his troops to Georgia and the Carolinas, he contracted the British defenses, abandoning many on the Westchester side of the Harlem River, but retaining Fort Number Four to maintain a bridgehead—literally—on the mainland side. Northern Manhattan continued to bristle with bastions and redoubts.

Most of these more defensive-minded redeployments occurred in 1780. But, in 1779, British and Tory units actively sought out the Continental troops and patriot militias, ranging deep into Westchester. Consequently, most of the county lay in a shifting no-man's land, leaving the inhabitants vulnerable to attack, robbery, and devastation from one side or the other, through scorched-earth measures. Defending the rebel areas from these raids was a major part of Tallmadge's responsibilities, and one which kept him from launching his own expeditions across the Sound.

Facing aggressive opponents like Banastre Tarleton, the young, ambitious commander of the British Legion, and John Graves Simcoe, capable leader of the Tory Queens Rangers, Tallmadge, with only 200 or so men, changed his camp at different times during the night to prevent being caught off guard and overrun.[2] In addition to his own growing experience—and appreciation of his opponents' abilities—he was also well aware of the fate of the Third Continental Dragoons, the previous year. In the early morning of September 27, 1778, British troops commanded by Major General Charles Grey found them encamped and unwary at Old Tappan, New Jersey. Grey ordered his men to attack only with bayonets, a tactic he had used with devastating effect against Anthony Wayne's men at Paoli, Pennsylvania, during the Brandywine Campaign. Again, he achieved near-total surprise and the ensuing action was more of a massacre than a fight. Of the 104 sleeping dragoons, 36 were killed or wounded and another 37 made prisoner.[3]

Tallmadge and his men also participated in the feint on the east side of the Hudson, which was intended to divert British attention from General "Mad Anthony" Wayne's successful assault on Stony Point in July 1779. The Stony Point offensive was Washington's counterstrike against Clinton's operations in the Lower Hudson region. Interestingly, Wayne ordered the no-shooting, bayonet-only method Grey had used against him and the Third Dragoons. This time the British were on the receiving end of the pointed steel, and their bastion on the Hudson carried and destroyed.

As if military operations were not sufficient for his energies, Tallmadge took the opportunity to check out the political scene. He visited Philadelphia in May, which gave him an opportunity to observe the Continental Congress in session. He was unimpressed, concluding that Congress wasted time with petty matters while letting crucial military issues and necessities slide.[4] His visit also reinforced his earlier opinion that the capital was "the sink of America, in which is huddled and collected Villains and Vermin from every quarter."[5] His attitude, common to many Continental soldiers, derived from his impressions of Congress, as well as the behavior of its residents who seemed driven only by profit and pleasure since the British evacuation.

Shortly after his Philadelphia visit, he became involved in more direct politicking when he was assigned to a committee of officers who were given the task of negotiating with the Connecticut assembly for bonuses for his dragoons. The bonus system, a precursor to that famously used during the Civil War, was used by both states and the Continental Congress to induce volunteering and keep veterans in the ranks. Congress attempted to shift the cost of maintaining regiments to the states that raised them, which led to Tallmadge's journey to Hartford to petition for increased bonuses. The Nutmeg State decided to allot $200 for each trooper, which was still $100 less than the bonus provided to members of the Continental line.[6] At almost the same time, Washington approved a Continental bonus of $200 for fresh recruits.[7] This raised the amount to $400 in United States and Connecticut currency, though the allure of the bounties was badly undercut by rampant inflation.

With the destruction of the British stronghold at Stony Point, the largest Revolutionary operation of the year in the region, the Continental Dragoons resumed their duel with the British units and "Cowboys"—Tory irregulars—operating out of Manhattan and southern Westchester. Not all of these contests ended favorably for the mounted rebels.

In June 1779, Washington suggested that the Second Dragoons establish a base at Bedford in northwestern Westchester to protect the Whig inhabitants from British attacks. Tallmadge thought Bedford, which was approachable by several roads, would be too difficult to defend with only the ninety men available, and the horsemen took up a position at Poundridge a few miles eastwards.[8] Sheldon, Tallmadge, and the other officers found quarters at the home of Major Ebenezer Lockwood, a member of the county Committee of Safety and militia officer. The troopers were barracked in the Presbyterian Meeting House across the road. Unbeknown to the dragoons, Clinton had received an intercepted letter from Washington to Tallmadge, revealing the dragoons' location in Poundridge. The British commander decided to act on the new intelligence and turned to Banastre Tarleton, an aggressive and ambitious cavalry officer who had served well under Simcoe. Together, Clinton and Tarleton planned to inflict on the Second Dragoons the same devastating assault that Grey had unleashed against their compatriots in the 3rd Dragoons the previous year.

At 11:30 p.m. on a stormy July 1, 1779, Tarleton led a large raiding party of about 360 men from their camp at Mile Square (near today's Mount Vernon). Tarleton commanded a mixed force of British regulars and Tory units including the Seventeenth Light Dragoons, Simcoe's

Queens Rangers, and the British Legion. The British raid did not proceed unnoticed. Indeed, Sheldon and Tallmadge had received warning of the British expedition from "the famous Kennicott of the Spies," who arrived on foot with reports of Tarleton's approach.[9] The "Kennicott" in question was Luther Kinnicutt, one of the most active patriot spies in the conflict, and allegedly James Fennimore Cooper's model for the protagonist of his novel, *The Spy*. On hearing Kinnicutt's report, Lockwood prepared to take his family and leave the village, but Sheldon managed to dissuade him, arguing that the British could never move in such wet weather, especially at night. Lockwood stayed put, but took the precaution of keeping his family dressed and their horses bundled and ready to ride.[10]

The next morning, as Sheldon was arranging for the horses to be set out to pasture, a vedette posted three miles from the village rode in "at great speed and reported a large party of cavalry advancing from Bedford."[11] Tarleton was on his way. Sheldon, persisting in his conviction that the British could not travel in the heavy rain, remained untroubled, and assumed that his pickets had seen a party of Moylan's troopers who were scheduled to join him at Poundridge. Tallmadge, who had more intelligence and combat experience than his commander, was less complacent, and took a small party to reconnoiter. About half a mile from Poundridge, he "suddenly met the British advance guard face to face. They had previously been hid from him by the winding of the road and the hills."[12] Immediately recognizing the peril posed by the oncoming British, Tallmadge wheeled his small group around, and galloped back to warn Sheldon and the unprepared dragoons as Tarleton's men screamed, "Surrender! You damned Rebels surrender."[13]

With the British charging hard behind them, the only recourse left to the dragoons could take was flight. "The onset was violent," Tallmadge remembered, "and the conflict carried on principally with the broad sword, until the [British] light infantry appeared on our flanks, when Col. Sheldon found it necessary to retreat."[14] Sheldon, Tallmadge, and most of the Continentals retreated southward on the Stamford Road, though a few followed Lockwood, who must have wondered why he had trusted Sheldon's assurances, eastwards towards Canaan. Though the dragoons were pressed two miles out of the village, some turned to fight when the opportunity arose, and "there were many fights in the wood."[15]

These were, for the most part, individual encounters which passed into local tradition. For example, a dragoon named Hoyt was being closely pursued by a British horseman, cursing and calling for the "damned rebel to surrender," when Hoyt, turning "in his saddle, fetched a backstroke which passed through his pursuer's mouth, cutting his face in nearly two parts from ear to ear."[16]

As the dragoons retreated, sometimes turning and fighting, help was on the way. A detachment of Continental infantry under Major Eli Leavenworth was stationed about a mile from Poundridge. Swelled by local militia, the massing rebels forced Tarleton to call his men back. Leavenworth hoped to cut off the British retreat, but the mounted troops had the advantage of speed and withdrew successfully, but not before torching Lockwood's house and driving off his cattle. As they returned to their camp, Tarleton's forces burned one dwelling in Bedford. Nine days later Simcoe returned with another raiding force and finished the job, burning the entire village.[17]

The British returned to their lines in triumph, with Tallmadge and the militia nipping ineffectively at their heels. Though he had the satisfaction of driving the rebels out of Poundridge—locals wryly dubbed the Pound Ridge-Stamford Road "Sheldon's Race Course"—Tarleton had failed in his primary objective, which was the capture or destruction of the Second Dragoons.[18] Though largely taken unawares, American losses were not heavy. Sheldon later calculated them at eight wounded, with four men and four horses missing. The Americans believed Tarleton lost one man to death, another wounded, and four captured.[19]

Though the American losses in manpower were light, the British captured considerable equipment, including a stand of regimental colors which they found encased in one of the houses. (This standard, along with several others Tarleton took from Revolutionary forces during the southern campaign in 1780–81, returned to the United States in 2007 when one of his descendants sold them at auction.[20])

Tallmadge's personal losses at Pound Ridge amounted to his horse and the 20 guineas he was carrying in his saddlebags. More significantly, the British discovered a letter from Washington to Tallmadge in which the general discussed the young major's espionage operations.

Fortunately, Washington did not know the true identities of the Long Island and Manhattan agents. The general's message, which made

Guidon of the Second Continental Dragoons. *Sons of the Revolution in the State of New York, 1904.*

its way to Clinton, discussed payment for the agents, and the necessity of speedy communication of information. Washington had written:

> I send you Ten guineas for C-----r, -----. His successor (whose name I have no desire to be informed of provided his intelligence is good & seasonably transmitted) should endeavor to hit [?] upon some certain mode of conveying his information quickly, for it is of little avail to be told of things after they have become a matter of public notoriety and known to every body— This new agent [Townsend/Culper, Jr.] should communicate his signature and the private marks by which genuine papers are to be distinguished from counterfeits.[21]

That Washington had agents at work in the area would have been no news to Clinton, who had probably also been aware that Tallmadge was one of his chief intelligence officers. But Washington also mentioned a Manhattan resident named George Higday "who, I am told hath given signal proofs of his attachment to us, & at the same time stands well with the enemy."[22] Washington urged Tallmadge to recruit Higday into his operations but warned that Higday's "name and business should be kept profoundly secret, otherwise we may not only lose the benefits desired from it, but may subject him to some unhappy fate."[23] Indeed, Washington's naming the potential spy was an uncharacteristic blunder, and Higday received an unwelcome visit from the British, though he managed to convince them that some nefarious rebel plot led to his being unjustly identified by the Continental commander.

The fight at Pound Ridge was not the only sizable action Tallmadge and the dragoons were involved in that summer. The Second and Fourth Dragoons, who were also stationed in Westchester in 1779, were sent to the Norwalk area to aid the local militia who were trying to save the town from a large British raiding party led by General William Tyron. The British were too great in number to attack directly, and the dragoons could do no more than cover the retreating militia and fleeing refugees as the British set Norwalk ablaze. The rebels got a taste of success when a 100 light horse from the Second and Fourth Dragoons buttressed with forty infantrymen surprised Oliver Delancey's men near Morrissania. The Continentals took 30 prisoners and considerable plunder before falling back to their lines. The success of the raid also convinced Delancey to pull his force back to a better protected site, near High Bridge.[24]

The success against Delancey strengthened Tallmadge's determination to take the fighting to the enemy. Sheldon received intelligence that the only Crown forces north of the Harlem River were Delancey's Tories, whose security arrangements seemed lax. Tallmadge organized an expedition with 60 horses and 120 infantry and set out into Westchester's Middle Patent—Cowboy territory—hoping to spring a trap between Eastchester and Williamsbridge.[25] His ploy was to draw the British out of the camps by having his horsemen scour the countryside while his infantry waited in concealed positions. While resting at Valentine's Hill below Yonkers on the evening of August 12, Tallmadge discovered that the British, who had their own network of spies and informants, were warned of his approach and had been reinforced. In fact, DeLancey had set up an ambush of his own on the very road Tallmadge was expected to use. Tallmadge countered by falling back, hoping his retreat would entice the British to follow, but they refused the bait, and Tallmadge returned to his base at North Castle, having gained nothing while "my brave Serge Major James Dole was shot by one of the Cow-Boys."[26] Despite Tallmadge's fears for his survival, Dole survived and lived into the nineteenth century. Tallmadge shrugged off his disappointment about the operation and set about organizing his descent on Fort Franklin. (See Chapter 5.)

Spring brought the return of campaigning weather and the inescapable resumption of raid and parry. From their positions in northeast Westchester, the Continental Dragoons watched the British in the lines which stretched from Phillipse Manor in Yonkers, southeastward to Mamaroneck on the Sound. In between was the bandit country prowled by the "Cowboys," Tory guerrillas whose fervor for rustling cattle from patriot farmers and selling them in New York gave them their name.

In the first week of July, Tallmadge led a force of 60 horse and 200 infantry to the vicinity of White Plains, deep in no-man's land.[27] Holding his main force at the ready, he sent out small patrols with which he hoped to lure the British back into an ambush by his main body. But the British were active as well, and on the early morning of July 10, a detachment of redcoats and Tories charged into one of Tallmadge's advanced patrols, forcing them back. Regrouping his men, Tallmadge returned to the site of contact and found about 30 enemy horsemen in Kings Street, a major thoroughfare which ran from the coast near Rye, deep into northern Westchester. Tallmadge tried to trick them into another ambush, but they suspected a trap and stayed in place, awaiting developments. Deciding to attack, Tallmadge sent 16 of his mounted men against the British, who turned and fled after an exchange of pistol fire. Tallmadge's men chased them six miles southward until they crossed the Rye Bridge and into their lines.[28]

Though he had the satisfaction of driving the enemy back into their defenses, he chaffed at his failure to capture their commander, Captain Nathan Frink, a long-term member of the Connecticut Assembly, who had recently turned coat and joined the Tories. "To have taken him would have been a great acquisition," Tallmadge stated, adding that "his Conduct in running from an inferior force (in number) & firing at more than ¼ of a mile Distance, proved him to be a Poltroon."[29]

Tallmadge's expedition remained in the lower part of Westchester for six days, hoping for an opportunity to punish their opponents, but could not maneuver them into a fight "by all my art."[30] Indeed, he was convinced that he had never seen "the Enemy so averse to fighting," and felt able to hold his ground or defeat "all the Horse they had," which he estimated between 300 and 350.[31] Nevertheless, Tallmadge could not operate indefinitely so far from support, and returned to camp on the Croton River, lamenting that the British would secure the abundant forage in the lower sections of the county.

Patrolling the "bandit country" in the Middle Patent, or Neutral Ground (as it was also called), was a relentless cycle of raid, retaliation, and deadly guerrilla encounters, all the while trying to suppress pillaging (or worse) by Tories and opportunistic bandits. Campaigning there in August 1780, Tallmadge claimed it was "the most rascally part of the country that I was ever in." He added that the "Refugees [Tories who had fled rebel territory] sometimes pick off our Sentinels, then firing on our Patroles, & at all times endeavoring to steal our horses."[32] Seldom clothed in uniforms, the Cowboys' guerrilla/plundering tactics left them on the wrong side of the rules of war, and Tallmadge, bitter at their deprivations, was not loathe to apply the penalties. "We have sometimes," he wrote to his friend Wadsworth, "scoured the adjacent Woods and taken a few of the rascals who have been hanged as Spys."[33]

On both Long Island and in Westchester, two of Tallmadge's most persistent opponents were members of the DeLancey family. Following the fall of New York City to the British, Oliver DeLancey raised three battalions of Tories, the third battalion recruited in Queens County, for the "suppression of the present unnatural rebellion."[34] DeLancey's Loyalists were initially intended for the defense of Long Island, although that mission was later altered, and the first and second battalions were transferred to the southern theater in November 1778. The third battalion remained on Long Island, sometimes with a detachment at Jamaica, although the bulk of them faced the rebel raiders from their bastion on Lloyd's Neck. At times, before being sent to the Carolinas, Delancey's first two battalions were posted near High Bridge and Morrisania, where they skirmished with Tallmadge and other patriot outfits. Oliver DeLancey attempted to inculcate a strong sense of professionalism in his regiment, and forbade his men from looting or destroying property.[35] Such was not the case with the other DeLancey unit.

Colonel James DeLancey, a cousin of the general, was commander of the Loyalist Refugee Corps, comprised of men who had fled patriot-held territory in Connecticut and New York, and who had frequently suffered at the hands of the rebels. His men, who roamed the Middle Patent or Neutral Ground, fought a pitiless, ruthless, and vicious war against their enemies. Tallmadge despised them and considered them no better than the Cowboys. This did not make them less formidable. James DeLancey, who had been a prisoner early in the war, and formed his Refugee Corps after being exchanged, was responsible for the burning of Bedford on July 11, 1779.[36] Fearing he would be strung up from the nearest tree if captured, DeLancey seldom rode at the head of his men, and was infamous for remaining out of danger. Nevertheless, he planned the attack on the First Rhode Island Regiment, which resulted in the death of their commander, Colonel Christopher Greene, cousin of General Nathanael Greene, at Pines Bridge, on May 14, 1781.

Not surprisingly, combat between the Refugee Corps and the Continental Dragoons was characterized by the brutality and ferocity common in civil wars where each side considers the other as traitors. In September, Tallmadge received reports of snipers lurking near the rear of his camp. Taking a few men with him, the major drove the enemy into a swamp, where he was able to capture two of them. "One was a Soldier in DeLancey's Corps," he wrote.

> I ordered them immediately put to Death, but their Cries and entreaties prevailed upon me to spare them, for a more exemplary Punishment. One of them has just been tried at our Quarters by a General Court Martial and sentenced to suffer Death, which has been ratified By the Genl.
>
> Last night a man was pursued from Middle Patent, almost to Kingstreet, when he was overtaken, cut badly on both arms, and after being half-hanged a few times; he acknowledged that he came from Newton, in Connecticut, and was bound to join DeLancy's Corps and that 14 more were on their way from the same Place, on the same rascally business. We have taken measures to intercept them, tho' I fear they will evade our utmost Vigilance. If I come across them, I think they will get cut a little.[37]

The "half-hanging" employed by Tallmadge was the eighteenth century equivalent of water boarding. A prisoner unwilling to divulge suspected valuable information was strung up in a noose, not to break his neck and execute him, but to strangle him for a brief time, before letting him down. The process might be repeated until the interrogators either got what they were looking for, or decided there was no actual intelligence to be gained. Both sides resorted to "half hanging," and Tory raiders in Westchester used it to force farmers to divulge the location of their money and valuables. Tallmadge certainly knew of their brutal behavior towards civilians, and showed no qualms about applying it to captured Loyalists.[38] He may have enjoyed the payback. Tallmadge captured two more Tories later, in September. He decided to treat the one who was enrolled in Delancey's Refugee Corps as a prisoner of war, probably because he was uniformed. The other, a guerrilla wearing civilian garb, was executed.[39]

Tallmadge's attitude towards his Tory opponents, formally enlisted or not, only hardened as the war lengthened. He despised them not only for their bushwhacking tactics, but held them largely responsible for the devastation which had been visited on much of Westchester. Observers new to the region were often appalled by the sights which greeted them. In the summer of 1782, a French officer, Clermont-Crevecoeur, noted the county's sorry state. "Casting your eyes over the countryside," he wrote, "you felt very sad, for it revealed all the horrors and cruelties of the English in burned woodlands, destroyed houses, and fallow fields deserted by the owners."[40]

In October 1782, Tallmadge reported capturing four men from DeLancey's Refugee Corps. He argued against including them in any prisoner exchange as their release would "give them a license to pursue their predatory practices."[41] Despite the growing evidence that peace was at hand and the war was coming to an end, the scouring of Westchester by Tories showed little sign of slackening. Expanding on his argument against prisoner exchanges for DeLancey's men, Tallmadge warned headquarters that "unless some very decisive measures are adopted, the lives and the property of the Good inhabitants in the Vicinity of these Lines cannot be protected."[42] He added, of course, that he would follow Washington's instructions regarding the Loyalist captives. Shortly after, he received a response from the commander-in-chief, which he acknowledged, though whether or not Washington agreed to hold the Tories prisoner indefinitely is not known.

Although Colonel Sheldon protested that the move further stretched his under strength command and lowered combat effectiveness, Washington charged the dragoons with yet another duty after the French became established at Newport. The regiment was to station an officer and a number of enlisted men every 15 miles along the Connecticut coast road to provide a communications link between the two armies. The dragoons would act as a Pony Express, conveying messages from Newport to Washington in his Hudson Highlands headquarters and back again. To prevent interception by British soldiers, Tories, or Cowboys, no permanent posts were established in Westchester.[43] Instead, the horsemen employed shifting rendezvous such as Tallmadge often employed to thwart surprise attacks.

But the ever-present shortage of money threatened to interfere with the line of communications as the civilians in the eastern sections of the network balked at accepting Continental currency or promises of future payment for supplies and shelter. Reporting from Fairfield on September 12, 1780, Tallmadge warned that a lack of forage and provisions would force the dragoons to abandon their stations along the Franco-American communications line. The horsemen stationed at the communication posts had been forced to forage for themselves—which meant requisitioning if not outright looting—after the civilians providing supplies refused to continue selling on credit. Tallmadge made personal pleas to the reluctant farmers, and convinced them to continue providing provender until he could lay the matter before Washington. Though he confessed he was sorry "Your Excellency should be troubled with these complaints," he saw Washington as the only person who could rectify the situation.[44] Whether the commander-in-chief was able to arrange acceptable payment for the dragoons' maintenance is not clear, though the line of posts connecting headquarters to Newport seems to have remained intact until the French moved south at the onset of the Yorktown campaign the following year.

But money problems would plague the Continental Army throughout the war. The difficulties Tallmadge faced in arranging payment for his men and civilian suppliers were echoed throughout the rebellious states. With their pay often months in arrears, and tendered in paper money of dubious value, the soldiers were often in desperate straits. The realities of the Revolutionary's financial distress were quickly perceived by the Comte de Rochambeau, commanding the French troops in Newport. "Send us troops and money," he wrote to Vergennes, the French foreign minister in Paris, "but do not depend upon these people or their means. They have neither money nor credit."[45]

Lack of pay, insufficient or inferior food and supplies, worsened the gap between soldiers and civilians in many areas. Civilians, at least in regions not directly affected by the war, often seemed intent only on making money, while resisting the taxes necessary for the army's welfare. "Continentals knew that the public's negligence lay at the heart of the army's hardships," historian Charles Royster observed. "Soldiers saw the agricultural plenty of a country that yielded them little pay and a marginal supply of food. They blamed not just the army's quartermasters and commissaries, but also the populace that had deserted the defenders of the cause."[46]

This dismal monetary situation, combined with what the troops saw as a lack of support from civilians even in pro–Revolutionary areas, often resulted in pillaging on the part of hungry, destitute Continental soldiers. This caused particular hardships on civilians attempting to survive in areas burned by the flames of war, but, wherever it occurred, it deepened mistrust and alienation between the army and the populace. While Tallmadge does not directly state that the dragoons on the Rhode Island–New York communication line engaged in looting, it seems likely given the circumstances. If so, their depredations may have resembled those described in a candid account of written by Lt. Col. Eben Huntington in August 1780. Referring to a foraging operation in New Jersey, just across the Kill Van Kull from Staten Island, Huntington declared that the "rascality of our troops was equal to the British."

> They plundered the inhabitants villainously; and I believe offered that violence for which the British are universally condemned. One from the Pennsylvania line was immediately hung up without ceremony.
>
> You will think it strange that the army at this season should be starving, but I can assure you that the troops previous to the time mentioned ... rec'd no meat.... We are now in a county in which paper money is not worth a shaw. We have nothing but what the Commissary Store affords us & God knows that is poor enough....You must change your Congress that a new system may be formed for your army. They can not exist as an army otherwise.[47]

Such was the reality faced by officers and men of the Continental Army fighting for the liberty and independence of their country. Interestingly, Tallmadge's friend Jeremiah Wadsworth had secured the position of commissary for the French Army, a highly desirable office since the French paid in hard coin. Tallmadge had developed a high regard for

Wadsworth's abilities, and an equally respectful one towards French money. On learning of Wadsworth's selection as agent for the French, he remarked that he wouldn't be surprised "to find thro' the Campaign that they [the French] are fed, and our troops starving."[48] His assessment of the situation was uncomfortably close to the mark.

7

Spycatcher

After two years of running the Culper Ring, Tallmadge had become an experienced, case-hardened intelligence officer. Yet, in early autumn of 1780, the young spymaster found himself embroiled in a different type of espionage affair, perhaps the most notorious of the war—Benedict Arnold's plot to turn over West Point, the key to control of the Hudson River, to the British.

Arnold was one of the heroes of the Revolutionary cause, having served diligently and heroically in the ill-fated Quebec campaign of 1776, and providing crucial, though officially unaccredited, leadership at Saratoga. The precise roots of his treason will probably never be entirely clear, but certainly the lack of what he considered due recognition ate away at his patriotism. He may also have been influenced by his marriage to Peggy Shippan, an attractive woman of Loyalist sentiments. At any rate, he was in contact with the British from May 1779 onwards, providing information about American plans and deployments.[1] Anxious for a position he could sell to the British for a substantial sum, Arnold lobbied Washington for the command of West Point, a post which included control over all American troops between Albany and Manhattan. On July 30, he received the assignment. Apprised of the posting, Sir Henry Clinton agreed to pay him £20,000 for the plans of the fortification which he hoped would allow the British to achieve their long-desired goal of securing the Hudson River. To seal the betrayal of West Point, Arnold insisted on passing the plans of the fortifications directly to his British contact, Major John André.

As part of his plans to ensure André's safe passage through American lines, Arnold wrote Tallmadge at North Castle that if a merchant named John Anderson, André's *nom de guerre*, came into his lines, he was to be escorted immediately to Arnold at West Point.[2] Tallmadge had known Arnold from his student days at Yale, when the future traitor was a businessman in New Haven. Referring to that time from a vantage point of over 40 years, Tallmadge wrote: "I well remember that I was impressed with the belief that he was not a man of Integrity."[3] However, Arnold's exploits at Quebec and Saratoga redeemed him in the eyes of the young dragoon and "we [the officers who had known him] all seemed, as if by common consent, to forget his knavish tricks."[4] In any event, Tallmadge had no reason to suspect the motives of his famous and highly regarded superior. Indeed, he was engaged in official correspondence with him, including information supplied by the Culpers.[5] When he met Arnold in early September, he assured him that if Anderson came his way he would be conveyed to West Point.[6]

On September 23, 1780, on the Tarrytown-Kingsbridge Road, three pro–Revolutionary guerrillas, John Paulding, David Williams, and Isaac Van Wart, captured a rider who called himself John Anderson. He was attempting to slip back to British lines after meeting with Arnold at the home of Joshua Hett Smith, near Haverstraw. The three bushwhackers discovered suspicious papers, including letters from Arnold and a plan of West Point, concealed in Anderson/André's boots. They refused his attempt to bribe them for his freedom, and brought him before Lt. Col. John Jameson of the Second Dragoons, who was the officer in charge at regimental headquarters, near North Castle.[7] The officious and strangely incurious Jameson, reading Arnold's written pass to André, decided to send him on to West Point with a letter of his own, explaining the details of his capture.[8] At the same time, he forwarded the papers found on Anderson/André to Washington, who was returning from a conference with Rochambeau in Newport.

Tallmadge had spent the day reconnoitering along enemy lines as far south as Eastchester, in the southern part of Westchester. When he arrived at headquarters that evening and was briefed on the situation, he was astounded by Jameson's decision to release André and allow him to return with the explanatory letter to Arnold. In what he later described as a "private and most friendly manner," he pointed out the "glaring inconsistency" of sending André on his way before Washington was apprised of the developments and could make his own determination.[9] As an experienced intelligence officer, Tallmadge knew the map and letters went beyond mere suspicion, and were, in fact, incriminating.[10] Tallmadge offered to retrieve both Anderson/André and the letter to Arnold, but Jameson balked. Tallmadge then suggested a course of action "which I wished to adopt, offering to take the whole responsibility on myself, and which he deemed too perilous to permit."[11] In his *Memoir*, Tallmadge does not reveal the nature of his suggestion that left Jameson "agitated." However, the manuscript of his "Reminiscences" contains a note stating, "This measure as stated to me by his granddaughter, Mrs. George L. Balch, was the capture of Arnold O. Crane, copiest."[12] Reluctantly, under Tallmadge's continued protests, Jameson agreed to have the prisoner returned, but stubbornly persisted in forwarding the letter—which revealed the discovery of the West Point plot—to Arnold. Tallmadge was baffled and frustrated by Jameson's punctilious behavior, but had to content himself with Anderson/André's return.

Once Anderson/André was back at dragoon headquarters, Tallmadge assumed custody of the prisoner. Before setting out for dragoon headquarters, he penned a short note to New York's governor, George Clinton, informing him that the patriot forces had taken a prisoner calling himself John Anderson "who was found with information of the utmost consequence & thus most dangerous to this army."[13] The items Tallmadge listed in Anderson's possession included "an accurate map of West Point & its Dependencies ... the nature & strength of the works... & the most probable mode of attack to carry [the base] and a concise account of our present military."[14] Summing up the situation, Tallmadge concluded: "I think we have in him a very important man."[15]

Tallmadge took custody of the prisoner and conveyed him to Sheldon's headquarters at Salem with a strong party of dragoons. Observing Anderson's demeanor, especially his manner of turning on his heel while pacing, Tallmadge determined that he had been "bred to arms." For his part, Anderson/André became increasingly anxious as the danger of his situation became clear, and he finally requested leave to write to Washington. Tallmadge agreed, and after André handed him the letter which he signed with his true name and rank, his worst fears were confirmed. "If the Letter of Information had not gone to Gen. Arnold, I should not have hesitated for a moment in my purpose," he later recollected, indicating that Arnold's arrest had indeed been his "perilous" suggestion, "but this I knew must reach him before I could possibly get to West Point."[16] Indeed, as Tallmadge later observed, Jameson's letter "was the first Information that this Arch Traitor recd that his plan was blown up."[17] Upon receiving Jameson's missive, Arnold had just enough time to flee his headquarters and make his way to the safety of the British warship *Vulture*, riding the tides in the lower Hudson.

Tallmadge and 100 of his men escorted André to West Point, and then to Tappan, where Washington had convened a court-martial headed by General Nathanael Greene. Washington himself did not participate in the proceedings though he was present in Tappan, where he temporarily established his headquarters. Nor did he ever interview or meet André. When Tallmadge first arrived at West Point with the prisoner, he asked his commander if he wanted to see André, and Washington declined.[18] Washington's motives cannot be determined, but as a man with a deeply rooted sense of what was honorable, he likely felt it was beneath the status of an army commander to dirty his hands with an enemy spy.

While traveling south to Tappan for the court martial, first by barge to Stony Point and then on horseback to the small village, André asked Tallmadge what he thought was the likely outcome. Tallmadge then related the story of his Yale classmate, Nathan Hale, who was executed by the British as a spy in 1776, predicting "similar would be your fate."[19] André's assumption of civilian garb on his return through Westchester to New York—pressed on him by Arnold and provided by Joshua Hett Smith—stripped him of the protection afforded by military uniform and rank, and he was sentenced to death as a spy.[20] The execution was carried out on October 2, 1780, with André in his full-dress uniform, which had been sent under a flag of truce from New York.

Tallmadge was in charge of André most of the time after his capture and became much taken with the British spy's polished, urbane, and engaging character. Some have argued that André was as wily as he was debonair, and he deliberately undertook to play his captors. He began by immediately describing the militia men who took him prisoner as freebooters who discovered the incriminating documents while searching for loot. He asserted that they would have released him if he could have provided more money.[21] Tallmadge swallowed this part of André's story entirely. André then proceeded to ingratiate himself to the American officers in charge. He may have hoped he could extricate himself from his predicament by winning an exchange, or even a release. In this, he was doomed to disappointment. But he clearly won the sympathy and affections of Tallmadge and many of his fellow officers.

Indeed, the veteran dragoon and spy master was deeply moved by the prospect of André's hanging. In a letter to Samuel Webb, he wrote:

> By heavens, Col. Webb, I never saw a man whose fate I foresaw, whom I so sincerely pitied. He Is a young fellow of the greatest accomplishments, and was the Prime Minister [aide-de-camp] of Sir Harry [Sir Henry Clinton, commander of the British Army in New York] on all occasions. He has unbosomed his heart to me, and indeed, let me Know almost every motive for his actions so fully since he came out on his late mission that he has endeared himself to me exceedingly. Unfortunate man! He will undoubtedly suffer death to-morrow, and tho' he knows his fate, seems as cheerful as if he were going to an assembly. I am sure he will go to the gallows less tearful for his fate, and with less concern than I shall behold the tragedy. Had he been tried by a Court of Ladies, he is so *genteel, handsome, polite* a young gentleman that I am confident they would have acquitted him.
>
> But enough of poor *André*, who tho' he dies lamented, falls justly.[22]

On the day of execution, Tallmadge was among the officers who led André up the small hill away from the village which led to the place of execution. Two battalions of about 500 men formed a square around the gallows, holding back an "immense multitude" of civilians who had gathered to witness the spectacle.[23] Having clung to the hope that he might die by firing squad, the prisoner was brought up short by the sight of the gibbet. Underneath stood a wagon on which was placed a blackened coffin. A grisly-looking executioner, who had smeared his face with grease to obscure his identity, intensified the macabre atmosphere of the event. André climbed up on his coffin, and pulled the rope down on his neck, drawing the knot above his right ear. He blindfolded himself with one handkerchief while another was used to bind his arms. When asked his last words he replied: "I have nothing more to say than this: that I would have you gentlemen bear me witness that I die like a brave man."[24] Brigadier John Glover, the officer of the day, gave the command, the wagon moved off, and André's body dropped "with a tremendous swing." After a sudden gasp, the assembled troops and civilians fell silent. André's body twitched at the end of the rope, and it seemed some time before he was totally still.[25]

Two days after the execution Tallmadge sent his own account of the event to his friend and mentor, Jeremiah Wadsworth.

[André's] conduct was unparalleled on the occasion. He went death with a smile, cheerfully marching to the place of execution, and biding with friends & those who had been with him farewell. He called me to him a few minutes before he swung off, and expressed his Gratitude to me for my Civilities in such a way, & so cheerfully bid adieu that I was obliged to leave the parade in a flood of tears. I cannot say enough of his fortitude—unfortunate youth; I wish Arnold had him in his place.[26]

Late in life Tallmadge stated that "no Circumstances during that eventful period made a deeper Impression on my mind than those which related to *Arnold*, the *Traitor*, & *Major André*, the Sufferer."[27] In both his correspondence and his *Memoir*, he returned again to the theme of André's engaging personality, and his fondness for him.

I became so deeply attached to Major André that I can remember no instance in which my affections were so fully absorbed by any man. When I saw him swinging under the gibbet, it seemed for a time as if I could not support it. All the spectators seemed to be overwhelmed by the affecting spectacle, and

Self-portrait of John André, drawn the night before his execution, October 1, 1780. *Yale University Art Gallery.*

many were suffused in tears. There did not appear to be one hardened or indifferent spectator in all the multitude.[28]

Such sentiments were not unique to Tallmadge. They were widely shared within the officer corps—though not by enlisted men. Indeed, most of Washington's officers—as well as the commander-in-chief himself—saw in the urbane and accomplished André a reflection of the type of gentleman-officer they assumed themselves to be.[29] Under different circumstances, the Continental Army command would likely have arranged an exchange for the captive who had captivated them. However, Arnold's treason had sent shock waves through the army, and the non-commissioned officers and privates looked suspiciously at the officer corps for signs of further disloyalty. Additionally, almost all enlisted men knew members of their own rank who had been sent to the gallows or firing squad for far lesser offenses than spying. Consequently, any sign of weakness or leniency was likely to have provoked a hostile reaction among the rank and file, with unfathomable consequences. However much they might sympathize with André, Washington and the board of officers he appointed to try the British courier understood the necessity for imposing the ultimate penalty. Alexander Hamilton, another of Washington's bright young men, laid his finger on the crux of the matter when he observed that either Arnold or André had to swing, and "the former was out of our power."[30]

Not all of Tallmadge's friends and colleagues shared his conflicted feelings and anguished sentiments towards the executed British espionage agent. From Setauket, where he was harassed, threatened, and plundered by the British and their supporters, Woodhull was less sympathetic. "I am sorry for the death of Major André," he wrote Tallmadge, "but," he pointedly noted, "better so than lose the Post; he was seeking your ruin."[31]

Perhaps the greatest mystery in the entire André-Arnold affair was the obstinate refusal of Lt. Col. Jameson to call back the letter informing Arnold of André's capture. The circumstances themselves were more than suspicious, and Tallmadge heatedly urged Jameson to wait until Washington had a chance to see the evidence before forwarding anything to Arnold. But the logic of Tallmadge's course did not persuade Jameson. Tallmadge, who had been baffled and frustrated by his superior's stance, discovered more about the situation in later life when he began a correspondence with Jared Sparks.

Monument at the site of André's execution and original burial place, Tappan, New York. *Author's Collection.*

Sparks, who was compiling a volume of Washington's letters, was particularly interested in any fresh light Tallmadge could shine on the conspiracy. In the course of exchanging information, Sparks informed Tallmadge that Jameson had written to Washington on September 27, 1780, apologizing for sending the letter to Arnold. Jameson attempted to explain that he had not expected the *Vulture* to be so far up the Hudson, though Continental scouts must have reported it. He also contended that Tallmadge and the other officers present agreed with him that sending the warning letter to Arnold was the proper course until Washington, en route from Newport, could be consulted. This was likely the first time that Tallmadge had heard of Jameson's letter, and he had already written his version of the events in the memoir he was in the process of completing. He totally refuted Jameson's account in his reply to Sparks. He went on to say that "altho' my views & Col Jameson's differed so widely concerning the disposal of John Anderson...I never entertained a Doubt of his Patriotism & Devotedness to his Country's Cause. In sending the Prisoner & his letter of Information to Arnold, his *Head* was in fault & not his *heart*. His confidence in his Commanding General outweighed the Influence of prudent precautionary measures."[32]

As for Washington's reaction to Jameson's apology, he accepted the explanations for the colonel's conduct, but excoriated it as evidence of "egregious folly, or bewildered conception."[33] The Continental commander, infuriated by both the plot and Arnold's escape, added that Jameson "seemed lost in astonishment, and not to know what he was doing."[34]

Tallmadge's assumption that he and André shared the status of gentleman was held by most Continental Army officers. The distinction not only led them to consider themselves as equals to their British counterparts, it formed the core of their sense of honor, a word which encompassed their self-esteem and integrity, as well as a need for public recognition and approbation. "Honor," in the words of Revolutionary historian Charles Royster, "was the most precious possession of a gentleman. It had no degrees—a gentleman could not lose a little honor."[35]

Yet the Continental Army officers were often insecure about their gentlemanly status. Many had come from modest or middle-class origins, and they were aware that their British counterparts often sneered at them as provincials or bumpkins. Their anxiety about their self-assumed gentility resulted in a heightened vulnerability to slights—real or perceived—any actions or words which declared or implied that they were deficient in quality. The hyper-sensitivity to criticism, or diminution or questioning of their status, resulted in an astounding rise in dueling among Continental Army officers. Significantly, the vogue for dueling appeared after the Valley Forge winter, when, under Baron von Steuben's tutelage, the officers came to see themselves as professionals as well as gentlemen—a separate class of men. In any event, the "duel became almost a cult in the Continental Army" as officers turned to deadly, formalized methods of resolving supposedly unbearable slights while proving their social status.[36]

Though the Continental Articles of War forbade dueling, commanders ordinarily refrained from either discouraging or punishing the contests of honor. The Continental officers' passion for dueling was not lost on foreign observers, including the Revolutionaries' French allies.

In 1779, Gerard de Reyneval, French minister to the United States reported: "The rage for dueling here has reached an incredible and scandalous point.... This license is regarded as the appendage of liberty."[37]

Tallmadge probably saw, and certainly knew, of many duels. But he was among those who were appalled by the practice, condemning it as wasteful of life and detrimental to the cause. Almost 50 years after the war, he concluded his memoir of the War of Independence with a denunciation of resorting to the sword or pistol as a way of settling disputes.

> Among the vices and false pursuits to which military life is liable, perhaps none is more prominent than *dueling*. Having early imbibed this sentiment, that no man had a right to expose his life in this manner, I openly avowed my opinion, and yet amidst all the clashing of interests and opinions to which we were exposed, I never was called upon to defend my honor by this heaven-daring resort. I always determined that I would never be guilty of this *murderous sin*, and yet I am not conscious that any man thought me to be a coward. For this early imbibed opinion and subsequent restraining conduct, I desire most humbly and devoutly to adore and bless God.[38]

Of course, it would have been absurd to charge a man with Tallmadge's combat record with cowardice. What Tallmadge might actually have done if called out, with his sense of honor clashing with his sense of sin, is impossible to know. Fortunately, he was never called upon to choose.

Returning to Westchester after the hanging, Tallmadge found his duties had become very "arduous, the late events having excited much rage on the part of the enemy. What with *cow-boys, skinners* and *refugees* [Tories], we had as much as we could turn our hands to, to keep from being waylaid and fired upon from thickets, and stony eminences, about Salem, Northcastle, and White Plains. Indeed, it was not an unusual thing to have our sentinel fired upon from parties who would crawl up in the darkness of night, and then disappear."[39]

Tallmadge was also concerned with his agents across the Sound. André's capture and the revelations of Arnold's treason sent waves of anxiety through Culper Ring, including its master operator. Tallmadge confessed that when Arnold turned traitor he "felt for a time extremely anxious for some trusty friends in N. York, but as I never gave their names to him, he was not able to discover them, tho' I believe he tried hard to find them out."[40] Nevertheless, Arnold's knowledge of Continental intelligence, combined with other sources available to the British, led them to redouble their attempts to roll up the ring, and British and Tory patrols intensified their activities across Long Island.

As the British redoubled their efforts to detect the Continental agents, the apprehensive Long Island-Manhattan spies reduced their activities, though they did not completely go "dark"—silent. Woodhull continued to forward information about enemy movements on Long Island, which played a significant role in Tallmadge's subsequent operations. He also warned Tallmadge to beware of supposed patriot George Howell, of Southampton, who was a double agent operating in Connecticut.[41] On October 17, the spymaster wrote Washington that the unnamed "person is a very dangerous man among us and from the charges adduced against him by C----- should suppose he might be apprehended."[42] He did let his commander know that General Parsons had given the "person" a pass to cross the Sound with Caleb Brewster, but Howell has "since been prohibited agreeable to your Excellency's order to me. I am confident General Parsons was much deceived in this man."[43] Tallmadge intended to arrest Howell, though the ultimate outcome of the incident is unknown. Whatever threat he posed was blunted by Woodhull and his commander. The incident further validates Tallmadge's wariness about Parsons' judgment in cross–Sound matters.

Arnold's defection coincided with a major British troop movement. On October 16, General Alexander Leslie embarked with several British and German regiments, and Washington, fearful that this signaled an attack in the Hudson region, turned to Tallmadge for information. "Be pleased to find an appointment as soon as possible of obtaining the following information, with accuracy," he wrote. The commander-in-chief needed to know the number and units involved in the British operation, and whether or not Clinton accompanied it. He was also anxious to find out if the British had sent new detachments to New York to replace those who were involved in the expedition. Lastly, he pressed his chief intelligence officer to discover the "manner the British Army is at present disposed—designating as nearly as possible the Corps which lay at the different places [.] I am anxious to receive intelligence of the foregoing particulars, and you will oblige me by obtaining it speedily."[44]

Whether or not Tallmadge was able to squeeze the Culpers for fresh intelligence, it soon became clear that Leslie's expedition was sailing southward in hopes that victory in the Carolinas would win the war by securing the most valuable (in terms of profitable products) of Britain's North American colonies. Clinton remained in New York, and though the heavy fighting of the war would henceforth be done in the South, the ongoing campaign of thrust, parry, raid, and menace continued unabated in New York.

Nothing if not brazen, Arnold sent a letter to Tallmadge, inviting him to desert the American cause and joins a new Tory unit, the American Legion, which he was recruiting.

> As I know you to be a man of sense, I am convinced you are by this time fully of the opinion that the real interest and Happiness of America consists in a reunion with Great Britain, to which effect I have taken a commission in the British Army, and invite you to join me with as many men as you can bring over with you. If you think proper to embrace my offer, You shall have the same rank you now hold in the Cavalry I am about to raise. I shall make use of no arguments to convince you to take the step which I think is right. Your own good sense will suggest anything I can say on the subject. I will only add that the British Fleet has just arrived with a very large contingent of troops.
>
> B. Arnold, New York, October 25, 1780, To Major Tallmadge.[45]

Exactly why Arnold thought he could turn Tallmadge remains unclear. Possibly, he thought that an effective and energetic officer like Tallmadge had experienced the same frustrations that pushed Arnold into treason. Or he may simply have hoped to score more points with his new masters by recruiting an aggressive dragoon officer who was Washington's major spyrunner to boot. Whatever his reasoning, he misjudged the man. Tallmadge certainly resented the ineptitude of Congress, the constant struggle to pay and equip troops, and the often-tepid support for the struggle by allegedly patriotic civilians. Nevertheless, his commitment to the Revolutionary cause was unswerving. He was both perplexed and, by his own account, "mortified" at finding himself the recipient of an offer to turncoat from the Revolution's most infamous traitor, the one he blamed for the death of the gallant André.[46] In any event, Tallmadge scorned Arnold's blandishments, and took the letter to Washington "who consoled me abundantly on the occasion."[47] Washington knew his man well, and Arnold did not.

8

Raider

The heightened British activity on Long Island and Westchester, an almost spasmodic reaction to André's execution, subsided with the advent of colder weather. Freed from immediate concerns with patrolling the shifting lines on the mainland, Tallmadge began to revisit his plans for Long Island. Earlier in the year, when the warm months—the campaigning season—returned, Tallmadge's eagerness to attack the foe on his native soil intensified. Writing from Bedford on July 18, 1780, Tallmadge reported that 40 British ships were "constantly passing and repassing the Sound transporting ... supplies."[1] He specifically identified Huntington and Lloyd's Neck as the major collection point for British supplies taken on Long Island, and suggested a naval expedition to destroy it. Moreover, he had obtained intelligence indicating the British planned to send troops into eastern Suffolk County to "sweep off their [patriots] Cattle, Provisions &c." Tallmadge suggested launching raids into the county to disrupt the British and Tories, and give the pro–Revolutionary population the excuse to hide their cattle. "Suffolk County," Tallmadge reminded Washington, "is in our interest, & would willingly assist us, but must have some colour for their conduct like compulsion, so long as we do not possess enough of the Island to protect them."[2] Combining circumspection and ardor, Tallmadge told his commander that if "any plan of this kind should be tho't on" he could recommend places for a landing, advise how far westward the raiders might strike, and concluded by stating, "I should be happy to serve in this or any other Expedition your Excellency may think me best qualified for."[3] But the opportune moment failed to appear, and he was soon absorbed in the Arnold-André conspiracy. But in the late fall, Tallmadge again turned his attention across the Sound.

While Washington pondered Tallmadge's suggestions, the young officer began devising plans to launch a major raid on Long Island. The question was exactly where this would take place. Tallmadge knew that the British had constructed a blockhouse east of Huntington, though the 150 men posted there were said to be vigilant. Woodhull thought an attack on Fort Franklin a better prospect.[4] Tallmadge, who had received a detailed map of Fort Franklin the previous August, rejected the suggestion, likely concluding that the fortification was too great an obstacle with his available forces. Instead, his attention shifted southeastward, across Long Island.

It was Woodhull who probably first alerted him about a new British base under construction on the South Shore.[5] Soon, Tallmadge was directing his agents to gather up-to-date information on Fort St. George, as the British dubbed their new stronghold. Located near Mastic on the Great South Bay, the fort was built on the estate of dispossessed patriot judge William Smith. Planned as the easternmost British stronghold, and erected at the point where the Carmen's River flowed into the Great South Bay, Fort St. George was perfectly situated for the collection of supplies and provisions as well as providing a base for British forces gathering provender in eastern Suffolk. One of Tallmadge's informants, William Booth, sent a plan of the fort, which consisted of a triangle-shaped stockade built of 12-foot-tall pickets enclosing several acres. Two strong, well-built houses and a bastion anchored the angles of the stronghold.[6] The interior bastion consisted of a high earthen wall protected by a moatlike ditch, which, in turn, was encircled by an abatis. The fort contained embrasures for six guns, but only two were mounted.[7]

Benjamin Tallmadge, by John Trumbull, c. 1783. *Sons of the Revolution in the State of New York, 1904.*

Armed with this intelligence,

91

Tallmadge rode to Washington's headquarters and presented him with a plan to reduce the fort. The commander-in-chief listened with interest, but ultimately decided the undertaking was too risky. Tallmadge and his men would have to cross the Sound, avoiding British naval patrols and Tory raiders, and then march across Long Island from the north to the south shore, all the while avoiding detection. Then, after taking the fort they would have to retrace their steps, evade any British units attempting to intercept them, and recross the Sound to safety.

Though disappointed, Tallmadge did not abandon his plans. While Washington's description of the dangers the expedition faced were real, Tallmadge likely believed the audacity of the raid worked in its favor. Undeterred, he set about to obtain further information in order to "overcome [Washington's] prudent course of operations" by convincing the commanding general that the foray was worth the risk and could be carried out successfully.[8] Consequently, in late October he conducted a personal reconnaissance on Long Island. Who sheltered him, or acted as guides on this and other scouting missions he undertook on Long Island, was something Tallmadge never revealed.[9] Back on his native turf, the young major made his way south from the Setauket area to the south shore. Reconnoitering around Mastic, he found the fort completed and already operating as a British supply depot. On his return across the island, Tallmadge discovered that the British had accumulated a large quantity of hay and forage at Coram in the center of Suffolk County, presenting an inviting second target for his proposed raid.

Having succeeded in penetrating deep into British occupied territory and returning unscathed, he renewed his proposal to Washington. This time the commander gave his approval. Tallmadge's personal scouting and the opportunity to deliver two blows against the British apparently caused the general to change his mind. Interestingly, though Tallmadge saw Fort St. George as the most desirable target, Washington thought otherwise. "The destruction of the forage collected for the use of the British army at Coram upon Long Island is of much consequence, that I should advise the attempt to be made," he wrote his eager subordinate. He added, "If the party at Smith's house [Ft. St. George] can be attempted without frustrating the other design, or running too great a hazard, I have no objection. But you must remember that this is only a secondary object, and, in all cases, you will take the most prudent means

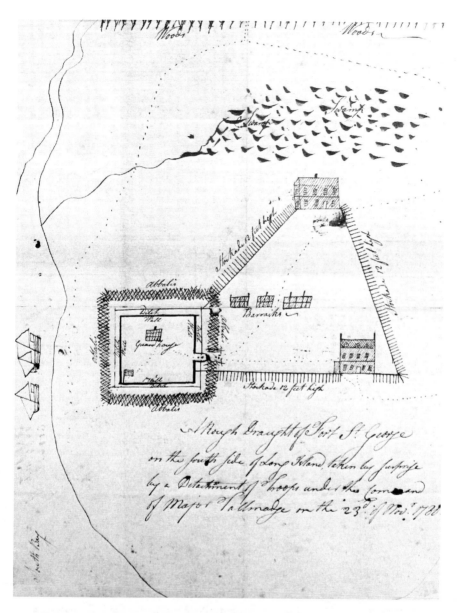

Map of Fort St. George by Benjamin Tallmadge, c. 1780. The fort, which sat on the shore of the Great South Bay, was bordered by woods and swamplands on its northern edge. The guard house, closest to the water, was connected to the other two houses by a 12-foot-high stockade. Abbatis surrounded the outer perimeter of the guard house, which was further protected by an interior ditch and wall. More than one version of this map exists. *Connecticut State Historical Society, Hartford, Connecticut.*

to secure a retreat."[10] Tallmadge had no doubt he could accomplish both objectives, and on November 16, 1780, he received the written go-ahead for the expedition.

It took almost a week to complete the preparations, and at four p.m. on November 21, Tallmadge marched a little under 100 of his dismounted dragoons—specifically selected for the operation—from their camps at Stamford to the awaiting whaleboats at nearby Fairfield, and embarked on the perilous voyage across the Sound. The crews tacked eastward across 20 miles of water to avoid the concentration of British troops concentrated in and around Huntington, and landed at Old Man's (Mt. Sinai) about five hours later.[11] A heavy rain forced Tallmadge to delay the cross-island march, and the raiders huddled under the cover of their boats which had been drawn up and hidden near the shore. The next evening, after detaching 20 men to guard the boats, Tallmadge led the remainder of the dragoons across Long Island, drawing within two miles of Fort St. George by three in the morning.

Tallmadge's plan called for dividing his force into three units. Two small detachments "under the command of subalterns of high spirit," Lt. Jackson and "Mr. Simmons," were ordered to get as near to the fort as possible without being seen and then remain in hiding until the main body—which Tallmadge would personally lead—began its attack. Simmons was detailed with preventing any of the defenders from escaping once the assault began. The van of Tallmadge's column was made up of a group of axmen under Caleb Brewster whose job was to hack an opening in the wooded stockade.[12] Borrowing a tactic from Anthony Wayne's successful attack on Stony Point, the aggressive dragoon leader ordered his men not to load their muskets. Fort St. George was to be taken with cold steel.

At four a.m., before the first flickers of dawn broke over the Great South Bay, Tallmadge sent his men forward. A British sentry shouted out, "Who comes there?' and fired. But, Tallmadge later reported to Washington, before the smoke from his gun "had cleared his vision, my sergeant, who marched by my side, reached him with the bayonet, and prostrated him."[13] At the sound of the firing, Tallmadge's supporting columns sprang from cover, and shouting, "Washington and Glory!" the surging Americans "seemed to vie with each other to enter the fort."[14] In less than ten minutes the raiders had taken the main part of the fort, and an exultant Tallmadge stood in the center of the grand parade, surveying the scene.

The stunned British in the fort struck their colors, but the defenders in one of the large houses fired a volley at the Americans, who quickly loaded their weapons, setting off an exchange of musketry. Tallmadge led his men to the house, and set Brewster and his pioneers to work, smashing through the wooden doors. The axmen made short work of the entrances and the Continentals burst through the shattered doorway. "As soon as the troops could enter," Tallmadge recounted, "the confusion and conflict was great. A considerable portion of those who had fired after the fort was taken, and the colors had been struck, were thrown headlong from the windows of the second story to the ground. Having forfeited their lives by the usages of war, all would have been killed had I not ordered the slaughter to cease."[15] With the British survivors taken as prisoners, the commandos turned their attention to a vessel along the Carman's River, loaded with forage and stores (including rum wine, sugar and glass) which was frantically attempting to get under sail. The dragoons trained the fort's guns on the ship, upon which the vessel's crew quickly surrendered.

As the sun rose, the raiders set fire to the fort's buildings, stockade, and the ship. Though Tallmadge reported capturing a "considerable Quantity of ammunition & Arms," he was forced to destroy most of them since his fatigued men could not carry them off.[16] At about eight a.m. the patriot raiders began retracing their route to Mt. Sinai. The Tory prisoners, tied two and two together, were forced to carry some of the confiscated clothing that Tallmadge intended to distribute to his men. As they neared the center of the island, Tallmadge sent the bulk of his troops and the prisoners under Captain Edgar ahead to a prearranged position, where he would join them later. Meanwhile, he and Brewster took about 12 men on horses which had been captured at Fort St. George, and galloped off towards the British forage dump at Coram. Tallmadge achieved total surprise again, and the Americans quickly seized the encampment and torched the accumulated supplies, which British sources later calculated at 100 tons, though Tallmadge believed that more than 300 tons had been collected there.[17] About two hours later Tallmadge and his men rejoined Edgar, and his reunited command resumed their march to the north shore. The local militia, controlled by the British or Tories, attempted a halfhearted pursuit, but, as Tallmadge put it, very "prudently avoided coming near us," though some fired ineffectually from a distance. By four o'clock, the dragoons and their prisoners, with spoils in tow, set off across Long Island Sound for Fairfield where they arrived sometime around ten at night.[18]

The operation was an unqualified success. Tallmadge's bold stroke had resulted in the elimination of a major British stronghold, the loss of at least one ship and supplies, as well as the destruction of forage that had been much needed by the British in Manhattan. Tallmadge tallied British losses as seven killed or wounded, most "of the latter mortally."[19] His prisoner returns listed one "half pay" lieutenant colonel, the commandant of Fort St. George, one "half pay" captain, a lieutenant, a surgeon, and 50 enlisted men.[20] In exchange, there was only one wounded American, who was safely brought back to Connecticut.

Tallmadge's raid no doubt raised the morale and hopes of the pro–Revolutionary inhabitants of Long Island, especially Suffolk County,

Monument to the Coram phase of the November 23, 1780, raid. Tallmadge was a major at the time. *Author's Collection.*

languishing under British occupation. Washington lavished praise on the operation, emphasizing that he "was particularly well pleased with the destruction of the Hay which must, I should conceive, be severely felt by the Enemy at this time," a reference to the onset of winter.[21] "I beg of you to accept my thanks for your judicious planning and spirited execution of this business," the commanding general continued, "and that you will offer them to the officers and men who shared the honors of the Enterprise with you."[22] Tallmadge received Washington's approbations "with the most singular satisfaction," pledging to "be particular in making known the favourable Sentiments imployed by the Commander in Chief to the detachment which I had the honour to Command."[23] The Continental Congress issued an official resolution lauding the participants of the Mastic-Coram raid:

> While Congress are sensible of the patriotism, courage and perseverance of the officers and privates of their regular forces as well as the militia throughout the United States, and of the military conduct of the principal Commanders in both, it gives them pleasure to be so frequently called upon to confer marks of distinction and applause for the enterprises which do honour to the profession of arms and claim a high rank among military achievements. In this light they view the enterprise against Fort St. George, on Long Island, planned and conducted with wisdom and great gallantry by Major Tallmadge, of the Light Dragoons, and executed with intrepidity and Complete success by the officers and soldiers of his detachment. Ordered, therefore, That Major Tallmadge's report to the Commander-in-Chief be published, with the preceding minute, as a tribute to distinguished merit and in testimony of the sense Congress entertains of this brilliant service.[24]

Tallmadge's descent on Fort St. George and Coram stung the British, who naturally took a different view of it than Congress and Washington. On December 2, 1780, *Rivington's Gazette*, a leading Loyalist publication in Manhattan, ran an article on the raid which probably drew (at least partly) on testimony from Long Island Tories, and the wounded survivors at Mastic whom Tallmadge had paroled and left behind. On the other hand, the *Gazette* frequently printed both rumors and outright fabrications designed to defame the rebels and buck up the declining Loyalist morale. Rivington correctly identified Tallmadge as the expedition's commander, and named a few other principals, such as Heathcoat Muirson, whom Tallmadge had singled out for praise in his report to Washington, as well as Setauket refugees Benjamin Strong and Caleb

Brewster, perhaps the Revolutionaries' most prominent whaleboat warrior. The Tory account credited the raiders' ability to escape detection to the aid they received from "their old friends on the Island."[25]

Rivington described the British garrison at Fort St. George as "a respectable body of [Loyalist] refugees from Rhode Island and vicinity." Refugees or not, they were enrolled in an American Loyalist unit, as their armament and Tallmadge's listing of their ranks attest. The article proceeded to charge Tallmadge's men with atrocities, including shooting, bayoneting and beating a Tory "in the very act of imploring quarter," who subsequently died of his wounds. Four other "refugees" were listed as wounded but recovering, among whom was "a poor woman ... barbarously wounded through both breasts."[26] Charges of atrocities were common during the Revolution, and whether or not any occurred at Mastic—and Tallmadge listed no women in his report—is difficult to assess.

Tallmadge and the raiders who fought at Mastic and Coram were unaware, and possibly never knew, that one small incident did mar their otherwise-stellar performance. A few of the men left to guard the whaleboats at Mt. Sinai took advantage of their situation to indulge themselves in a bit of freebooting. In 1786, Joshua Davis of Fairfield, who was stationed under John Sutton with the boats, revealed that Sutton and David Dickinson went to James Smith's home, took a quantity of goods from him "and Secreted them on board Sutton's boat for fear Tallmadge's men would discover them."[27] Sutton then sent Davis back to Smith's to obtain a blanket, which he claimed to have bought. Davis returned with the blanket and stashed it with the other items taken from Smith "& all was performed before Lt. Brewster returned to Said boat."[28] No doubt, in the excitement and exultation of reembarking for Connecticut, and the subsequent landing of the troops, prisoners, and contraband seized at Mastic, Sutton was able to spirit away his plunder without notice. However minor, the robbery of Smith makes clear that the principal officers and men were not involved and would have prevented it, testifying to Tallmadge's effective discipline and leadership—not to mention his empathy for the inhabitants of his distressed homeland. It also explains why Long Islanders felt apprehension at the presence of armed parties from Connecticut, even when they were ostensibly (and, in this case, genuinely) on their side.

General Oliver DeLancey, who commanded the British garrisons closest to Mastic, was especially enraged by the raid. His first measure was to ask for reinforcements to secure more effective control of Suffolk County. When he was informed that none were available he vented his frustration by destroying the homes of some well-known Whigs, imprisoning the men, and turning the women and children out to fend for themselves.[29]

Following his raid on Fort St. George, Tallmadge sent the prisoners to West Point while he encamped his men in winter quarters around Simsbury and Windsor, Connecticut. But he remained preoccupied with Long Island, and often rode to the coast hoping he "might find some spot where the common enemy might be annoyed."[30] On a clear day, Tallmadge could observe unconquered Fort Franklin on Lloyd's Neck, defiantly projecting British power in western Suffolk.

But, as usual, winter was dominated by the necessary and frustrating need to recruit, rebuild, and replenish. While his men went into quarters, first in Litchfield County and then western Massachusetts, Tallmadge joined other Connecticut officers in what was becoming the annual petitioning of the Connecticut assembly to raise the troops' pay to offset the continual depreciation of Continental currency. Again, the army officers met with success and the legislators agreed to the pay increases, the money for which was to be garnered from the confiscation of Tory-owned estates.[31]

Tallmadge remained busy with the outfitting of his men well into the New Year. On January 16, he reported that the troops were short of virtually all necessary equipment—swords, pistols, bayonets, cartridge boxes, curry combs, and horse blankets.[32] The lack of supplies, and uncertainty over the amount and worth of currency, continued to lower the morale of the soldiers. There were other problems as well. With the reorganization of the regiment into legions, many of the men who thought they were enlisting in the horse service found themselves assigned as infantry, and some felt they had been deceived by the recruiters. Regimental returns in early 1780 showed the dragoons had suffered only three casualties, but lost another 21 from dischargers. Even worse, 39 men deserted.[33] Indeed, in early summer, as Tallmadge was still preoccupied in trying to obtain supplies and mounts around Litchfield, the regiment counted only 60 men on horseback.[34]

Fort Franklin still dominated his thoughts, and Tallmadge was soon concocting plans to reduce the post. He also began casting his eyes towards Fort Slongo, a British blockhouse erected near the Sound, about eight miles from Huntington. In a letter to Washington, dated April 6, 1781, Tallmadge broached the idea of a descent on Franklin. Impressed by the effectiveness of Tallmadge's forays of the previous autumn, Washington's response was positive. He did caution, however, that "the success of the proposed enterprise must depend on the absence of the British fleet, the secrecy of the attempt, and knowledge of the exact situation of the enemy."[35] Washington went on to instruct Tallmadge that "if, after you have been at the westward, the circumstances ... shall still appear favorable" he should proceed to Newport to obtain the aid of the French army and navy, as any sizable movement by the Continental Army would tip off the British and "effectually frustrate the success" of the attack.[36]

On April 19, Tallmadge again sailed to Long Island to do some reconnaissance. His informants provided him with plans for the two forts as well a return of Crown land and naval forces in the area.[37] In his report to headquarters, Tallmadge estimated Fort Franklin's garrison at about 800 men, chiefly "refugees and deserters from the American Army," of whom about 500 were properly armed.[38] The British stronghold was further protected by a naval force of one 16-gun vessel, two small frigates, and a galley. Another 150 British soldiers were stationed further east, at Fort Slongo.[39] The dragoon major reckoned that two small frigates could clear the Sound of any British naval defenders for the time necessary for him to destroy both forts.

Satisfied that the "circumstances" were favorable for the assault, Tallmadge set off for the French headquarters in Rhode Island, carrying a "very flattering" letter of introduction from Washington to the French. Both Count Rochambeau, commander of the French troops, and his naval counterpart, Chevalier Destouches, were receptive to Tallmadge's proposal, but the ships necessary for the attack were away on duty, forcing him to shelve the proposed attack. Once again, the bastion on Lloyd's Neck had thwarted Tallmadge's designs. The following July, when Tallmadge was engaged in acquiring horses and supplies in Litchfield County, a small Franco-American force attempted to subdue Fort Franklin. Heathcote Muirson, whom Tallmadge had praised for his conduct in the capture of Fort St George, led the assault with about 450 men, mostly French.[40] The attackers landed on the east side of Lloyd's Neck, and advanced to about 400 yards of the fort. Grapeshot from the fort's two 12-pounders caused the force to abandon the attack and retreat to their ships.[41] Another expedition against Fort Franklin was proposed for late October, but was never carried out.

Though Tallmadge was disappointed about the inability of the French to furnish aid for his descent on Lloyd's Neck, his visit to Rochambeau awakened the idea of enlisting the French to bolster another of his many challenges. While he may have gotten the idea from Wadsworth, his own careful assessment of the French headquarters led him to conclude that the European Allies had the requisite specie to keep an agent constantly employed in New York. Tallmadge was particularly keen on gaining the funds since both Townsend and Woodhull had effectively suspended their activities in the wake of Arnold's treason, and he hoped hard cash would revive their spirits, or allow him to recruit new agents. For their part, the French were anxious to obtain reliable intelligence about the common enemy, and were impressed by the enthusiastic young dragoon officer. An arrangement was devised by which Tallmadge would make duplicates of reports he received from his agents and forward one copy to Washington and another to Rochambeau.[42] Exactly how much the French paid for his services he did not say, but it certainly made Tallmadge's espionage operations much easier.

On one of his clandestine missions to Long Island, Tallmadge had met a "gentleman" he believed was "peculiarly favored" to provide information to the rebels. He also obtained a plan of the British fortifications at the Brooklyn ferry from an agent called "SG."[43] Whether or not "SG" and the "gentleman" were one and the same is unknown, but Tallmadge's continued recruiting of agents provides further evidence that his espionage activities were not limited to the Culper Ring, whose effectiveness declined after 1781.

"SG," who has never been identified, became an active "asset" in Tallmadge's network of spies, informants, and couriers. Despite the similarity between SG and Samuel Culper's initials, the former seems to have been a different man, as Tallmadge always referred to the Culpers by their *noms de guerre* in his letters and reports. In August 1782, Tallmadge reported to Washington that he had met again with "SG," explaining Washington's current intelligence needs, though he also sent a similar request to Woodhull.[44] At the same time, the dragoon/intelligence officer boasted that he had made contact with someone "in great repute among the [Tory] Refugees, and very intimate with Col. Upham, ADC to General Carleton [who] would be very glad to render important services to the States & Army.... I have great hopes from his services—"[45] Like much of Tallmadge's intelligence activities, the ultimate result of these plans is unknown, but they all required money, and hard specie at that. What is certain is that Tallmadge never lost sight—or control—of his espionage networks, and showed no signs of relaxing his operations, even as the rumors of peace began to spread.

9

Yorktown, Slongo, and Huntington

In the summer of 1781, as Tallmadge chafed at his inability to get at Fort Franklin, Washington and the French began the hunt for larger prey. The British campaign in the South, led by Lord Cornwallis, had been thwarted—if not shredded—by General Nathaniel Greene's Fabian tactics, and the exhausted British and Germans were slogging down the York peninsula in Virginia, where they expected to be either resupplied or evacuated by the Royal Navy. The key ingredient in any Allied plans was the French Navy. Rochambeau had informed Washington that a major fleet, under Admiral DeGrasse, was being sent to the Americas in an attempt to secure a decisive victory. Indeed, Washington understood that 1781 would probably provide the last opportunity for significant French participation in the war—and with it the prospects of American independence. If nothing decisive was gained in the ensuing campaign season, the French would likely cut their losses and settle for a negotiated peace which might well result in a rump United States, consisting of New England and parts of the Middle States.

As for the Continental Army, Rochambeau put his finger on the crux of the matter in a letter to DeGrasse, dated June 11, 1781:

> These people are at the very end of their resources. Washington will not have at his disposal half the number of troops he counted on having. While he is secretive on the subject, I believe that at present he has not more than 6,000 men all told.[1]

Washington and Rochambeau met at a council of war at Wethersfield, Connecticut, on May 21–22, 1781. Washington pressed for a French commitment to attack the British at their New York base and secure a decisive and morale-shattering victory over the Crown. Rochambeau eyed the vulnerable British army at Yorktown as a more likely prospect for a successful offensive—if the French fleet could prevent the British Navy from intervening. In the end, the two generals split the difference: while New York was declared the primary objective, both agreed to keep the Virginia option open if "circumstances and a naval superiority might render [it] more necessary."[2] In the meantime, the French would march from their Newport encampment for Westchester, where they would link up with Washington's army. Rochambeau was in motion on June 10, and by July the two armies were positioned in the Lower Westchester Encampment, the largest aggregation of Allied forces in New York during the war.

As the French army neared the Lower Hudson Valley, Washington devised a plan to snip off Fort Knyphausen on the mainland, just across the Harlem River, from Manhattan. The operation called for the Second Dragoons to join the Duke de Lauzon's French legion in a surprise assault on the works. If all went as planned, the garrison, comprised of men from DeLancey's regiment, would be cut off from the river and destroyed. Unfortunately for the attackers, the Loyalist pickets detected the American approach, and began firing before the French could get in position. DeLancey pulled his men into the fort, leaving the Continentals with little to do but skirmish with his rear guard.[3]

The American position in the new encampment was anchored at Dobbs Ferry, on the Hudson, with the camps of the Continental Army extending eastward to the Sprain Brook. The French held the ground from the Sprain River eastward to White Plains. All told, about 4,500 American troops and 5,000 French massed in central Westchester, a force which intimidated the Cowboys, and kept Clinton behind his defenses in New York, wondering what the Franco-American force might do. Later in July, the Second Dragoons, who were positioned on the high ground overlooking Dobb's Ferry, saved two rebel supply sloops from pursuing British vessels at nearby Tarrytown, an action Tallmadge missed as he was with his squadron on the Connecticut coast.

On July 21–23, Washington and Rochambeau undertook a reconnaissance in force along the Harlem River from Spuyten Duyvil eastward to Long Island Sound. Brushing aside occasional Tory attacks, the two commanders scouted out British defenses in northern Manhattan.[4] They then made similar calculations from the Jersey side of the Hudson. While

Washington noted possible sites for an attack, he reluctantly concluded that, even if DeGrasse arrived on the scene with reinforcements, the Allies would still lack the strength to carry the British stronghold. Tall-madge rode with Washington during the reconnaissance, drawing close enough to the British lines that he could observe how "the red Coats got under Arms, & seemed to act as if they expected an attack. We continued in view of each other through the day, and then retired for repose. The next day the same maneuver took place, and I presume there were many in both Corps [French and American armies] who wished the British to leave their Strong Entrenchments beyond Kingsbridge, and give the Allied forces an opportunity to pay their respects to them. But," the pugnacious young major added, "Sir Henry Clinton very prudently kept within his own fortified Encampment."[5]

In the end, as Washington and Rochambeau had expected, the French Navy determined the course of the campaign. On August 1, Washington received word from the French that DeGrasse's fleet was off the Virginia capes, ready to cooperate with the Franco-American armies. The window of opportunity was limited, however, and DeGrasse would leave the area by October 15. Though not Washington's first choice—he had hoped to drive the British from the island they had forced him from in 1776—he recognized the practicality of Rochambeau's plan for a southern campaign. Speed and deception were of the essence to prevent Clinton from attacking the combined armies at their most vulnerable point while they were crossing the Hudson, or strung out along the 400-mile journey southward. When the Continental Army was put in motion on August 19, Tallmadge recollected that "the common opinion was that our movement was to be towards Kingsbridge, where some very serious work was expected."[6] Instead, the armies marched northward to Kings Ferry, about 20 miles from Dobb's Ferry, where they began crossing the Hudson. To convince Clinton that New York was still his target, Washington took his army south to New Jersey, and made a show of advancing along the shore opposite Manhattan. Falling for the ruse, Clinton prepared his men to defend against an impending Franco-American attack. As the British braced themselves for combat, Washington and Rochambeau broke away, and hurried the Allied armies southward to Virginia.

Clinton was also misled by a piece of intercepted intelligence. Due to the turbulent situation in Westchester, the Second Dragoons express rider communications network from Rhode Island to Washington's headquarters kept no permanent station west of Connecticut. The dangers of communicating across the contested area were brought home in early June when dispatches from Washington and Rochambeau to Congress and Lafayette in Virginia were captured and delivered to Clinton. Ironically, the letters revealed the initial thinking of the two generals which emphasized plans for a projected attack on New York, with only cursory mention of Virginia as an alternative. The letter convinced the British commander that he, not Cornwallis, was in imminent danger of being overwhelmed by the Allies.

The intercepted messages also included a letter from Washington to Tallmadge, discussing his New York espionage network. The letter from Washington to his key spy runner helped assure the British commander that the letters were authentic, and confirmed his fears that the Allied army was about to launch an attack on New York.[7] The Allies' campaign of deception and misinformation, along with Clinton's mistaken confidence that he knew Washington's plans, resulted in the British high command doing nothing to reinforce Cornwallis, and even caused them to reject suggestions to disrupt Washington and Rochambeau's plans through spoiling raids. By the time Clinton realized the true objective of the Franco-American armies it was too late.[8]

Washington and Rochambeau reached Cornwallis's lines at Yorktown on September 28, and soon invested the exhausted British and Germans, whose hope for rescue by the Royal Navy was dashed by the French fleet's victory over the British off the Virginia Capes. After American and French forces captured two key British redoubts, Cornwallis was forced to capitulate on October 19, 1781. The surrendered British army, the second lost by the Crown in the war, amounted to about 11,000 men, 75 pieces of brass cannon, and 169 pieces of iron artillery. The victors also took 7,794 muskets.[9] All in all, the Virginia campaign was an unmitigated disaster for the British and a crucial triumph for Franco-American arms. Reacting to news of this, on February 28, 1782, the House of Commons passed a motion calling for an end to the war. A new ministry, headed by Lord Shelburne, soon entered into negotiations with Benjamin Franklin and the other American statesmen in France to draft a peace treaty based on American independence.

While Washington and Rochambeau executed their destruction of the British in Virginia, Tallmadge remained on station in New York. Upon receiving Washington's report of the triumph at Virginia, Tallmadge hurried off a letter to Barnabas Deane in Hartford conveying "the glorious news which has this moment come to hand. I have a letter from Col. Humphrey, and other letters have arrived at this place from the Southward, which announce the surrender of Lord Cornwallis to the Allied army on the 19th inst."[10] In reporting British troop losses, Tallmadge explained they were "inclusive of about 2000 Negroes, Tories and Devils."[11] The "Negroes" in question were escaped slaves who had joined the British Army as soldiers or laborers, it having been British policy to offer freedom and refuge to slaves who fled patriot plantations, but not those who escaped from Tory bondage. It is less certain to whom he was referring by the term "devils." Possibly, he meant the British and Hessians in general. Or he might have been thinking of opponents like Banastre Tarleton—who had trounced him at Poundridge—whose fighting in the Carolinas, especially the destruction of Patriot horse at Monck's Corners, South Carolina, in April, 1780, resulted in the rebels dubbing him "Bloody Ban."

Tallmadge's command was part of a force commanded by General William Heath which included 17 New England regiments, the Corps of Invalides, the Third United States Artillery, and the New York militia. The duty lacked the drama and climax of Yorktown, but it was essential in keeping Clinton distracted and off-balance and forestall any dispatch of reinforcements to the beleaguered Cornwallis. In September, Tallmadge returned to the coast under orders to watch for an expedition commanded by Benedict Arnold, which Clinton was believed to have sent to force the Allies to detach men from the South. Tallmadge arrived too late to catch sight of Arnold's expedition, which attacked and burned New London, a haven for American privateers, on September 4, 1781. Though he missed any chance for intercepting the traitor, Tallmadge was happy to return to the coast where "my former plan of annoying the enemy on the Sound, and on Long Island, came fresh to my recollection."[12]

With the French fleet operating in concert with the Franco-American forces in Virginia, Tallmadge knew his plan for an assault on Fort Franklin was impractical. But if Franklin was too formidable for the means at his disposal, Fort Slongo, a strong blockhouse fronted by a moat, appeared ripe for the taking.[13] As usual, the Continental spymaster had received detailed intelligence regarding the British bastion, situated about eight miles east of Huntington, from his Long Island agents. A rebel sympathizer who lived near the fort drew a sketch of the position and passed it along to Lieutenant Henry Scudder, a local resident who had fled to Connecticut after 1776, but who sometimes returned to his home. He returned to the mainland and delivered the drawing to Tallmadge. With the advantage of the map and other intelligence—he boasted that he knew "even where the sentinels stood"—the dragoon leader made his arrangements, including the selection of guides, local Long Island men who would conduct the troops to the British outpost.[14] Breaking with his previous practice, he did not lead the expedition himself but gave that honor to Major Lemuel Trescott of the Ninth Massachusetts Infantry. "Having determined on my plan of attack," he later told his daughter, "Major Trescott requested to lead the Lt. Infantry which I had always done myself. The Fort being but small I consented to it, & he performed the service to my entire satisfaction."[15]

Although Tallmadge acceded to Trescott's request to lead the raid, he took care to provide precise guidelines for the operation. Though the subjunctive tense was heavily employed, his instructions, which covered several contingencies, were clear.

> I should recommend you to land your troops at least two miles to the Eastward or Westward of the fort, to avoid any guards which may be advanced on the bank next to the Sound. The guides will point out the most proper place for this purpose. When you advance near the Fort, if you should find the Garrison alarmed & under arms—I cannot advise you to attempt a Storm, as the strength of the work seem not to warrant the [repulse?]. In this case it may not be amiss to endeavor to draw out the troops by some proper Maneuver. If you find the Garrison pretty much off their guard, from the draught of the works herewith given you, I should I suppose you had better make two attacks at the same time—the one directly against the sally Port or gate, & the other against the south within the abattis—If you succeed in the former you will affectually cut off the Garrison from entering the Fort, and by the latter measure they will be prevented from escaping—However if from a more accurate Survey & enquiry, you should judge any other mode of attack more likely to ensure success, you will be at liberty to adopt it— you must by all means endeavor to accomplish your business so as to be ready to re[em]bark your troops on or before daybreak, to avoid being cut

off in the Sound by any of the Enemies boats or guard ships. Wishing you Success.[16]

On October 2, Tallmadge conducted the raiders to the Saugatuck River near Norwalk, where Trescott assumed operational control. The expeditionary force consisted of 50 Connecticut infantry under Captain Richards, and 50 dismounted dragoons commanded by Captain David Edgar. Edgar's men were selected to surprise the garrison and carry the works, while Richards and his company surrounded the position and prevented any of the garrison from escaping. Ten specially selected dragoons, led by Lieutenant Rogers, were chosen to spearhead the attack, with Edgar and Trescott himself following close behind. Cornet William Pike was to bring up the rear.[17] The raiders launched their boats at about nine p.m. and reached Long Island about four the next morning, probably near a small body of water, lying just south of the beach, called Fresh Pond. They moved silently into position and, once in place, Trescott gave the word, and the Americans surged towards the blockhouse.

The Americans achieved total surprise, perhaps aided by the absence of Major Valentine, the fort's commander, who was in New York. The raiders also benefitted by the absence of some of Slongo's officers, who were busy carousing at the Milford House, a local inn.[18] As Trescott sent his men forward, a British sentry got off a quick shot, but fled so quickly in the face of the attacking Americans that he failed to shut the fort's gate behind him. The Continentals quickly overran the bastion, captured its defenders, and then set fire to the blockhouse and any stores they could not carry off. The Americans returned to Connecticut with a stand of colors and 21 prisoners, including two captains and a lieutenant. The number of prisoners might have been greater, as Tallmadge was forced to concede, but "notwithstanding the greatest exertions of captain Richards and his officers, some of the garrison jumped over the works and escaped."[19] Trescott reported two British troops killed inside the works, with two others mortally wounded and left behind.[20] The raiders also captured 70 muskets and a brass three-pound cannon as well as considerable ammunition.[21] Two iron double-fortified cannon, deemed too heavy for the boats, were destroyed at the fort.[22] In addition to military stores, Trescott took "a considerable quantity of English goods & Cloathing" among the spoils of the attack.[23]

Although he regretted missing Major Valentine, Tallmadge was highly satisfied with the expedition. He wrote Washington that he presumed the "plunder," the British goods brought off from Slongo, could be distributed among the troops and boatmen who made the raid, a standard military practice. "The piece of brass artillery, I shall annex to my command for the present."[24]

The only American casualty was Elijah Churchill, a veteran of the Mastic raid, who received a slight wound. In 1782, when Washington instituted the "Badge of Merit" for conspicuous service, Churchill, on Tallmadge's recommendation, became one of the first recipients. Tallmadge had forwarded his name for his actions at Ft. St. George, in which he killed the sentry, which prevented the British from shutting the fort's gate, as well as for his distinguished conduct at Fort Slongo, where he was among the advanced guard who pushed their way through the abatis and into the fort.[25] The entire raiding party received a more immediate and tangible reward in the form of a cask of rum which Heath sent from West Point to celebrate the victory.[26] The destruction of Fort Slongo was

Remnants of Fort Slongo, New York. The site is on private property. *Author's Collection.*

a relatively minor incident compared to the triumph at Yorktown, but it constituted another piece of bad news arriving at British headquarters, bringing home the reality that the Allies were on the offensive everywhere.[27]

Tallmadge himself led a small party on an extended reconnaissance/espionage foray on Long Island in November. His primary motive was to "effect an interview with certain persons who had been previously directed to make discoveries on the N[orth] River near Fort Washington."[28] As he arrived on the island, Tallmadge received word from the unidentified "SG" that he could carry out his mission, but as he was returning from New York he was arrested, and though no incriminating papers were found, he was held for several days on suspicion.[29] Tallmadge spent over a week on Long Island, apparently his longest stay during the war, successfully eluding British patrols and informers, obtaining intelligence, engaging in sabotage, and subsisting largely on clams before returning unscathed to Connecticut.

By then Washington's army returned triumphantly from Virginia and took up its default position in the Hudson Highlands. Tallmadge was recalled to northern Westchester after a raid by DeLancey's Tories, which probed as far as the Croton River. In addition to parrying DeLancey, the dragoons resumed the task of breaking up bands of "Cow-Boys" and "Skinners." These were ostensibly groups of guerrillas, the "Cow-Boys" supposedly professing loyalty to the Crown, while the "Skinners" were their Revolutionary counterparts. In reality, their allegiances were elastic and, like many of the whaleboat raiders along the Sound, they acted more like bandits, robbing and harassing anyone who had the misfortune to lay across their path. Among their other duties, elements of Tallmadge's legion were charged with suppressing the freebooters and providing some semblance of law and order in the region.

As the year drew to an end the prevailing mood in the army, despite the ever present shortfall of pay, was upbeat as it settled into winter quarters. Most of the dragoons were camped in interior Connecticut, but Tallmadge and his legion were again on the Sound, near Fairfield. The recent victories, great and small, had instilled a sense of confidence in the Continentals, who had come to believe they were the equal, or better, of the British in an open fight, and that peace and independence were in sight. Indeed, they would come, though the process sometimes seemed uncertain and many small and bloody engagements remained to be fought. The civilian population, especially rebels under British occupation, had cause to wonder whether success was really in the offing.

For Tallmadge, the winter–spring of 1781–1782 were consumed with the regular, often tedious, tasks of keeping his men fed, equipped, and paid—none of which was easy to do. In pursuing his duties, and probably personal interests as well, Tallmadge was often on the move, visiting points as distant as Springfield, Massachusetts, and the Continental capital at Philadelphia. Intelligence from Long Island continued to arrive regularly. In July, Woodhull reported that Tallmadge's nemesis on Lloyd's Neck, Fort Franklin, was in a deteriorated condition, containing only about 200 men whose dwindling numbers were "without discipline."[30] The fort was receiving no supplies from the British commissary and the garrison had to "subsist entirely by trading to your shore [Connecticut]."[31] Nevertheless, Franklin was protected by an armed brig and galley which rendered any seaborne attack risky. About a thousand British and Germans remained posted in nearby villages, with many more in Kings County.[32] But the dilapidated situation at Fort Franklin was prophetic, and when the British dissolved the Associated Loyalists who manned the post in 1782, they abandoned the fort as well, though Tory whaleboats continued to lurk in the coves and harbors around Lloyd's Neck.

Whatever thought Tallmadge might have given to taking another shot at Fort Franklin, changing circumstance soon led him to alter his plans. In November 1782, he received word that 600 British Light Horse and infantry, under the Tory commander Benjamin Thompson, had moved into Huntington village, apparently intending to make it their winter encampment. Thompson forced the local militia to tear down the Presbyterian church and use the wood to erect a fort on the town's burial grounds. He then demanded that the militia provide carpenters who were to prepare the bastion's defenses, ordering them to work every morning until the position was finished to his satisfaction.[33] Thompson's dismantling of the church and desecration of the burial grounds, accompanied by the destruction of orchards, fences, and the callous treatment of civilians, was a calculated act of destruction and oppression. With the war ostensibly coming to an end, Thompson's vandalism seems both unnecessary and vindictive. Possibly, the Tory commander had become embittered by what he accurately saw as the impending rebel victory.

Realizing he had no future in an independent United States, and having lost his home, possessions, and status, he determined to exact as much revenge as possible on the pro–Revolutionary town and village.

Tallmadge had an answer for Thompson's brutal occupation: attack. He first broached a plan for an assault on Thompson's fort in writing, and then pressed it in person. Washington agreed that it was "a very desirable thing for the Corps of Cavalry … to be cut off," but added that "under the peculiar circumstances of the present moment I should not wish the Enterprise to be undertaken unless there should be a certainty of success."[34] Washington's "peculiar circumstances" referred to a projected operation of his own which he wanted to launch in tandem with Tallmadge's descent on Huntington. The commanding general, who never ceased in his hopes of driving the British from New York, envisioned a two-pronged assault on the British in their northern Manhattan defenses. The first would consist of an amphibious landing below Fort Washington to the south, while a larger body of Continental struck Fort Independence and Kingsbridge. If successful, the operation would collapse the Crown's defensive perimeter, opening the way to the city. In any event, after urging Tallmadge to be sure he had everything in order, the commanding general requested Tallmadge's "further Sentiments."[35]

The eager dragoon major was happy to furnish his "sentiments" on the raid. He was apprised of Thompson's activities by a stream of reports from "a person who has been on the spot," later referred to by the initials "D.M."[36] Though it was late in the year—past conventional campaigning season—Tallmadge refused to let Thompson's outrages go unanswered. He calculated that the lateness of the season was an argument in favor of a raid as the British would have considered it most unlikely and be caught off guard. "I cannot but believe that an Enterprise might be conducted against that [Thompson's] Corps with Success," he assured Washington. "The Naval Guard in Huntington Harbor consists of only one Brig, a sloop and two small gallies. I think we should have no fear from them."[37]

Tallmadge sent Washington a map and specifics of Thompson's positions from information supplied by "D.M.," a resident of Stamford, whose visits to Huntington were probably made under the guise of illegal cross–Sound trade. The key British position in the village was the redoubt, approximately two acres in size, facing north, with a gate or sally port on the side. This wooden fortification stood above an earthen work six-feet high, fronted by a ditch from which the dirt had been excavated. Thompson's force, remnants of the Queen's Rangers and British Legion, comprised 550 men.[38] Those Tories not sheltered in the fort were quartered in houses and barns nearby, or given huts along the fort's sides. "D.M." further reported that "the inhabitants of Huntington do suffer exceedingly from the treatment they receive from the troops who say the inhabitants of the County are all Rebels, and therefore they care not how they suffer."[39]

Washington had signaled that he looked favorably on a possible raid against the British in Huntington, but he had intended to coordinate it with his own attack, and, as usual, insisted that all contingencies be addressed, and the prospects for success made as favorable as could be arranged. Determined to demonstrate that he was again prepared to execute a stinging defeat against the British on Long Island, Tallmadge wrote the most detailed proposal for an operation that he penned in the war. His November 25 letter listed all the positive results to be gained through the raid. The British would lose most of their cavalry, at least on central Long Island, while Thompson's defeat would throw their bases in Jamaica and Brooklyn into confusion. The destruction of the British stronghold in Huntington would also deal a heavy blow against the "London Trade," the illegal commerce between Connecticut and Long Island. With the British drastically scaling down their New York operations, Thompson had been almost wholly dependent on receiving provisions and forage from across the Sound. His removal would destroy a major market for Yankee black marketers. Lastly, Tallmadge reiterated "D.M.'s" description of the miseries Thompson was inflicting on Huntington's residents. The good Whig citizens deserved succor.[40] To add to the weight of support, Tallmadge sent more information and another map of Thompson's positions three days later.

Washington was convinced. After dispatching infantry and dismounted dragoons to augment the raiding force, the commander-in-chief set December 5 as D-Day for expedition, unless an accident should intervene to prevent it. "In conducting the business," he told Tallmadge, "you will be governed entirely by your own discretion."[41]

Tallmadge's intended assault on the Huntington encampment was even more daring than his Fort St. George raid, and he later described it as "to have been the most brilliant of my military Career."[42] He planned to land his men on Eaton's Neck, an irregularly shaped peninsula on the east side of Huntington Harbor. By launching his attack from the Neck, he would avoid British ships in the harbor, and ensure a safe retreat if necessary. The core of his strike force consisted of four companies of light infantry—all hand-picked men—plus the dismounted dragoons, who were expected to seize horses from the British on Long Island. The Continentals were reinforced by Connecticut militia, giving Tallmadge about 700 men in all.[43]

Tallmadge may have intended, or at least hoped, for an even more ambitious operation than he appears in his published memoirs or in the correspondence of the time. Writing to his daughter long after the war, he explained that he "had a large force, much above my rank to Command, & was to have landed at Huntington on L.I., where I had to take about 500 B[ritish] Troops, horse & foot, the move down to hell Gate, cross over to Harlem, & cooperate with our Army under gen'l Washington, in capturing 8000 of the Enemy, & thus close the War."[44]

It is hard to know what to make of this more audacious plan. Hell Gate is a narrow, turbulent choke point on the East River, and Tallmadge would have had to march deep into western Queens to reach it. Crossing to Harlem (then a village in upper Manhattan) would have required a number of boats for both horses and men. Even with 700 men, Tallmadge would be venturing deep into British-controlled territory, where he would be outnumbered by both land and sea forces. The British Navy could easily cut him off while the army trapped him against the East River.

The objectives of the expedition, as presented in this accounting, were daring to the point of recklessness, and could easily have resulted in a "bridge too far" situation. Any chance of victory depended on Washington, whose own plan of attack was equally ambitious. A successful assault on Manhattan would have likely drawn British troops from Long Island, presenting some possibility that Tallmadge might have been able to range deep into Queens (at least for a time) without being destroyed or captured. Conversely, a major American incursion into western Long Island would present the British with difficult choices regarding deployment and reinforcement, if they were simultaneously facing Washington's waterborne operation. This was likely in Washington's mind as he made his calculations. Under the circumstances, it appears probable that Tallmadge and Washington discussed the possibilities if both their attacks went as planned, but nothing quite as brazen as Tallmadge's penetration of Queens and landing in Manhattan appears in the letters written at the time. It may be that the old soldier was conflating his most optimistic hopes with the actualities of the situation. In any event, the raid did not take place. As Tallmadge put it, "A kind Providence prevented my crossing the Sound."[45]

Having made all his preparations, Tallmadge mustered his troops near Stamford, and marched them to Shippan Point, where the whaleboats were waiting. As usual, Tallmadge had laid his plans carefully and thoroughly, but there was one critical element he could not control: the weather.

As the troops began climbing into the boats, a violent winter squall swept up Long Island Sound. Before half of the men had embarked, Tallmadge was forced to order them off the boats and postponed the crossing, hoping for better weather the following day. The men spent a rainy, miserable night huddled under their boats along the beach. The rain ceased by morning, but the Sound roiled with chop, preventing any daylight voyage. As dusk fell, Tallmadge ordered his men back into the boats, but a stiff wind again defeated his efforts, forcing all to endure another wet, chilly night under the upturned whaleboats.

As Tallmadge chafed in frustration, he received reports that three Tory whaleboats had crossed from Long Island, and were waiting out the winds in the shelter of the Norwalk Islands. Forced to delay his own operation, Tallmadge made haste to snag the Tories before they could escape. But before he could reach them, the wind softened, and the Tories pushed off into the Sound. Determined not to let them escape, Tallmadge ordered his six best boats and crews after the fleeing loyalists.

Tallmadge placed his little fleet under the command of his most experienced whaleboat captain, Caleb Brewster, an eager participant in many of Tallmadge's raids, and the key conduit of Culper messages from Setauket to Connecticut. Three of the American boats were forced back by contrary winds, but Brewster pressed on and caught up with the Tories in the middle of the Sound. The Americans closed in on the two heaviest British craft, and the ensuing fight was hot and short. All the

Tories were killed or wounded in the first volley of musketry, although Brewster himself took a ball in the chest, which passed through his body.[46] Despite the wound, Brewster captured two of the British boats, though the third escaped to the protection of British outposts on Lloyd Neck. Brewster returned victorious, though Tallmadge and most of the soldiers feared his wound fatal. But the redoubtable warrior proved them wrong, recovered, resumed his service, and lived to be almost 80 years old.

The capture of the Tory boats was heartening, but the one which escaped jeopardized the larger objective—the raid on Huntington. The escaping Loyalists would have noted the strong American force massing near Shippan Point, and reported as much to Thompson, who would readily recognize the significance of the Patriot concentration. Reluctant to abandon his plan to destroy the Huntington encampment, Tallmadge decided to give it one more try, and once again prepared his men to embark. Again, the wind turned so severe that he was forced to abandon the effort, and, considering the likelihood that the British were thoroughly alerted, aborted the entire expedition.

On December 8, 1782, more "mortified and chagrined than I had ever been in my life," Tallmadge submitted his report of the failed expedition to Washington.[47] "I feel as completely unhappy as disappointed military ambition can make me," he went on, venting his frustration. "It adds much to the misfortune that so important a blow would have been given the enemy, with almost a certainty of success."[48] Tallmadge's depressed mood was somewhat alleviated by the fact that unforeseen events—the presence of British warships off upper Manhattan—had forced Washington to cancel his own assault.

Washington expected much from his young protégés, and did not refrain from chastising them if he felt they had underperformed. But he had developed a keen appreciation of the vicissitudes and uncertainties of war, and further appreciated the need to buck up the spirits of young officers when necessary and appropriate. "Tho' you have not met with that success you deserved and probably would have obtained had the Enterprise proceeded," Washington consoled the dispirited dragoon major, "yet I cannot but think your whole conduct in the affair was such as ought to entitle you still more to my confidence and esteem."[49] The commander-in-chief went on to explain that "I have accustomed myself to judge human Actions ... by the manner in which they are conducted, more than by the Event; which it is not in the power of human foresight and prudence to command.... Another time you will have less opposition from the Winds and Weather, and success will amply compensate you for this little disappointment."[50] Washington concluded his letter by instructing Tallmadge to remain on his post along the Sound and concentrate on his intelligence operations. Perhaps, the commander-in-chief wrote encouragingly, another "favorable moment" to attack Huntington—or another tempting target—might appear.

Washington's empathetic letter greatly soothed Tallmadge's wounded feelings. He became more philosophical about the aborted raid when he later learned that a preliminary treaty of peace had been concluded between the Crown and the United States during the time he was preparing his assault on Huntington. Under the circumstances, the casualties incurred in the expedition would probably have been in vain, though bloodying the odious Thompson would have been some compensation.

10

Enterprises, Financial and Military

The lessening pace of combat, along with the generally defensive stance adopted by the new British commander, Sir Guy Carleton,[1] was accompanied by a spike in the "London Trade." The commerce across the lines of war was originally licensed by New York State, but all such legal permissions were revoked in April 1779. Following the victory at Yorktown, the powers that be in New York tried to squeeze the British further by declaring all goods received from British-occupied territory as contraband. This blanket proscription was modified in April 1782, to apply only to British manufactured goods.[2] These increasingly stricter prohibitions had little effect in Connecticut and the Long Island Sound region, generally. By 1780, importation of British-manufactured goods into New York City had reached prewar levels, indicating a market far beyond British-controlled territory.[3] Following the victory in Virginia, many (if not most) Revolutionary civilians assumed the war was over, and the growing demand for British goods could not be stopped. And neither could the "London Trade."

Not that those Continental forces stopped trying. Positioned along the Connecticut shore facing Long Island, Tallmadge became increasingly involved in suppressing the commerce, a task which consumed more and more of his energies during the last winter of the war, 1782–1783. The task was daunting. As he explained to Washington, the small number of vessels at his disposal, coupled with the long, indented coastline, meant "we can check it but in part." Moreover, the trade was winked at by many who were charged with interdicting it. Tallmadge believed that the few captures made among the many vessels engaged in exchanging contraband stemmed from the fact that vessels licensed by the Continental and Connecticut governments "connived at the trade."[4]

Tallmadge's men seized at least one Connecticut-commissioned vessel, confiscating its cargo, which was probably sold and the profits distributed among officers and soldiers.[5] The dragoon major would soon have a more intense, personal encounter with an American, playing a double role in the "Devil's Belt," as Long Island Sound was often called.

Early in 1783, Tallmadge received a report that a large American sloop, the *Suldham*, commanded by Captain Hoyt, was using its assigned duties to suppress illicit commerce as a cover to smuggle British goods into Connecticut. One of Tallmadge's agents secured a copy of the *Suldham*'s manifest, which included a large number of proscribed goods. Tallmadge had both the manifest and a search warrant in hand when Hoyt docked in Norwalk harbor. Armed with these documents, Tallmadge introduced himself and explained the reason for his visit. Rather than protest his innocence, Hoyt threatened to throw Tallmadge into the harbor. Tallmadge replied that wasn't going to happen, and that the captain had better comply with the orders of a superior officer. Instead, taking Tallmadge by surprise, Hoyt ordered his crew to hoist canvass, and catching a "smart wind," quickly sailed out into the Sound. Tallmadge demanded Hoyt turn back, but he refused, repeating his threat to throw Tallmadge overboard. Tallmadge countered that if he went over the side, he was taking Hoyt with him.[6]

Despite his bluster, Hoyt made no attempt to lay hands on his unwilling passenger, but steered a course towards Lloyd Neck, where the British and Tory ships, rocking on the waves, waited menacingly. When Tallmadge asked Hoyt where he was heading, the renegade ship's master swore he would hand the dragoon major over to the British. Tallmadge told him that if he did, he would see the smuggler court-martialed and executed. Hoyt claimed he didn't care what happened, and Tallmadge heatedly warned him that he would "have him hanged as high as Haman hung, if I ever returned, as I did not doubt I should."[7] The situation for Tallmadge was reaching the crisis point as the *Suldham* drew ever closer to the British ships. But Tallmadge's threats had begun to take effect, and the growing reality that the war would end on the terms of American independence no doubt began to weigh on Hoyt, who realized that swinging from a gibbet was guaranteed if he delivered a prominent American officer to the British. Hoyt suddenly ordered his men to reverse course. Upon sailing into Norwalk, Hoyt quickly fled the *Suldham* in a small boat, leaving Tallmadge in possession of his sloop. Tallmadge searched the ship and quickly found the English-made goods listed on his manifest. The contraband was immediately condemned—seized as spoils of war.

In February 1783, Tallmadge turned his attention to yet another irritant along the "Devil's Belt." Tallmadge's energetic attempts to halt illegal trading had led the British to employ more armed vessels in the business. Among the most active of these was a British privateer, the *Three Brothers*, commanded by Captain Johnstone. Late in the month, Tallmadge received word that Johnstone had landed European goods near Stratford Point and was expected to return for a shipment of beef. The dragoons quickly made arrangements to prepare a different kind of exchange.

The *Three Brothers* was heavily armed for its operations, bristling with a formidable complement of 11 carriage guns, and four swivel guns. An estimated 25 small arms were available to its 21-man crew.[8] Though a dragoon officer, Tallmadge's Setauket upbringing had provided him with a solid knowledge of the Sound, and he never hesitated to conduct combined or even purely naval operations. In order to take the *Three Brothers*, Tallmadge enlisted the aid of Captain Amos Hubbel, who usually sailed a Bridgeport–Boston route. Hubbell's ship was central to Tallmadge's plan, and he arranged for the captain to receive a portion of the prize money raised from the British ship's capture as compensation for damage to his own vessel, which was unlikely to emerge from the operation intact. Tallmadge then organized the boarding of 45 light infantrymen from his legion under immediate command of Lieutenants Rhea and Hawley. The always-ready Caleb Brewster was placed in command of Hubbel's vessel, which was manned by his veteran whaleboat men.[9] Hubbell himself was to sail the vessel under Brewster's orders.

When the *Three Brothers* reappeared off Stratford on February 20, 1783, Tallmadge sprung his trap. Brewster, his men, and the dragoons—functioning more like Marines or Seals than soldiers—were loaded on Hubbell's ship, under strict orders to remain out of sight below deck until the decisive moment arrived. Hubbell pushed off from Bridgeport about four PM, and quickly came within shouting distance of the British vessel. Johnstone unleashed both cannon and swivel guns at what he perceived as a coastal trader, causing severe damage to the hull, masts, and rigging. Undeterred, Hubbel pressed on and steered his bow directly towards the side of the enemy. As the ships drew within a few yards of each other, Brewster and his men sprang up from below, and poured a volley into the startled British seamen. Hubbell then rammed the British vessel, and the dragoons and whaleboat men then leapt aboard the *Three Brothers*, taking it at the points of their bayonets.[10] Most of the British crew were killed or wounded in the fighting, Johnstone himself being among the dead.

Among the items seized by the Americans was Johnstone's letter of marque and reprisal issued by British Admiral Digby, which conferred privateer status to the *Three Brothers*. Digby's letter also revealed some of Johnstone's trading connections. The triumphant Americans, having suffered no casualties, then sailed both ships back to Blackrock Harbor.[11] In addition to seizing the privateer's ship, its cargo and remaining crew, Tallmadge's men also freed a few American troops who had been taken by Johnstone before the fight. Tallmadge proudly sent a report of the action to Washington, who expressed his thanks in a letter of February 26, 1783. Along with his commendation, Washington authorized the condemnation (sale) of the prize, with proceeds divvied up among the troops.[12]

The sale of captured enemy vessels and property for "prize money" was a common practice in the eighteenth century and provided an additional incentive and reward for troops. For the rebels, it could be especially important as their pay, usually in vastly depreciated currency, was often in arrears. Tallmadge, who often drew from his own funds to supply his men or finance the Culpers, was happy to seize an opportunity of making a legitimate profit from the war.

Money worries had bedeviled Tallmadge throughout the war, though he had plenty of company in that regard. As an officer he was responsible for providing his uniform and food from his pay. The latter was ordinarily provided in state or Continental paper currency, which had depreciated so badly by 1780 that a captain's compensation was often little more than a pair of shoes.[13] As a major, Tallmadge would have been only marginally better off. Most of the hard currency which went through his hands was intended for his espionage agents who needed specie to grease their operations. Though Washington provided the required gold and silver for intelligence work, and New York and Connecticut sometimes provided him with their more dubious currency to equip and maintain his men, Tallmadge frequently reported paying for supplies and equipment from his own pocket. Even the specie Washington dispensed for secret service activities was sometimes less than intended, as unscrupulous parties "shaved" the coins, depriving them of their proper weight—and value.[14]

An astute Yankee, the young major never overlooked opportunities for pecuniary advancement (such as investing in privateers), nor did he ignore the cash rewards obtained through capturing British vessels and selling them and their cargo for prize money. Nevertheless, personal solvency was a constant challenge. In March 1780, Tallmadge sought to take advantage of insider knowledge to improve his financial situation. While conferring with the Connecticut Assembly at Hartford he learned that Connecticut had decided to pay off the £10 notes they had issued in 1777. Apparently, these were to be redeemed at full value, though whether in hard coin or new, presumably better-valued paper, is unknown. These had floated through the northeastern states for three years, and had, along with most paper currency, depreciated greatly. Tallmadge encouraged his friend Samuel Webb to buy up as many of the £10 notes as possible at their discounted value, a practice he clearly intended to follow himself. Having bought the £10 notes for a fraction of their face value, Tallmadge, Webb, or anyone who possessed the fiat currency, could then redeem them in Connecticut at full value.[15] Considering that pay for the Continental army was often badly in arrears, and the currency in which it was made was barely a half-step above worthless, Tallmadge's willingness to use every opportunity to improve his cash balance seems reasonable, and certainly well within acceptable eighteenth-century practices, though not everybody had the advantage of his connections.

Tallmadge continued to seize opportunities to benefit from financial dealings, and relied heavily on his connections with Wadsworth and Deane to provide him with the expertise to do so successfully. In August 1780, he purchased Massachusetts State notes for Wadsworth, who wanted them either for purchases, or, more likely, the chance to make a profit by trading them.[16] The following year he was involved in another currency arbitrage involving different issues of Continental dollars. Again, Wadsworth was central to the plan. Tallmadge sent the Hartford financier $246 in "new Contl Dollars for which I expect bills of Exchange on the terms you mentioned this day. If I rightly understood you, I shall be entitled to receive of you 164 Dolls for the inclosed new Contl which is at present all I have on hand."[17] Although Congress's new currency had a greater face value, it was more advantageous to convert them into bills of exchange, probably those issued by the French, whose real value was greater.

Indeed, the war provided the young major with an education which stretched far beyond military affairs. Although he was considering a legal career when he first joined the army, friendships with Jeremiah Wadsworth and Barnabas Deane, who battened on government contracts during the war, opened his eyes to lucrative returns provided by business and investing. In addition to taking his share from seizures such as the *Suldham* and the *Three Brothers*, Tallmadge invested in American privateering voyages. Several of the Connecticut River towns such as Middletown, Wethersfield, and Hartford served as bases for the construction and outfitting of such vessels which plagued British and Loyalist shipping. Commencing his interests in privateers, Tallmadge turned to his experienced friend Wadsworth, writing him "that some of us young Lads who were just beginning in the World, are spending our time and exposing our lives and health for but the paltry Consideration in the pecuniary way. I have for some time been determined to try my luck at Privateering."[18] Tallmadge was joined by two other members of his regiment in the gambit and informed Wadsworth that he and his partners could put up $1,000, relying on Wadsworth's judgment as to which ship and captain would receive the investment.[19]

Tallmadge's first foray into privateer investment must have been successful, for the following May (1778) he acted as attorney for a partnership, including himself and three members of his regiment which invested in the armed sloop *Wooster* and the ship *Mars*.[20] While the privateers were often successful, and their profits large, they also suffered their losses from the Royal Navy and their Tory counterparts. Indeed, in late 1778 and early 1779, Tallmadge's luck changed and he lamented the loss of "the 5th Vessel in which I have been concerned that has been taken by the Enemy. This branch of business I am determined to quit, and must turn my attention to matters on which a more certain profit may be made. To find this out is the grand point."[21] Whatever his chagrin at the time, Tallmadge continued placing some of his money in privateering enterprises. In August 1781, for example, he enjoined Peter Colt, Wadsworth's partner and another member of the Hartford military-industrial complex, to act as his agent regarding the booty taken by the privateer, *Jay*.[22]

But Tallmadge began to diversify his financial interests. He used insider knowledge to buy heavily depreciated Connecticut currency which he knew was soon to be redeemed for a new issue payable in gold and silver, and called upon his Hartford friends to secure French bills of exchange—notes payable on European banks—which often circulated as currency. He also had the specie payments made by the French for his intelligence reports. While a substantial part of these revenue flows may have gone into purchasing supplies for his regiments and running his intelligence network, much of it contributed to the capital he had at his disposal for investment. He also seems to have been involved in a company owned by Wadsworth which had obtained a contract from the French to furnish them with necessary supplies.[23] His investment income allowed him to purchase a 60th part of the Vermont town of Enosborough, on Lake Champlain, which he sold at a handsome markup in 1798.

Tallmadge found the time to concentrate on his financial concerns in the colder months when the pace of the combat slackened. In the last year of the war, as rumors of peace negotiations grew in intensity, both armies refrained from major actions, allowing Tallmadge to increase his preparations for his civilian pursuits. In August 1782, he backed his brother, John, in a store located in Bethlehem, Connecticut, not far from the county seat of Litchfield. Tallmadge had become familiar with Litchfield during the war, and had come to appreciate it for both its economic potential and the site of a future home. Even as his efforts to suppress the London Trade kept him often along the coast, he entered into a partnership with Litchfield merchant Miles Beach, establishing a firm which was to do business under the name "Benjamin Tallmadge & Company."[24] The company controlled the Bethlehem store that John Tallmadge had been operating, which was relocated to Litchfield in 1783. By this time, Tallmadge had decided to make the village his postwar home, purchasing from Thomas Sheldon a large house that was situated conveniently near the new store.

The Tallmadge store accepted a variety of currencies—as well as produce—for the "best of European, East or West India Goods." The source of much (if not all) of the store's imported items was probably captured London Trade vessels. Tallmadge's rank and fame helped make the new venture a success. Towards the end of the war, and into the uncertain days after its conclusion, some officers who had private capital or arrangements with speculators set up operations in camp or in the soldiers' home states, buying their land grant certificates, state currency—effectively, promissory notes redeemable after the war—or the late war notes issued by the Congress.[25] Tallmadge was one of these officers. Members of his Second Dragoons frequented the store, where he often acted as a banker, cashing their pay vouchers for cash or credit. In a like manner, he was able to acquire the land grants given to discharged soldiers as compensation for their service.[26]

Tallmadge, and others like him, were taking a risk with government currency, but their confidence that the government would make good on its paper paid off when the United States redeemed the issues. The same was true of state currencies—effectively promissory notes—which generally matured with interest after peace had returned. Most soldiers needed cash immediately, and sold their notes for a fraction of face value. Speculators, like Tallmadge, could make several hundred percent if they could wait until peace was fully returned.[27] The land grants—the only thing of value states could immediately offer their veterans—were almost a sure thing. Such manipulations allowed Tallmadge to build up his own wealth and to speculate successfully in western lands following the war. But the practice revealed a class divide: well-placed officers and speculators on the one side, and enlisted men and their families on the other. A significant part of the politics of the early republic was driven by this gap in circumstance and status.

Though Tallmadge's

Hard Money for Paper.

All Kinds of
CONTINENTAL AND CONNECTICUT
STATE SECURITIES,
SOLDIERS' BOUNTY LANDS, &c.
Bought and Sold, by

Benjamin Tallmadge, & Co.

Litchfield, Jan. 19, 1790.

Tallmadge and Company newspaper advertisement, 1790.

legion took several other vessels that winter, the seizure of the *Three Brothers* proved to be the last notable military operation. "After this event," he wrote, "we captured several boats, some belonging to the British, & some to our Side, for we served all that we found carrying on this trade pretty much alike."[28]

Talk of peace had been building from the summer of 1782, even as Tallmadge planned his attack on Huntington, and sent his "navy" into the Sound to suppress smuggling. Washington, however, remained skeptical of British intentions, suspecting that the rumors of peace emanating from Britain were designed to lull Americans into a sense of complacency while they recovered from their defeat at Yorktown.[29] But the British were in earnest. On July 11, 1782, they evacuated Savannah, and began the withdrawal from Charleston two months later. Those troops not sent to Halifax or Europe were concentrated in New York, which was to be the last Crown stronghold evacuated. On August 2, Carleton informed Loyalist leaders that a treaty based on American independence was in the works. On the same day, the British commander sent the same news to Washington, who forwarded it to Congress, which was largely unaware that such a treaty had been negotiated.

In this fluid situation, the still-unconvinced Washington was hungry for information regarding British intentions in New York, especially if they provided any hard evidence regarding the peace treaty. Writing from Croton, New York, on September 17, 1782, Tallmadge forwarded information which had been relayed to him by "T. [or J] C." The identity of this agent is uncertain. It might have been an alternative form of Culper, Jr., though such a sudden alteration of Tallmadge's code system seems unlikely. In any event, after referring to Washington's repeated requests for information about peace prospects, Tallmadge related that the Loyalists in New York had learned that an agreement was in the works in which the "Independence of America is acknowledged. Nor will there be any conditions insisted on for those who have joined the King's standard."[30]

The report grew more positive—from the American point of view. Tallmadge's informant had spoken with one of Sir Guy Carleton's aides, who told him that troops then embarking from New York were headed for either the West Indies or Halifax, signaling a further diminution of the Crown's forces. Another naval expedition was sailing to Charleston to remove the British garrison there, while yet a third fleet was preparing to convey Tories to the Bay of Fundy [St. John's, Canada].[31] "Sir Guy himself," Tallmadge informed his chief, "says he thinks it not improbable that the next packet may bring orders for the evacuation of New York."[32] Whatever the feelings of the British military, the Loyalists were stunned by the ensuing developments. Quoting his news-rich operative, Tallmadge wrote, "I have never seen such general distress and dissatisfaction in my life as is painted in the countenance of every Tory at New York."[33] In fact, the exodus of the Loyalists had been noticeable ever since the British defeat at Yorktown, and the numbers of Tories leaving their native shores would swell as the stages of British withdrawal became public.

The rumors of an impending treaty between Britain and the United States, and the general terms of the agreement, were accurate enough but no definite confirmation as to its completion would arrive for several months.[34] In the meantime, though no major military operations were undertaken, Washington attempted to hold the Continental Army in readiness for further action should the reports of peace prove premature. His task was made difficult by widespread dissatisfaction in the army over lack of pay by Congress. Washington broke one incipient mutiny by some of his officers by sheer weight of his prestige and authority, and was forced to send reliable troops to Pennsylvania to halt a mutiny of the Pennsylvania line guarding British prisoners. With word of the end of the war circulating through the army, the commanding general knew he couldn't keep his men under arms and control much longer. Appropriately perhaps, Tallmadge's networks provided Washington with the first hard, definitive, evidence that a peace treaty had been concluded. On March 29, 1783, he wrote the commanding general that "we are informed from N York that a general Peace has actually taken place," and that he intended to cross over to Long Island to secure more information. Two days later he was able to elaborate. "From every Enquiry, & a variety of Information, it appears to be reduced to a certainty that a general Peace has been concluded on in Europe, an authenticated account of which great Event, I hope Your Excellency has rec'd before this time."[35] He hadn't, but he soon would.

Congress proclaimed a cease-fire and approved the preliminary treaty at the end of March, recalling all warships and suspending enlistments. On April 6, Carleton declared a formal cessation of hostilities.

While Washington would have preferred to wait for confirmation of a permanent treaty, not to mention signs that the British were evacuating New York, the course of events and the growing demands of his men for pay and discharge, forced his hand. On April 19, he officially acknowledged the preliminary treaty of peace recognizing American independence, and the subsequent cessation of hostilities. The army was demobilized rapidly, with the troops given certificates promising their pay at some future time. Between April and June 1783, the Continental Army shrunk by four-fifths, falling from about 8,500 soldiers to 1800 fit for duty.[36]

Little remained for Tallmadge to do except for winding down the network's operations and settling accounts. This meant dealing with the painful issue of money again. On June 14, he asked Woodhull to furnish an accounting of his expenses as a Revolutionary agent. Culper, Sr., responded three weeks later with his statement, explaining that he couldn't supply particular dates for his expenditures as he kept only "the most simple account that I possibly could for fear it should betray me."[37] Nevertheless, the Setauket spy hastened to "assure you I have been as frugal as I possibly could," and asked Tallmadge to "explain to the general [Washington] the circumstances of this lengthy compendium that he may be Satisfied that we have not been extravagant."[38] In particular, Woodhull reminded Tallmadge that he "was directed to keep a House at N York which in about a month or a little more cost me £25."[39]

On August 16, 1783, Tallmadge forwarded Woodhull's statement to Washington, averring that the Setauket agent "has been as attentive to the public Interest as his Circumstances & peculiar situation would admit."[40] In addition to the money due the Culpers, Tallmadge also requested that the sums he had personally laid out be reimbursed as well. He went on to explain that he would be at the paymaster general's office shortly and hoped Washington would make arrangements for the disbursement of the monies due him and his intelligence agents so that all accounts could be squared.[41] While no record seems to have survived indicating that Tallmadge was paid the money owed him, his silence on the matter indicates it was. Washington, however, responded with unexpected irritation at Woodhull's request for reimbursement, maintaining that the network's usefulness in the previous year was minimal, an attitude which discounted the long, dangerous, and pertinent service they had given the patriot cause since 1778. Nevertheless, the Culpers received their monetary due.

Washington's ungenerous and ungrateful reaction to the Culpers' request for reimbursement probably derived from the critical situation he faced at Newburgh. Urgent requests, even petitions, that Congress provide promised pay for officers and enlisted men had generally gone unanswered throughout the war. Though the troops were being discharged with formal promissory notes of back pay, the reality was that they were being returned to civilian life without adequate (and promised) compensation for their service—basically broke. Washington himself had to formally request that sums he had laid out from his personal accounts for the war effort be repaid. Under the circumstances, a bill from yet another operation may have triggered a flare-up of his famously volatile temper. If Tallmadge made any comment on his commander's disparagement of the men upon whom he had relied so heavily for intelligence throughout the war, it has not survived.

11

Endings and Beginnings

Like most of the officers in Washington's circle, the young dragoon major became devoted to his commanding general during the war. As the fighting wound down, and the army gradually demobilized, Tallmadge was unsure whether or not he would meet with the commander who, in many ways, had become a father figure to him. In one of his last wartime reports to headquarters, Tallmadge, writing in the florid yet formal manner of a Yale-educated eighteenth century gentleman, was effusive in praise and professions of gratitude. Though the language seems stilted by modern standards, Tallmadge's sincerity rings true.

Should I not have the opportunity to pay my personal respects to Your Excellency before you retire from the army; Give me leave at this time, with the warmest Gratitude, to assure Your Excellency that I shall ever entertain the liveliest sense of the many marks of attention which I have recd from Your Excellency's hands. Whatever may have been the result, it gives me great pleasure to reflect that during my Service in the army it has ever been my highest ambition to promote the Welfare of my Country & thereby merit Your Excellency's approbation. In the Calm retirements of domestic life, may you continue to enjoy health, & find increasing satisfaction from the reflection of having conducted the arms of America thro a War so particularly distressing to the obtainment of an honorable peace, & of having been the Instrument, under God, in obtaining the freedom & Independence of this Country—Adieu, my Dear General, & in every Situation of Life I pray you to believe that my best wishes will attend You, & that I shall continue to be, as I am at this time, with every sentiment of respect & Esteem, Your Excellency's most Obedt & very H.ble Servt. B. Tallmadge[1]

Washington replied to Tallmadge a few weeks later. After requesting records of the money advanced to the Culpers so they could be paid, he reciprocated his loyal dragoon's admiration and best gratitude.

I cannot conclude without offering you my sincere and affectionate thanks for your good wishes, and the favourable Sentiments you have been pleased

131

to express of me. The ready obedience, and the polite attention which I have ever experienced from the Officers of the Army, over whom I have had the honor to preside, fills me with the most pleasing Sensations; the reflection of which will contribute not a little to my future happiness.—To none, am I more indebted for these than to yourself and with great truth I can assure you that at all times and in whatever place I may be, I shall have pleasure in seeing you.[2]

As the Continental soldiers began their return to civilian life, a group of officers founded the Society of Cincinnati as a fraternal organization to preserve their ties, and celebrate their service. The society, which is still in existence, took its name from the legendary Roman general Cincinnatus who relinquished the political and military power given him and returned to civilian life after defeating Rome's enemies. Tallmadge was chosen as the society's treasurer, and was later elected president. Washington, of course, served as the organization's first president. The society became a matter of controversy among some of the more ardent Revolutionaries who smelled the foundation of an incipient aristocracy. Such fears proved unfounded, and the society endured primarily as a social organization, though its members benefitted from economic and political networking.

The war sputtered out. The Provisional Treaty of Peace, signed in November 1782, was followed by George III's declaration of a "cessation of arms" in February, a development which depressed and infuriated New York's Loyalists who, seeing themselves abandoned to their enemies, began to leave in droves. Many sold off their property for ready cash in an 18th-century version of a tag sale. The political situation became increasingly confused as prominent Revolutionaries, and even Continental Army officers, appeared on New York streets fraternizing with their British counterparts.[3] In the fluid, semi-chaotic situation, crime spiked, and British sentries policed the streets to prevent brawls between Whigs and Tories.[4]

Though Washington remained vigilant, the course of events slowly convinced him that the Crown had had enough. In April, as he began "furloughing"—effectively discharging—his men, the British began releasing American prisoners of war held in makeshift prisons in Manhattan, along with those languishing in the fetid British hulks anchored in Wallabout Bay. After the permanent Treaty of Peace was signed on

September 3, 1783, Washington happily anticipated the British withdrawal from New York. The commander-in-chief's last official act at West Point headquarters was the discharge of the Second Continental Dragoons.[5]

Though Tallmadge was no doubt delighted with a last-minute promotion to lieutenant colonel, his mind was preoccupied with the impending British withdrawal from New York City. He requested that he and the officers of his legion be included in the official entry of American forces into the city, a moment of triumph especially savored by those who served through the dark days of the war when the Revolutionary forces were driven from Manhattan. Thinking of the Culpers and his other agents and informants, Tallmadge wrote his commander urging "that particular attention is paid to certain Characters in N.Y. who have served us very essentially, & who may other ways be treated amiss—It is a favor which they will by all means expect, & some of them will not wish to have the nature of their services divulged."[6] His greatest fear was for those of his agents who had feigned loyalty to the Crown as a cover for their real work. To ensure his "emissaries" suffered no reprisals on this account, Tallmadge proposed that he undertake a special mission to New York.

Washington readily acceded to Tallmadge's request, and arranged for him to enter the still British-occupied city under a flag of truce. As he rode south into Manhattan from which the Continental Army had been driven six years before, Tallmadge found himself "surrounded by British troops, Tories, cowboys, and traitors."[7] Nevertheless, the young dragoon major, spy master, and commando was well treated by the British army and navy officers he encountered, although they were certainly aware of his prominent role in the Revolutionary cause. Sir Guy Carleton, the British commander-in-chief, invited Tallmadge for dinner, at which he was introduced to other high ranking officers of the Royal Army and Navy. Tallmadge took a grim satisfaction in the entreaties of Tories who came to him seeking protection against revenge-seeking patriots. "It was not a little amusing to see how men, Tories and Refugees, who a little before uttered nothing but the term Rebels and Traitors to their King against all officers of the American Army, could now come around me in N York and beg my protection against the dreaded rage of their countrymen. But I knew them too well to promise them any protection."[8]

Tallmadge contacted his agents and informants, and took measures to provide for their security and safety. Exactly how he did this is unclear. Possibly, he visited the political leaders of the patriot faction in the city, and apprised them of the crucial and dangerous service given by the putative Tories. Or he might have left written documents testifying to their deeds. In any event, he was happy to later record the lack of even "one instance occurred of any abuse [of American agents], after we took possession of the city, where protection was given, or engaged."[9]

Tallmadge returned to the American lines and briefed Washington on the situation regarding his informants. He also conveyed his impressions of the British high command, which Washington was anxious to learn. With most of the troops already discharged—as much for economic reasons as anything else—Washington prepared to enter New York with a largely symbolic force. On November 21, Carleton withdrew all Crown troops from Long Island, ending the seven-year British occupation. On November 25, 1783, long after celebrated as Evacuation Day, the British ferried their forces from Manhattan to Staten Island, where their transports awaited them. As the British embarked on their vessels, Washington and the remaining Continentals triumphantly marched down rural Manhattan to the city which still occupied only the southern tip of the island.

With the bulk of the soldiers already streaming home, the American forces were led by a small, select corps of American troops under General Henry Knox. Washington and New York governor George Clinton followed close behind, tailed by the army's officers, including Tallmadge, and various politicians. "It was indeed a joyful day to the officers and soldiers of our army," Tallmadge recalled, "and to all the friends of American independence, while the troops of the enemy, still in our waters, and the host of Tories and refugees were sorely mortified. The joy of meeting friends, who had been separated by the cruel rigors of war, cannot be described."[10]

One of the Washington's first acts upon reaching New York was to publicly recognize and reward the services of some ostensible Tories. Whether this was deemed an additional necessity, or because Tallmadge was unaware of their activities and hadn't made provision for them, remains unclear. Washington first breakfasted with Hercules Mulligan, a tailor who had passed on intelligence to his former Kings College classmate, Alexander Hamilton. Most startling—at least in the view of the unsuspecting patriots—the victorious commander-in-chief visited James Rivington, whose *New York Gazette* had functioned as a major mouthpiece for British propaganda during the war. Apparently, Rivington switched sides at some point, possibly because he had become offended by British censorship, or disgusted by the venal conduct of the British military in New York. On the other hand, he may simply have been playing a double game and working for both sides. But Washington clearly considered his covert services of great value—he had secured the British navy flag codes which contributed the victory of the French fleet in the Yorktown campaign—and publicly handed him a bag of gold coins.[11] However stunned they might have been, the public benediction bestowed by the nation's greatest hero redeemed Rivington in the eyes of the patriots. The gold coins, a precious commodity in the cash-strapped infant nation, and used only for the most crucial tasks, were no doubt happily received as well.

Later that night, Governor Clinton threw a dinner for the principal officers and political figures; the following day, victory and independence were celebrated by what Tallmadge declared "a splendid display of fireworks, at the lower part of Broadway, near Bowling Green. It far exceeded anything I had ever seen in my life."[12] The most moving event following the American liberation of the city (though the Tories no doubt viewed it otherwise) occurred on December 4, 1783, when Washington, preparing to return to Mount Vernon, took leave of his officers at Fraunces Tavern in New York. Tallmadge left the only account of what transpired.

> We had been assembled but a few moments, when His Excellency entered the room. His emotion, too strong to be concealed, seemed to be reciprocated by every officer present. In almost breathless silence, the General filled his glass with wine, and turning to the officers he said: "With a heart full of love and gratitude, I now take leave of you. I devoutly wish that your latter days may be as prosperous and happy as your former ones have been glorious and honorable." After the officers had taken a glass of wine, Gen. Washington said: "I cannot come to each of you, but shall feel obliged if each of you will come and take me by the hand."[13]

Led by Knox, Washington's officers came to bid him goodbye, grasped his hand, and kissed him as a token of affection. Not a word was spoken, though many were teary-eyed and some were openly weeping. Reflecting on his own emotions, which were clearly shared by all present, Tallmadge wrote, "The *simple thought* that we were then about to part from the man who had conducted us through a long and bloody war, and under whose conduct the glory and independence of our country had been achieved, and that we should see his face no more in this world, seemed to me utterly insupportable."[14]

Washington waved his hand to his "grieving children," signaling that the time had come for him to depart. He left the tavern, passed through a detachment of light infantry, and walked to Whitehall where a barge was waiting to transport him across the Hudson. A large crowd joined the officers who accompanied the general to the shore and watched as he took a seat in the craft. As the barge slipped into the current, Washington waved his hat in a silent farewell.

The Revolutionary Army's officers soon followed their leader's example and departed for their homes. Tallmadge joyfully journeyed to Setauket, from which he had felt "banished" for seven years. Though he had certainly been in or near the village during some of his reconnoitering excursions, it is doubtful that he ever dared enter, or even approach, his boyhood home. But the renowned major's return following the victorious conclusion of the war was a signal to celebrate. The Setauket residents, excepting the Anglicans, were largely supporters of the Revolution, and they celebrated the homecoming of their most illustrious citizen with a public feast on the village green, featuring a roast ox. Happily surrounded by friends and family, including many he had not seen in years, Tallmadge acted as master of ceremonies. Following his father's invocation, he carved the beast for distribution to the happy villagers.

Tallmadge did not record any conversations he may have had with Roe, Woodhull, or any other members of Culper ring or his other agents, though they surely occurred. Indeed, his involvement with the Culper Ring was a secret he never revealed. But Tallmadge took note of who was absent from the victory festivities in Setauket. "A *Tory* could not have lived in that atmosphere [the celebratory feast] one minute," he recollected. "The joy of the Whig population through the island was literally unbounded, nor could it be expected that their Tory neighbors would escape, unnoticed, through such a scene of rejoicing after victory. In some instances private satisfaction was taken in a pretty summary manner, but in most cases the milder process of law was resorted to and maintained."[15]

Tallmadge's own attitude towards the Tories was complicated. In 1777, with the war well underway but the outcome far from certain, his attitude towards the Loyalists was bitter and unforgiving. "Plague on 'em," he wrote, and then added a thinly veiled threat. "I protest against their coming into any part of America again (they must leave it) which Directions if they think not proper to take, they must abide the Consequence."[16] Combat against the detested Delanceys and the other Loyalists, in Westchester and elsewhere, did nothing to soften his attitudes. Nevertheless, as the war wound down and victory was secured, he began to reassess the wisdom of driving all former Tories from what had been their homeland as well as his. His shifting stance derived from his increased understanding of finance and economics, and he came to see that the new nation was losing a sizable amount of capital—both human and monetary—with the flight of the 30,000 Loyalists who left with the British. In May 1783, he admitted that "with all my Zeal to oppose and punish this race of Delinquents, I cannot but believe there is the greater part of them, the readmission of whom would be the soundest policy the United States could pursue."[17]

Nor was Tallmadge alone in thinking most of the common Tories could be assimilated into the new order. His contemporary Alexander Hamilton was also dismayed by the Loyalist exodus in the last months of the war. "Many merchants of second class," the future secretary of the treasury wrote, "characters of no political consequence, each of whom may carry away 8 or 10,000 guineas have, I am told, applied for shipping to convey them away."[18] Hamilton clearly viewed the departure of money and business acumen as a loss to the nation. Tallmadge and Hamilton were not alone in their assessment of the Tory question. Indeed, it took little time for the more moderate, educated, and wealthier Whigs to reach a détente with the remaining Tories—as long as they had not served in British or Loyalist military units or were prominent in the British occupation administration. In many ways, the moderate Whigs, denounced as "Buttermilk Whigs" by the less-affluent, more radical— and vindictive—"Warm Whigs," shared the same economic and social interests as their Loyalist counterparts. And many former Tories learned how to adjust and prosper in the new republic.

In the days following the victory feast on the Setauket green, Tallmadge toured the east end of Long Island, whose inhabitants' steadfastness to the cause of independence often left them on the receiving end of British and Tory retaliation. Tallmadge's exploits were as well known in the east end villages as they were in Setauket, and he was greeted by public and private officials with respect and gratitude. The dashing dragoon officer also spent some time at Mastic, not far from Fort St. George, where he stayed at the home of William Floyd, a signer of the Declaration of Independence. Floyd had been forced to flee with his family to Connecticut following the British victory at Brooklyn. Tallmadge visited the Floyds at their refuge in Middletown, Connecticut, where he became acquainted with Floyd's daughter, Mary. The Floyd girls were considered great beauties, and James Madison, who had become besotted with Mary's younger daughter, Catherine, was devastated when she broke off their engagement and married another suitor.[19]

Tallmadge must have had a similar response to her older sibling. Despite his numerous flirtations, his relationship with Mary deepened during the war, and shortly after the restoration of peace, with the Floyds back at their Suffolk County home, the couple announced their engagement. Before the wedding, Tallmadge crossed to Connecticut to check on his business interests and prepare his house in Litchfield for his bride to be. Tallmadge had spent much of his young adult life in the Nutmeg State, first at Yale, then as a teacher in Wethersfield, and then in Connecticut regiments in the Continental Army. While he never severed his Long Island ties and affections, he and Mary decided that their future lay in Connecticut.

Benjamin and Mary were wed on March 18, 1784, at a ceremony conducted by Benjamin's father, at Mastic. The wedding, especially after the hard years of the war, was a major event. The estate's grounds and animals had been destroyed or looted by the British, who had used the house as a stable.[20] Floyd's efforts to restore his holdings following his return to Mastic were proceeding smoothly, and Tallmadge happily recollected that his father-in-law had provided a "sumptuous entertainment" to the large gathering of well-wishers. Following the ceremony, the newlyweds visited friends in New York, and then took a lengthy "farewell tour" of Long Island before setting off for their new life in Litchfield.

Later in life, looking back on his service in the Revolution, Tallmadge wondered at the sheer audacity of the Revolutionaries in challenging the British Empire. "It looks almost like madness to have ventured on the mighty conflict." He added that it was "a little less than a miracle that we were sustained through such a bloody war, and finally came out of it victorious."[21] On a purely personal level, Tallmadge was also amazed that he had emerged from the contest without receiving either a life-threatening wound or even a broken bone, despite his practice of leading his men from the front. For that happy circumstance, he thanked divine providence. Tallmadge was not reluctant to reminisce and discuss his wartime exploits, and he was clearly satisfied and proud of his service. Nevertheless, he expressed a sentiment well-known to combat veterans when he wrote his daughter in 1817: "I bless my God that I have not the Occasion, nor the Inclination, to act over these scenes again."[22]

12

A New World

As a young, politically connected war hero, with a healthy amount of capital (probably enhanced by his wife's dowry), Benjamin Tallmadge was well poised to make his mark in the new nation he had helped create. Settling in his expansive, Georgian-style house on Litchfield's South Street, Tallmadge assumed the role of a Federalist squire. He and Mary soon started a family, which ultimately extended to seven: five sons, William S. (1785–1822), Henry Floyd (1787–1854), Fredrick Augustus (1792–1869), Benjamin (1794–1831), and George Washington (1800–1835); and two daughters, Maria (1790–1878) and Harriet Wadsworth (1797–1856), the latter named for his friend and partner, Jeremiah.

In 1790, Tallmadge decided to memorialize his family and commissioned the artist Ralph Earl to paint two large portraits. Paradoxically perhaps, Earl had been a Tory and spent most of the war in London, where he studied under Benjamin West. Whatever his politics, the resulting production is impressive. One picture presents Tallmadge's wife, Mary, attired in fashionable federal-style dress, with children Henry Floyd and Maria Jones. The second features Tallmadge himself with his eldest son, William. The two are posed in what seems to be the library, Tallmadge sitting and Fredrick standing beside him. Tallmadge gazes confidently towards the viewer, the small boy's hand resting on his father's forearm. Tallmadge holds a document, a symbol of his education, if not his status, as a prominent businessman. He conspicuously wears the medal of the Society of Cincinnati, the Revolutionary officers' fraternal organization. While not exactly a badge of rank, the decoration marked him as one of the young republic's proven leaders.

As he began his peacetime career, Tallmadge pursued several financial and business ventures. The store was up and running before the war even ended, and was highly profitable. Tallmadge also served as a private

The Federalist Gentleman. Benjamin Tallmadge and his son, William Smith Tallmadge, by Ralph Earl, 1790. *Benjamin Tallmadge Collections, Litchfield Historical Society, Litchfield, Connecticut.*

banker to his community, providing mortgages and other types of loans.[1] He later assumed more formal banking services, becoming the president of the Phoenix Bank, which became the First National Bank of Litchfield. Nor were his financial activities confined to northwestern Connecticut. He real estate ventures, which began in New Hampshire and New York, soon expanded westward. In 1786, he joined a number of New England Revolutionary War officers in the Ohio Company. The company, founded by Rufus Putnam, purchased a large section of eastern Ohio from the federal government, which it intended to resell to settlers. Nine years later Tallmadge joined with 36 other speculators in purchasing the entire Western Reserve of Ohio for one million dollars.[2] The Western Reserve had originally been claimed by Connecticut for its veterans, but the state later ceded its interest to the federal government. Tallmadge himself made a journey to Marietta, Ohio, in 1795 to see his properties firsthand. He sold off sections of his substantial holdings at different times to generate further cash flow, and deeded parcels of his real estate holdings in Ohio (and elsewhere) to his children and grandchildren.[3] Indeed, he was still involved with the Ohio Company as late as 1834, a year before his death. Tallmadge, Ohio, founded in 1805, is an enduring monument to his western interests.

Tallmadge was a seemingly happy and devoted family man, very much involved with the raising of his children and grandchildren. Throughout his business dealings, investments, and speculations, he made sure they were as well provided for as he could arrange. He also became close to John Cushman, who had married his eldest daughter, Maria, in 1812. Cushman, who was elected to Congress as a Federalist in 1818, had studied law at Litchfield where he met Maria. Tallmadge had full confidence in his son-in-law's financial abilities, and sometimes entrusted him to act as his financial and business agent, investing in stocks and bonds, and carrying out Tallmadge's business on Wall Street and elsewhere. When Judge Tapping Reeve, a close friend of Tallmadge who had established a well-respected law school in Litchfield, wished to invest $2,000 in a safe and steady venture, Tallmadge turned to Cushman and asked, "Can you invest that sum for that good man in the way you have done for me?"[4]

Tallmadge's total worth is difficult to ascertain. Sizable amounts of it were in stocks, bonds, and property, which he converted into cash at

A Lady of the Republic. Mary Floyd Tallmadge and son, Henry Floyd Tallmadge (left), and daughter, Maria Jones Tallmadge, by Ralph Earl, 1790. *Benjamin Tallmadge Collections. Litchfield Historical Society, Litchfield, Connecticut.*

various times. An indication of his assets can be gleaned from a letter he wrote to Cushman in 1820, in which he proposes setting up an investment account of $10,000, while mentioning that he expected to received a draft for an additional $2,000 shortly afterwards.[5] These figures reflect only a slice of his total investments, yet would be at least $238,000 today.[6] However calculated, Tallmadge was a wealthy man.

There was no doubt where Tallmadge would stand politically. He followed his wartime commander, George Washington, in supporting the new Constitution in 1788, and became a member of the Federalist Party, which advocated the creation of a stronger and more effective central government. While many of the Federalists had served in the Continental Army or Congress, they also assumed that the hierarchical socio-political system that operated during the colonial period would continue in place. The Federalists believed that wealth, social and political prominence made natural leaders. As former Revolutionaries, they,

Benjamin Tallmadge House, Litchfield, Connecticut. *Author's Collection.*

of course, supported the right to vote and hold office for freemen and property holders. But they also believed in a "deference democracy," that the "middling sort"—small farmers, craftsmen, minor professionals— would naturally defer to, and elect, those who had proven their ability to lead through visible achievement, perhaps with a little genteel birth thrown in. While Tallmadge never seems to have deeply analyzed the political culture which shaped his world and his thinking, as a young, ambitious man from a respected ministerial family, he saw no contradictions between deference democracy and republicanism. Surely, he had demonstrated his claim to leadership in the new American Republic.

Tallmadge had the opportunity to meet his former commander-in-chief on several occasions in the 1790s. His business and family connections sometimes took him to New York, then the nation's capital, and Washington visited Tallmadge in Litchfield during one of his excursions into the countryside. Washington presented Tallmadge with a portrait painted by James Sharpless, depicting him as president. The portrait remained in the family until Tallmadge's grandson, Frederick Samuel Townsend, bequeathed it to the Sons of the Revolution in New York upon his death in 1904.

How often Tallmadge communicated with Washington after the first president left office and returned to Mount Vernon is uncertain. The two men were clearly in contact with each other, however indirectly, in the year before Washington's death. In 1798, France, then governed by the Directory (a five-man board) which took power in the aftermath of the Reign of Terror, adopted an imperious and confrontational policy towards the young nation. American ambassadors were demeaned, bribes were demanded for the Directory's personal use, French privateers were set upon American commerce, and pro–French factions in the United States were encouraged to attack the policy of neutrality adopted by the United States when Europe erupted into war in 1792. In the spring and summer of 1798, the John Adams administration took steps to prepare for war, laying down frigates for the navy, and making preliminary plans to enlarge the army. Instinctively, they turned to Washington to command the newly proposed "provisional" army of 10,000, which was to be mobilized in the event of a French invasion.[7]

Washington, feeling his age (he was 66 in 1798), was reluctant to take on the responsibility, but accepted the position out of a sense of duty, and unwillingness to stand aside in the event of a French invasion which many, especially Federalists, believed imminent.[8] Washington, however, stipulated that he should "not be called into the field until the Army is in a situation to require my presence, or it becomes indispensible by the emergency of circumstances."[9] In the meantime, having previously advised the administration not to activate the army until "the emergency becomes evident," Washington began planning for the organization of the intended force, consulting with Adams, James McHenry, Secretary of State Charles Pickering, and his old confidant, Alexander Hamilton, who was the primary force behind the agitation for an expanded American military.

Washington dismissed most of the "old generals" as unsuited to the task at hand: "Some on account of their age or infirmities; some from never having displayed any talents for Enterprise; and others from their general opposition to the Government, or their predilection to French measures, be their present conduct what it may."[10] Not all of the Revolutionary generation was rejected out of hand. Despite his controversial political reputation, Washington intended to appoint Hamilton as inspector general, with the rank of major general. Charles Pinckney and Henry Knox were also slated for major general commissions.[11]

Beyond the new force's high command, Washington drew up a "Proposed Arrangement of General & Other Officers." The once and future commanding general based his evaluations on his recollection of "the most intelligent and active Officers in the late American army."[12] Washington divided his list by states, regional politics being a consideration. A total of 49 officers were included in the listing, five being from Connecticut. Elisha Sheldon, Tallmadge's old commander, was included without comment. Only Tallmadge was described as "very good."[13]

Washington had clearly been impressed by Tallmadge's abilities as a combat leader and horse soldier. When the time came to nominate a head of the Cavalry Corps in the proposed army, he wrote the following to Secretary of War McHenry: "I have no hesitation in declaring it as my opinion, that Major Tallmadge (formerly of Sheldon's horse) would not disgrace it, and is to be preferred to his former colonel."[14] Apparently an offer of the cavalry command was made to Tallmadge. Surprisingly, he declined, and requested a higher position—adjutant general of the army. On learning of Tallmadge's response, probably from McHenry, Washington replied that he "did not imagine that Major Tallmadge's expectations would have soared so high. To have commanded the cavalry I should have thought would have been gratifying, and I believe he is better qualified for *that*, than Adjutant General. Not that he *might* do for the latter, altho' it so happened that he was little with the Army (being chiefly deployed on detached parties), and of course less acquainted with a roster."[15]

Washington clearly saw Tallmadge as a man of action, a field commander, and not a staff officer, which was the role of an adjutant general whatever the grade. Why Tallmadge declined the command of the Cavalry Corps and pushed for the adjutancy is puzzling. Tallmadge was always ambitious and, secure in his Revolutionary record, he might have thought he deserved a more prominent position. Although he was only 44, he might also have concluded that a front-line command was too arduous, and, as a successful businessman, he was entitled to greater rank and prestige as compensation for leaving the private sector and reentering the unpredictable whirlwind of warfare. Interestingly, André had been adjutant general of the British Army.

While Washington may have been taken aback, and perhaps offended, by Tallmadge's reaction, he did not alter his appraisal of Tallmadge's military worth. In October 1798, commenting on a projected force of six troops of Light Dragoons for the Provisional Army, Washington noticed that a commandant of dragoons had yet to be appointed. He knew who he wanted: "If Major Tallmadge would accept command of this Corps, I know of none who is more preferable."[16] Whether or not Tallmadge ever received an official offer of the command, or if he ever heard or read of Washington's evaluation of his abilities, is unknown. Whatever his response to the proposal might have been, there is little doubt that he would have taken Washington's evaluation of his talents as the highest accolade of his wartime career.

In the end, it all came to naught. Much to Washington's relief, at least, the expected open war with France did not occur, and the proposed army was never called into being. Instead, the Adams administration fought the Undeclared Naval War with France, unleashing its new frigates and warships against the French until they held off on their attacks on American commerce. War was avoided. For a time.

Though he and Washington differed on his potential place in the projected army, Tallmadge's affection and respect for his Revolutionary commander never diminished. Shortly after Washington's death in 1799, Tallmadge wrote the Rev. Manasseh Cutler, a colleague in the Ohio land speculation deal, voicing his assessment of the man he had devoutly followed in war and peace.

> Our Country seems to be clad in *real mourning* for the loss of our great Benefactor, Patriot and Friend, the illustrious Washington. I can truly say that the loss of my own father did not so sensibly affect me as the death of this peerless Man. While he lived I was fully satisfied that his equal was not on earth, and since he has died, the public testimony to his worth has exceeded even the most sanguine expectation.[17]

The one area where Tallmadge thought Washington slightly less than he might have been concerned religion, a subject which became increasing important to him as the new century progressed.

> Although from a long and tolerably intimate acquaintance with him, I have been abundantly convinced of his attachment to the *Christian system*; yet had he been explicit in his profession of *faith in* and *dependence* on the finished *Atonement* of our glorious Redeemer for acceptance and pardon, what a conspicuous trait it would have formed in his illustrious character.[18]

Tallmadge received the position of postmaster, in Litchfield, in 1792. Washington was in his first term in office and the post was a government gift. By the end of the decade, however, Tallmadge decided to pursue an active role on the national stage. He ran for Congress as a Federalist, and was elected in 1800. It was not the most fortuitous time to take office as a Federalist. Washington had left office in 1797, and died two years later. His successor, John Adams, became the second and last Federalist president, losing to Thomas Jefferson in the year Tallmadge won his seat in the House of Representatives. Jefferson was the leader of the Democratic-Republicans, who derided the Federalists as arrogant aristocrats. Despite being led by wealthy Southern slave owners, the Jeffersonian Republicans adopted the rhetorical device of extolling the "common man," which resonated among a growing segment of the population. Indeed, the rival party partisans, in and out of the press, grew increasingly vituperative in their attacks, often engaging in what the late–20th century would term "politics of personal destruction." The pro–Democratic-Republican press, never shy about vilifying their opponents, grew ever more hostile with the arrival of British, Irish, and French radicals, who quickly joined their cause.[19]

In 1813, during a debate on army expansion, Tallmadge rose in a House committee to denounce his party's adversaries. Although he opened his remarks with the statement that "this is no time to indulge the bickering of party," he must have realized the point had long passed when such an Eden—if it ever existed—could be revived.[20] He then referred back to his idea of a Golden Age when he asserted, "I should consider it the most auspicious event of my life if I could see every gentleman on the floor determined to take and maintain *the true old American ground, occupied by the patriots of '76.*"[21] The veteran colonel then laid out his political and patriotic credentials by pointing to his Revolutionary War service, and declared that, after 1776, he had "never changed my political creed to the present day."[22] In other words, Federalism was the embodiment of the Revolutionary tradition.

Taking a swipe at the Jeffersonian editors and writers, he castigated the "foul presses of our country for the odious epithets of *monarchists, foreign agents, Tories,* and the like," which had been derisively hurled at the Federalists. Tallmadge took special notice of the belligerence of recent immigrants among the Democratic-Republican supporters. Such persons, he claimed, had grown "weary" of toiling in their native homes, and had fled to the United States, sometimes one step ahead of the law. Although they were but recent arrivals in America, Tallmadge sarcastically claimed the immigrant Republicans now intended to "instruct [Americans] into the true principles of *liberty and equality.* To this set of newly hatched politicians, and men of a similar stamp, is this once happy country indebted to one half of the miseries, and much of the disgrace which it suffers."[23] This was a heavy charge, essentially denouncing the immigrant Democratic-Republicans as French agents, who had pushed the United States into war with Britain, with all its attendant miseries and costs. Tallmadge was hardly alone in his disdain for the immigrant radicals and Democratic-Republicans' foreign and economic policy in general. Indeed, his arguments hewed to the Federalist line, just as the newspaper editors, who assailed the Federalists as anglophile aristocrats, supported theirs.

Tallmadge may have feared Jefferson and his party as an organization of radical levelers, but he also abhorred the use of slave labor on which the wealth of the Democratic-Republican's Southern leadership depended. The Revolution and its insistence on liberty and freedom had caused soul-searching on the part of many of those advocating American independence. Immediately following the war, the states north of Maryland began emancipating their slaves, some gradually, others relatively quickly. While over 80 percent of the nation's slaves lived in the South, the system was practiced in New York and Connecticut, and Tallmadge would certainly have been familiar with the sight of slaves on Long Island. There is no evidence that his family owned slaves in Setauket, nor that he possessed any in Connecticut before the institution was outlawed there. In 1797, however, he did buy the contract of two indentured servants who were bound to work for him for three years.[24]

The only time Tallmadge mentioned slavery during the Revolution was after his raid on Lloyd's Neck in 1779 when he captured a man described as being one of the Tory officers' slaves. He did not explain the slave's ultimate fate. However, in 1819, as the controversy over the admission of Missouri as a slave state embroiled the nation, Tallmadge voiced his disapproval of the willingness of some Northerners to seek a compromise: "I am sorry to learn that by the votes of any of our Northern Members, slavery should be perpetuated in any part of the Country. But I have long since learned to expect disappointments from the Conduct of men, from whom a very different Course of Conduct might have been hoped."[25] A compromise was reached, avoiding a collision between the free and slave states, a "course of conduct" which was pursued into the 1850s when the disagreement about slavery could no longer be negotiated away. Tallmadge was also a supporter of the American Colonization Society, which encouraged slave owners to manumit their slaves and transport them to Africa.[26] The west African nation of Liberia was founded by such liberated slaves, though the society's hopes to free and repatriate all slaves ultimately foundered on the growing profitability of cotton, and the reluctance of most free blacks to move to a continent they had never seen.

Among the major events which Tallmadge dealt with as a congressman was the War of 1812, the nation's second war with Britain and one to which Tallmadge was deeply opposed. In 1808, Jefferson and his secretary of state, James Madison, persuaded the Democratic-Republican majority in Congress to pass the Embargo Act, effectively economic

sanctions, which they hoped would lead Britain and France to stop seizing American ships and seamen. The act, which prohibited American
international trade, created a depression in New England. At the same
time suggestions were made to strengthen the United States Army in
the event of war. Rumors floated that Tallmadge, whose military career
was well known, would be appointed a colonel of light dragoons, though
there is no evidence he was seeking such a command. In any event, the
Washington Federalist quashed that scenario: "Judging from the appoint-
ments already made we see no reason for supposing that Jefferson and
his man [Secretary of War] Dearborn will bestow a commission on so
meritorious an officer, and gentlemanly a man as Colonel Tallmadge."[27]
As far as the Federalist press was concerned, Jefferson, despite his plan-
tation and slaves, was no gentleman, and Dearborn was of even lower
status.

Federalist opposition to the Jeffersonians, especially their economic
and diplomatic policies, became heated, and some, though not many,
may have flirted with taking New England out of the union. For their
part, the Democratic-Republicans doubled down on their campaign to
brand the Federalists as elitists, aristocrats, and even would-be monarchists. Years later, looking back on the political warfare which dominated
his eight terms in Congress, Tallmadge, stated that he had "some opportunity of noticing the changes which took place in *men*, as well as some
of the *measures* of government."[28] He was particularly bitter about the
defection of some Federalists—especially John Quincy Adams—to the
opposition: "Whether their conversion from Federalism to Democracy
was by agreement of the parties as to *time* and *fact*, has not yet been disclosed. In one thing no one can be mistaken:—their malice against their
former friends seems to be unbounded."[29]

While the drift into war inflamed the passions of the opposing parties, their animosity was present from Washington's second term, and
was well established when Jefferson captured the presidency in 1800. As
early as the 1803–1804 Congressional session, the Democratic-
Republicans charged the New England Federalists with secessionist
intentions, an allegation which they denied at the time, and which Tallmadge refuted when it was dredged up in 1829. He had roomed with the
Connecticut delegation during those years, he remembered, describing
his colleagues as "Federalists of the old school." He went on, stating that

he would certainly have remembered "so solemn a subject" as secession being "spoken of without leaving a deep impression on my mind. For myself, I can say I have no recollection of any [secessionist] conversation having taken place, among my Federal friends ... advocating the necessity of forming a separate government in New England; or having a meeting in Boston, of the leading Federalists, to consult on such a measure; or that General Hamilton had consented to attend such a meeting."[30]

Tallmadge's mention of Alexander Hamilton was telling. Until his death, resulting from a duel with Aaron Burr in 1804, Hamilton was the leader of the high (or ultra) Federalists, and the bête noire of the Jeffersonians. Hamilton's aspiration for a powerful central government overseeing a commercial/industrialized nation was anathema to the agriculturally minded Democratic-Republican leadership, and he was often charged with seeking some sort of American monarchy. When the charges were revived in 1829, Tallmadge set about to defend his old colleague and party leader from the posthumous allegations of the "Democracy." Tallmadge was acquainted with Hamilton during the war, and met him occasionally while he was Secretary of the Treasury during the Washington administration. "Yet I had not the honor of a free intercourse with him," he insisted, "and do not remember ever to have received a letter from him in my life." He had, however, called on Hamilton alone or "in company of our mutual friend, Colonel Wadsworth ... yet have I never heard an expression from him favoring the project of forming a separate government, which would thereby jeopardize the Union of these States."[31]

Like most Federalists, Tallmadge opposed the declaration of War with Britain over the issue of the impressment of sailors and seizure of American shipping. Tallmadge and his party were outraged by the paradox—if not hypocrisy—of the Democratic-Republicans, dominated by members from the West and South, breaking with Britain over issues which did not affect them, but which the Northeast, which bore the pain of the British policies, opposed. At least once during the war, Tallmadge voiced his condemnation of the conflict, fully and publicly. On January 7, 1813, a new bill authorizing an increase in American forces was introduced in the House of Representatives Military Committee. Before explaining his opposition to the bill, he laid out his objections to the war itself:

Because I deprecate this war, as pregnant with great evils, if not ruin to my country, I will therefore take all constitutional measures to bring it to a speedy and honorable close, and because I have no confidence in the executive department of our government, nor the subordinate agents who have been appointed to conduct the war, I am in conscience bound not to vote for this bill, which if adopted, will intail greater evils on this devoted country.[32]

Tallmadge proceeded to identify three major causes of the war: the British attack on the American frigate *Chesapeake* during peacetime; the British Orders in Council which authorized the seizure of American shipping on the grounds that American trade aided France; and the British impressments of sailors on American ships, claiming they had deserted from British service. Tallmadge disposed of the first cause quickly by observing that the British did (finally) make "atonement" for the *Chesapeake* attack, and might have done so sooner if the Madison administration, which had succeeded Jefferson in 1809, had not attached other issues to a settlement.[33] While Tallmadge maintained he did not excuse the "great and heavy" grievances the United States had against both belligerents, he argued that Madison had ignored French infringement on American neutral rights while driving the nation to war with Britain for their similar behavior. He added, correctly, that the British had repealed the Orders in Council, which authorized the capture of American ships, five days after the United States had declared war. Due to the month-long trans–Atlantic communications lag, neither side knew what the other had done. Nevertheless, the Orders in Council, which were "ostensibly the most prominent cause of war," had been repealed, and yet the Madison administration chose to ignore their removal and continue the conflict.[34]

Tallmadge's take on impressments simultaneously downplayed its effects and implicitly accepted the British position. In the years leading up to the war, the Royal Navy began stopping American ships to search for sailors among the crews who were British subjects and/or deserters from the British navy or merchant fleet. To a large degree, the British were driven by a need to man their powerful navy, and Tallmadge noted that the British were unlikely to change their policy while at war with "the most formidable power on earth." But there was also a collision in concepts of citizenship. American law held that foreigners could become naturalized citizens, while the British maintained that anyone born a subject of the Crown remained so. Tallmadge remarked that Britain had always held this outlook, suggesting that the United States should accept their policy as valid in the case of *naturalized* American citizens. This was an odd attitude for a prominent Revolutionary War veteran, the irony of which he did not care to notice or pursue.

Turning to the issue native-born Americans impressed by Britain, Tallmadge claimed that their number was greatly exaggerated. He cited 6,257 American citizens that the government claimed Britain had impressed, but contended the number was scarcely 5,000, though how this removed the essential grievance was unstated.[35] Tallmadge went on to posit a two-tiered system of American citizenship. Native-born Americans were fully entitled to all the rights, responsibilities, and protections of the nation. This, however, was not the case for naturalized citizens. He believed they should be treated hospitably and accorded government protection while they were within United States territory. On the other hand, if naturalized citizens choose

> to go upon the great highway of nations, the risqué and choice are their own, as will be the peril. Put the case fairly to the yeomanry of the country, and let them understand the subject, that this war is to be carried out for the purpose of protecting foreigners while sailing on the high seas, and I much incline to the opinion, that they would dismiss the authors of this war from further service, or oblige them to bring it to a close. Sir, I will not consent to waste one drop of pure American blood, nor extend a single dollar, to protect on the high seas all the vagabonds of Europe. Valuable as may have been the acquisition in obtaining many great and good men as emigrants from Europe, still I maintain the opinion that all the blessings of liberty and domestic government which are secured to them in common with our native citizen ought to be ample compensation. I know it is no easy matter to draw the precise line where protection shall cease.[36]

But war with Britain was clearly crossing it.

This narrow, ungenerous, and unRevolutionary viewpoint,—which would have made Lafayette, von Steuben, Kosciusko, and like second-class citizens—is difficult to square with Tallmadge's Revolutionary experiences and the ideology it invoked. It likely sprang from the vicious politics of the times, and fears that French Jacobinism was threatening the liberties and tranquility of the country in the guise of the Democratic-Republicans. It also didn't help that they were clearly ascendant.

Having finished the administration's decision to go war, Tallmadge then explained his reasons for opposing the bill creating an expanded military force. He described the newly proposed regiments as short-term troops who would be both expensive and "useless in offensive war." Tallmadge argued that if the army were to be expanded, the regular, existing regiments should be brought to full strength. "If this bill is to be supported because the ranks in your regular army cannot be filled, I say you should begin to seriously think about a peace, or disgrace and discomfiture will be the consequence."[37]

Tallmadge also criticized those Democratic-Republicans, mostly from the South and West, who saw war with Britain as an opportunity to invade and seize Canada. Tallmadge charged that the proposed military increase as a means of promoting this objective and damned it as "truly anti-republican and dangerous to the liberties of this people. The history of the world and the principles of our own government call loudly for us not to jeopardize our safety by foreign conquests."[38] Foreign conquests, Tallmadge warned, harkening back to his old Whig roots, resulted in large standing armies, those "engines of despotism." "I cannot too strongly reprobate the doctrine of foreign invasion, for the purpose of annexing great districts of country to the territory of the United States."[39]

Tallmadge was also concerned what the leader of a large army might do if victorious. He recounted the Newburgh Conspiracy at the end of the Revolution when anonymous notices appeared, encouraging a military coup if the army's grievances—primarily lack of pay—were not met. These calls for a military march on Philadelphia were only defeated through the intervention of Washington, that "illustrious chief, who now sleeps in his humble tomb in Mount Vernon [who] saved the army from disgrace; and perhaps the country saved from bloodshed and ruin."[40] And a man like Washington, Tallmadge had no need to remind his listeners, was a phenomenon. Would a lesser man in command of a large, powerful, and victorious army, follow the example of the American Cincinnatus, relinquish his power, and resist the temptation to seize control of the nation? Tallmadge had his doubts.

More prosaically, Tallmadge contended that the new appropriations were simply too expensive. "I fear gentlemen have not sufficiently attended to this circumstance in their zeal to conquer Canada," he acerbically remarked.[41] In the end, the Federalists, in the minority, were out-voted. The party continued to criticize, if not outright oppose, the war. Feeling almost besieged in their last bastion in New England, many avoided supporting the government, and some, also in the minority, worked to impede the war effort. When the war ended in 1815, almost simultaneously with Andrew Jackson's one-sided victory over the British at New Orleans, the Federalists seemed obsolete, unpatriotic, and possibly seditious. They were soon extinct.

Perhaps worn down by all the wartime politics, possibly recognizing that his party was fading into history and his political career ended, Tallmadge declined to run for re-election in 1816. Continued service, he advised the voters, would "be incompatible with [my] views."[42] Upon returning to private life, he professed, probably sincerely, to be relieved to have left Congress. "My domestic circle & fireside have more charms for me than all the pageantry of the Drawing room & law, nor would I exchange my quiet abode, for the best office the Gov't could bestow on me," he stated.[43] He may have left political life, but a man of his intellect and energies would not remain "quiet."

13

Senior Statesman

In or out of office, Tallmadge took a keen interest in the welfare of the Revolutionary War veterans. Though he had returned to private life in March 1817, he maintained many contacts in Washington, especially with his son-in-law, John Cushman, who was the Federalist representative from the Troy area of New York. In 1818, concerned that the War of 1812 veterans were being well compensated for their service while the Revolutionary veterans were ignored, Tallmadge raised his concerns to Cushman.

> I am pleased to find that the House of Reps. begins to believe that they ought not to lavish the whole Revenue of our Country, & all the new lands also, upon the late army. I am for performing our Contracts most faithfully, although I opposed most of the extravagant promises of the Govt.... As for the revolutionary Army, I have but small expectations that anything will be done for them.... The hardships of the late war [1812], would sink into almost nothing if they could be contrasted with the services & sufferings of the revolution; & yet our modern Politicians can vote pensions, & bounties to any Extent to the Agents of the former, while the hoary headed veteran who served in the latter, & sacrificed his health to achieve the Independence of this Country, may beg his bread, or suffer under the gripping hand of penury & disease without public relief. I ask nothing for myself, although I know my Country has not fulfilled her Engagements, solemnly pledged to me in the hour of her need; but I do implore some assistance for my indigent Brethren in arms.[1]

Tallmadge remained an advocate for his generation of soldiers throughout his life. In 1828, he solicited support for efforts by the Society of Cincinnati to lobby Congress to grant half-pay pensions to surviving Revolutionary War officers.[2] Yet, his concern for the veterans was not limitless. Indeed, he dramatically and publicly prevented one small group of veterans from winning an increase in their pensions—the militiamen who captured John André. As a result of their capture and the exposure of Arnold's treachery, John Paulding, Isaac Van Wart, and David Williams became instantaneous heroes in the pro-independence population and the army. In addition to the expressions of appreciation from Congress, they received pensions of $200 from the United States government, and tracts of land from New York State. Like many Revolutionary War veterans, they sought to gain an increase in the pension allotment, and likely assumed the memory of their service would win the raise. Tallmadge, on the verge of his own retirement from the House of Representatives in early 1817, protested that they had not acted out of patriotism, and denounced them as freebooters who went back and forth between American and British-held territory. He further charged that the only reason they had taken André prisoner was that he hadn't offered them enough of a bribe.

On the face of it, Tallmadge's allegations seem perplexing. The three militia men, who soon gathered testimonials to their adherence to the rebel cause during the war, had refused André's clumsy attempt at bribery, whatever the amount. Tallmadge was also at odds with his hero, George Washington, who was publicly grateful for the crucial roles played by Paulding, Van Wart, and Williams in exploding the conspiracy. He awarded each of them the nation's first military decoration, a specially ordered silver medallion bearing the title "Fidelity," and bestowed the medals on the men in a ceremony at West Point. Tallmadge's unexpected behavior can best be seen as a demonstration of the enduring affection he felt for André. While he never doubted André had to be executed, he always lamented its necessity, believed the wrong man suffered for the treasonous plot, and now attempted to defend André's posthumous honor by denying it to the men who had taken him. A class element was likely present as well. Tallmadge and André were bound by a shared status of "gentlemen," and the militiamen were not.

Tallmadge's implicit invocation of class in his denunciations of André's captors did not go down well among the mechanics, farmers, minor professionals, budding industrialists, and smaller merchants— men who had absorbed the Jefferson-Jackson principles of the fundamental equality of all Americans—at least regarding white men. Paulding, Williams, and Van Wart had become not just Revolutionary War heroes, but heroes in which the more average Americans could see themselves—militia men, small farmers, part-time soldiers, men who had left their homes in service of their country and acted diligently and splendidly. "Col. Tallmadge," the *New-York Courier* declared in a widely reprinted article, "has endeavored to tear the fairest leaf from our history, and to deprive the yeomanry of our country of a theme in which they gloried."[3] The paper called upon Tallmadge to demonstrate the truth of his accusations, and ridiculed him for having accepted André's account of his captors "because André said he was of that opinion! Upon such ground the Col. employed the weight of his character, and the authority of his place, to consign to infamy the three men who saved West Point and the army."[4] Tallmadge succeeded in blocking an increase in the militiamen's pensions, but the blowback probably stunned the aging dragoon, whose judgment was apparently clouded by both personal feelings and eighteenth century values, neither of which fit comfortably in the new America.

The Arnold-André affair remained a badly healed wound which ripped apart at various times in Tallmadge's life. In 1822, a few years after he had left Congress, Tallmadge received a letter from Timothy Pickering stating: "I remember that you once stated to me some interesting circumstances concerning Arnold's flight, by which it seemed to you that you would have arrested him, but for the scrupulocity or weakness of lieut. Col. Jamisson [sic]. I am very desirous of obtaining your details of this matter."[5] Tallmadge begged off. He pointed out that there were "only *four Officers* of our Army who knew all the Circumstances relating to the Capture and detention of Major André, with the other incidents above hinted at, & of this number *I am the only survivor.* The Question presented to my mind is simply this; what benefits can result from a full statement of this interesting event?"[6]

Regarding the course taken after André was delivered to the dragoons, Tallmadge declared that a "full disclosure of all that was said and done on that occasion would appear almost incredible, and could have no other Effect but to wound the feelings of the friends of the deceased, and no public benefit to result from it."[7] The same was true of his discussing "the proposals made for the Detention of General Arnold." Tallmadge confessed he was still smarting from the hostile public reaction which greeted his intervention in the militiamen's pension request. "I have too high a relish for tranquility & peace," he informed Pickering, "to expose myself to the malignity of every party–Scribler and time serv-

MAJOR JOHN ANDRÉ hung as spy at Tappan, N. Y. Oct. 2, 1780 brought to a stand by John Paulding, Isaac Van Wert and David Williams. André had been commissioned to buy with gold what steel could not conquer; to drive a bargain with one ready for a price to become a traitor.—His remains were afterwards transferred and buried in Westminster Abbey. General Arnold's treason revealed Sept. 26. Washington writes, Arnold's conduct is so villainously perfidious, that there are no terms that can describe the baseness of his heart.

MAJOR JOHN ANDRÉ

General Arnold

LANGE, Serie II.   No. 35.
I. SCHWALBACH, Plessigrapure.

ing Editor, who would glory in such a subject for abuse. In addition to all, I should be considered the Hero of my own Tale, without a living Witness to corroborate the Story. The result of all is, after weighing all Circumstances, that I have deliberately concluded never to disclose the Circumstances which relate to that interesting Event."[8]

Tallmadge's response to Pickering is intriguing and frustrating. Though he declined to state directly all he knew of the affair, he clearly implies that the botched capture was caused by Jamieson's refusal to allow him to secure Arnold until Washington could determine his involvement with the British major. Tallmadge's reticence at the time likely stemmed from a desire to shield Jamieson's reputation, the man himself having died in 1810. Arnold was one of the great devils in the American republic's creation, and had Tallmadge clearly stated the traitor could have been taken but for Jamieson's obstinacy, his name would have been held in contempt to the detriment of his family.

In the early 1830s, while working on his memoir, Tallmadge corresponded with Jared Sparks about André, and had recovered from the shock of being pilloried in the press for his remarks on Paulding, Williams, and Van Wart. Tallmadge opened up somewhat about the events of September 1780. A careful reading of his memoir, correspondence, and the remarks he made to his daughter, leaves little doubt that Tallmadge grasped the nature of the plot and Arnold's role in it. Jamieson failed to do so and rebuffed Tallmadge's arguments and entreaties to hold Arnold under guard until Washington returned to West Point. (See Chapter 7.)

A happier reminder of the war appeared with the visit of the Marquis de Lafayette to the United States in 1824. Lafayette had been the most notable of the foreign officers who had volunteered to aid the Continental Army, and he was probably Washington's favorite among his officers. Lafayette's visit gave the nation the opportunity to celebrate the Revolution by welcoming the revered Frenchman with elaborate public displays and celebrations. In August, Tallmadge traveled to New Haven to meet Lafayette, whom he had known during the war, though probably

Opposite: **Heroes of the Republic. Patriotic postcard, c. 1900, celebrating the capture and execution of André. Paulding, Van Wart and Williams are credited with foiling Arnold's plot.** *Author's Collection.*

not intimately. Lafayette, who had arrived from New York, was greeted by a large crowd at the harbor, and escorted into the city. He was first greeted by the politicos, the mayor, city corporation and governor, and then the sheriff escorted Tallmadge and a group of waiting Revolutionary officers to meet him. "Being senior officer in rank," Tallmadge related, "it fell to my lot to introduce my brethren one by one. As soon as we reached the Door I caught the General's Eye, when he came forward & clasped me in his arms & embrac'd me with much affection, kissing both cheeks repeatedly. Our embrace was mutual & cordial, & both of us were very much overcome. As soon as this salutation was over, I introduced my fellow officers, all of whom the Genl recd with peculiar regard. Then followed the citizens male & female without number. In fine I never witnessed such a scene."[9]

Another pleasant reminder of the halcyon days of the Revolution appeared in the guise of the exhibition of Rembrandt Peale's portrait of Washington as president, in 1826. The public response was enthusiastic, and many compared it favorably to Gilbert Stuart's dour portrait which appears on the dollar bill. Tallmadge, who viewed the portrait in New York, was equally adulatory. In a letter to Peale published in the *Connecticut Herald*, he wrote:

> Having served under the immediate command of Gen. Washington through the Revolutionary War and having been often with him during his subsequent political life, I think I have had opportunities to see him in almost all conditions of his variegated life. Although many excellent portraits have been taken of him, I have never seen one, until this day, that seemed to combine a good likeness of his person, with that peculiar expression of countenance which never failed to impress every one who beheld him. I am free to acknowledge, that your portrait of Washington, in his presidential costume, embodies more character, with a good likeness, than I have ever yet seen on canvas. When I first beheld your portrait, it excited in my mind that peculiar feeing of veneration and respect, which his presence never failed to inspire.[10]

An officer and a gentleman, Tallmadge was justifiably proud of his Revolutionary War service. Nevertheless, from time to time he expressed suspicion of overly ambitious military men. His concerns, he once wrote, stemmed from his "knowing something of human Nature, & having often seen that men cloathed with military power, far removed from controul, are very liable to abuse it."[11] As he returned to private life, Tallmadge's tranquility was troubled by the rising star of national politics, the hero of the Battle of New Orleans—Andrew Jackson. Tallmadge likely sniffed a demagogue in the frontier-born, violent-tempered, populist politician in the making. He was particularly concerned with Jackson's willingness to take aggressive action with little or no governmental sanction. In 1819, provoked by raids into the Southern states by escaped slaves, Seminole Indians, and garden-variety outlaws, Jackson invaded Spanish-owned Florida. Declaring that the Spanish had not exerted proper control over the territories' inhabitants, he occupied Pensacola and St. Mark's. He carried out his campaign largely on his own authority as military commander in the South, and basically informed Washington of what he was doing as he unleashed his forces.

Tallmadge was among those who saw Jackson's actions as an act of international outlawry, and an usurpation of the Constitutional authority of the president and Congress, carried out by a man with Caesar-like aspirations. Fearful of Jackson's ambitions, Tallmadge wrote to his son-in-law, John Cushman, his hopes that "there may be many men who will not be disposed to offer up the liberties of our country on the altar of military Despotism. I hope some proposition may yet be submitted to Congress that will test their opinions on the conduct of Genl Jackson."[12]

Tallmadge's hopes in this regard were doomed to disappointment. While Jackson's seizure of the two key towns and forts in Florida were not ordered by the government, both the president, James Monroe, and his Secretary of State, John Quincy Adams, considered them useful leverage in negotiating with Spain for an overall boundary agreement from Florida to the Louisiana Territory–Texas border. "I take it for granted the Administration and Gen Jackson are to be supported," Tallmadge wrote resignedly to Cushman. They were. Realizing Jackson was not going away, and valuing their Mexican territories more than Florida, Spain agreed to sell the entire territory to the United States as part of a general treaty. The Spanish had not much time to relax as revolutions soon drove them from all of their mainland colonies.

Jackson went on to parlay his dramatic military career into an equally successful political one, winning the presidency in 1828. Tallmadge and the aging former Federalists, along with others of similar political disposition who eventually formed a new opposition party, the Whigs, watched impotently as Jackson proceeded as victoriously in politics as he had in war. Tallmadge probably applauded Jackson's defense of the Union and the Constitution during the tariff-nullification crisis with South Carolina when that state threatened the sovereignty of federal law. As an experienced businessman and banker, he was unlikely to have supported Jackson's destruction of the Bank of the United States. Originally created by Hamilton during Washington's administration, the institution had functioned as a central bank which issued sound currency and kept a rein on state and local banks. As an experienced businessman and financial figure, Tallmadge understood the bank's important role in maintaining stable economic conditions. Jackson's blocked renewal of the Bank's charter led to its collapse, and the subsequent "Panic"—depression—of 1837.

Tallmadge, and many of the Whigs in New England, opposed yet another of Jackson's primary initiatives—the removal of the remaining Indian tribes east of the Mississippi. Jackson's formative years were spent in the South Carolina backcountry during and after the Revolution, where conflict with the Indians was a common occurrence. During his second term in office, Jackson supported the campaign by the state of Georgia and other Southern land interests to oust the Five Civilized Tribes from the South, and open up their lands for settlement, especially the increasingly lucrative cotton economy. Despite his democratic rhetoric and political stance, Jackson had made himself a wealthy planter, allied with the Southern land interests. "John Marshall has made his decision. Now he can enforce it," he is reputed to have stated after the Chief Justice of the Supreme Court gave Indian tribes special status and declared Georgia's impending seizure of their lands invalid. Instead, Jackson pushed the Indian Removal Act through Congress.

Many Northern politicians, such as ex-president John Quincy Adams, protested the impending dispossession of the Indians, especially the Cherokees who seemed the most advanced (i.e., they had created a lifestyle very much like the majority population). Tallmadge added his voice to their cause. Though he hadn't been in office for almost 14 years, he called upon Connecticut representative Asa Huntington to organize a petition supporting the attempts by the Cherokees to keep their lands, for "however desperate their case may have appeared," he argued, "we cherish the hope that Deliverance may yet be found for them."[13] Jackson destroyed many of Tallmadge's hopes, and he crushed those of the

Cherokee as well. In the winter of 1836–37 the Five Civilized Tribes were forced out of their homes, and escorted by the army to what would one day be Oklahoma and Kansas, in what the Indians remembered as the "Trail of Tears."

One of the striking developments in Tallmadge's life after 1800 is the growing prominence, almost predominance, of religion. Though he was raised in a ministerial household, and was certainly exposed to further Calvinistic instruction at Yale, there are few (if any) direct references to religion in his wartime letters. Some of this may just reflect a youthful attitude, and the turbulence of the time. It also suggests that, like many educated, late-eighteenth century Americans, Tallmadge was influenced by Deism, a fashionable philosophy which held that while a Supreme Being may have created the universe and everything in it, this force takes no action in its operations, including the work of human beings.

In any event, as the new century opened, Tallmadge became increasing involved with the contemplation of God, religion, and the spiritual state of his family, his nation, and, not least of all, himself. Increasingly, the three most common subjects in his personal correspondence were business, family, and religion, the latter two often being combined.

His newfound, or renewed, ardor may have simply been a function of age and status. The appearance of children, and later grandchildren, may well have stimulated thinking about the future, the perpetuation of his lineage and, as the children grew and formed their own families, his inevitable exit from this world. Tallmadge may have also

The Lion in Winter. Benjamin Tallmadge by Ezra Ames, c. 1825. *Benjamin Tallmadge Collections, Litchfield Historical Society, Litchfield, Connecticut.*

turned to religion for solace from personal loss and sorrow. His wife, Mary, died on June 5, 1805, and two of his sons predeceased him. His first-born, William, died on August 15, 1822, and Benjamin, Jr., died at Gibraltar on June 20, 1831, while serving on the USS *Brandywine*. Three years after Mary's death, Tallmadge married Maria Hallet, a woman 22 years his junior. No children resulted from this second marriage.

It seems clear that Tallmadge's religious sentiments were heavily influenced, if not triggered, by the Second Great Awakening. The Second Great Awakening, like the first of the eighteenth century, was a major religious revival which spread through the nation. The revival, promoted by itinerant preachers, emphasized an emotional/spiritual connection with the divine and a commitment to Christ as the means of salvation. This resignation to God's will was accompanied by a rejection of sin and immorality, making one "born again" in a new life devoted to virtue and God.

Tallmadge's "born again" conversion to the doctrines of the Awakening came through the work of Lyman Beecher, one of the leading Protestant preachers of the time, and father of Harriet Beecher (later Stowe), and Henry Ward Beecher. Beecher, also a graduate of Yale, had been the Presbyterian pastor of East Hampton, Long Island, before transferring to Litchfield in 1810. He remained in Litchfield for 16 years before moving on to Boston. Wherever he preached, his sermons galvanized his listeners, and Tallmadge was no exception. Indeed, Tallmadge was so impressed by the minister that he sometimes invited Beecher to his home for dinner so other members of his family could meet the renowned clergyman.[14]

Tallmadge's involvement in Revival activities seems most intense between 1817 and 1822, though he carried his devotion to his religion and resignation to God's omnipotent judgment to the end of his life. A letter to Cushman, in January 1819, exults, "The Lord has vouchsafed to visit Litchfield once more, with new Tokens of his mercy. Mr. Beecher has been watching the attention of his people in the western part of this town. Yesterday he announced to us, in a pretty full meeting of the male Members of the Church, that the Holy Spirit had manifestly begun a work of divine power on the hearts of a number in the western part of the Town."[15] Exactly why the eastern section of Litchfield was excluded from divine grace is not explained.

Beecher, who sometimes delivered several sermons on a given Sunday, was clearly the driving force in religious excitement in Litchfield. In 1822, Tallmadge wrote his favorite daughter, Maria, his delight that "the revival in this place seems to progress with greater power. By this I do not mean it is intended with any peculiar noise or Enthusiasm [fanaticism].... But it seems attended with a deep & heartfelt Conviction of divine truth; a wonderful discovery of the depravity of the heart, & its native opposition to God ... an humbling sense of unworthiness & Guilt, followed by an overwhelming sense of the Glory of God in the plan of Salvation by Jesus Christ."[16] He then went on to describe how several people had "emerged from Darkness into light ... rejoicing in God."[17] Tallmadge described himself as being moved to tears by the scenes of such conversions, enjoining his daughter to "bow before the God of the whole Earth, & adore his amazing Goodness to this people. Surely our God has come, & he will carry on his own work, in his own best way."[18]

Similar views punctuated his other correspondence with family. In March 1822, he recounted how 37 new converts "publicly devoted themselves to the Lord & several of them recd the Ordinance of Baptism. This is peculiarly a solemn transaction to me."[19] Tallmadge's religious fervor induced a longing to experience the divine, and he wondered if it would be so bad to leave this world if the glory of the next was the reward. "It would seem as if it would even be desirable to depart from a world of Sorrow and Sins," he mused, "& to enjoy the holy Society of the blessed, & to behold Christ in his glorified State. When I am favored with even feeble views of these divine Subjects, it seems as if I could be willing to leave all my earthly connections, & depart & be at rest."[20]

Nor did Tallmadge confine his fervor to family and friends. In a letter to the editor of a New York State paper, he marveled that "the Lord is shaking the earth in different ways, but all his footsteps mark the wisdom of an infinite mind."[21] The Revival, he approvingly observed, "appear[s] to be rapidly spreading over our country, as well as thro' the Protestant world."[22] Unsurprisingly, when Tallmadge's granddaughter, Maria Cushman, died in July 1824, he urged her parents to accept the consolations of religion and resign themselves to God's will. When his grandson, Tallmadge, also seemed to be on death's door later in the month, he again called upon religion for guidance, though he also expressed some skepticism about one of the standard medical practices of the time—bleeding the sick to remove bad "humors" in the blood. Writing to the Cushmans he diffidently remarked, "I dare not find fault with the medical treatment pursued towards him [Tallmadge] but I can not withhold the remark that I fear he will be so debilitated by the loss of blood that he can not be raised up."[23] But despite the best efforts of the medical professions, the little boy survived.

Tallmadge put his money behind his convictions. He supported the American Bible Society, and several missionary organizations. He also backed the American Temperance Society, a major turnaround for the man who had delighted in toasting in his youth.

Around 1833, prodded by his family, and conscious that his time was running out, Tallmadge began writing his own memoir of the War of Independence. The Revolution, its drama, horror, excitement, tedium, personalities—notable and villainous—victories and defeats were never far from Tallmadge's mind. While he was less directly involved as he grew older, he never abandoned his interests in the Society of Cincinnati, and the welfare of the Revolutionary War veterans. He clearly enjoyed meeting and reminiscing with old comrades as his happy meeting with Lafayette attests. The memoir was also a way to revisit his youth and his role in the creation of the republic. Perhaps, like many elderly men and women, it allowed him to re-enter—temporarily and mentally—a world he understood, as opposed to the unfamiliar landscape of Jacksonian America.

There are no indications of any decline in Tallmadge's mental acuity as he aged, and he likely relied a great deal on memory when he committed his military career to paper. These were prodded by correspondence with Jared Sparks, who was preparing a volume of Washington's letters. Sparks particularly wanted Tallmadge's account of the Arnold-André conspiracy, which Tallmadge readily provided. These exchanges both augment and illuminate the shorter account that he included in his reminiscences. Tallmadge kept up a voluminous correspondence throughout his life, and it seems clear he had retained letters sent to him during the war, and may well have made copies of some that he sent. Comparisons of his wartime letters with the memoir demonstrate the accuracy of the latter. Of course, the numerous letters to Washington, the Culpers, friends, colleagues, and superiors, contain far more material than the memoir itself, which runs to 104 pages in most editions. They also reflect the immediacy of events more than the memoir written almost fifty years later, in calmer and more reflective times. The memoir was first published by his son, Frederick Augustus Tallmadge, in 1858.

Tallmadge completed his reminiscences, and gave the handwritten account to his children. It was good he did, as he did not long survive this last journey into the nation's past. Recognizing that his time was growing short, Tallmadge, good businessman that he was, prepared his will carefully, and then sent a letter to his wife, explaining the provisions he had made for her. The letter reveals his state of mind at this late juncture of his life. The astute entrepreneur is there, but so are the devoted husband, and the religiously enthralled believer. "I have consulted your happiness in disposing of my property as a primary object," he explained. "In doing this it has not been so much my desire to make you rich, as to make you comfortable and happy."[24] Tallmadge gave Maria his house, not theirs (there was no communal property at the time), as well as the lot and outbuildings. Other land in Litchfield was also given to Maria, in addition to "all the hay, grains, meat, liquors, farming utensils at home, household furniture, plate, two cows, and one-third of my library." He enclosed a separate letter with a listing of all the bank stock and other property he intended for her.[25] Lastly, Tallmadge bequeathed a special fund of $500 to be used for charitable donations, an amount he had reserved for that purpose himself.

Having disposed of the property and financial arrangements, Tallmadge went onto more personal matters, thanking God that he had not only "permitted" their union, but had given them such a lengthy marriage. "I have loved and cherished you as my wife," he declared, "but do feel as if I prized you more as a Christian." Though he knew he and Maria would have to "part for a season," he hoped they would meet in a happier world and "mingle with that happy throng who shall sit down at the marriage supper of the Lamb, [when] how rapturous will be our interview, and how interminable our bliss." Declaring that the best legacy he could give Mary was the "perfect example of our glorious Redeemer," Tallmadge concluded with his hopes that God would preserve her from all evil and that they would meet in heaven.[26]

Tallmadge was also running down physically. In 1831, he mentioned "my late severe attack of bodily indisposition."[27] The old soldier died at

Benjamin Tallmadge's tomb, Litchfield, Connecticut. *Author's Collection.*

his home in Litchfield, on March 7, 1835, and was buried in the East Cemetery nearby. An imposing box tomb was erected over his grave, on which was emblazoned an epitaph expressing the religious convictions and hopes of his later years—"As the hart panteth after the water brooks, so panteth my soul after thee, O God."

14

An Accomplished Man

News of Tallmadge's death spread quickly beyond Litchfield. As was to be expected, obituaries appeared first in the Connecticut papers, but they were soon picked up by the press in Rhode Island, Maine, New York, Baltimore, and Washington, D.C., where many people remembered him from his years in Congress. Death notices also ran in Southern cities, including Alexandria, Virginia, and Charleston, South Carolina. The notices were adulatory, remarking on his governmental, mercantile, charitable, and religious activities. But almost all began by noting his distinguished record in the War of Independence. Several included references to his "advanced age." Indeed, by 1835, the number of living Revolutionary War veterans was dwindling rapidly, and the commentators of the time were alert to inform their readers of the passing of another member of the first and most indispensible "greatest generation."

As new generations made their appearance and the nation's interest turned to different concerns, the children of the Revolution passed into history. While their memory and accomplishments were revered and commemorated, many faded from public consciousness, and even major figures, especially Washington, were transformed into preternaturally wise and noble national icons, frozen in marble and stiff portraiture. Tallmadge was among those whose exploits became largely unknown by the larger public.

Not that he ever slipped entirely from view. His memoir, in fact, became a staple primary document for scholars, especially his account of the final meeting of Washington and his officers at Fraunces Tavern, which was often repeated or drawn upon by various writers. In 1939, Morton Pennypacker identified the principals of the Culper Ring, and revealed Tallmadge's role as a spy master, which Tallmadge opaquely alluded to in his *Memoir*. Indeed, the story of the Culpers has been revisited by several historians since Pennypacker, most recently by Alexander Rose in *Washington's Spies* (2006). Inevitably, Tallmadge's crucial role in the operations of the network made him a key figure in these works. Tallmadge's operations as a dragoon and legion commander in the various battle and campaigns from 1776–83 have received less attention. As for his postwar life, Charles Swain Hall's *Benjamin Tallmadge: Revolutionary Leader and American Businessman*, published in 1943, was the only volume to examine Tallmadge's later years. In the ensuing 70 years, new material has surfaced, and archives have become more readily accessible, advancing the project of filling in, rounding out, expanding, and reassessing the remarkably variegated life and activities of an unusually accomplished man.

Tallmadge left strong evidence as to what he saw as important in his life. Certainly, his post–Revolutionary War interests grew increasingly varied. Financial, mercantile, legislative, philanthropic, and familial roles all fell within his purview. Religion in particular became a major concern in Tallmadge's life after 1800. In all cases he played his parts responsibly and well. His myriad financial and economic enterprises contributed to the commercial revolution that swept much of the North in the early republic, a phenomenon which resulted in a burgeoning and politically assertive middle class. Tallmadge may have harbored reservations about the boisterous, ambitious, and self-consciously democratic society which emerged after the War of Independence, but he himself had played an active role in its birth.[1] Yet, as voluminous a writer and correspondent as he was, when it came time for him to write an account of his past, none of those subjects was covered. Instead, he tuned to the great adventure of his youth, his distinguished role in the seminal event of American history, the Revolution.

Intelligent, brave, and devoted to his cause, Benjamin Tallmadge carved out a distinguished record in the struggle for American independence. He carried out his assignments with skill and dash, and aggressively pushed his superiors—Washington included—to allow him to launch expeditions of his own design, often against the odds and in areas of great danger. His drive, skill, and effectiveness earned him promotion in rank, and the respect and confidence of Washington, who entrusted him with missions of great importance to the Revolutionary cause. Ultimately, Tallmadge became a master of what later became known as "combined operations." His battle experience covered almost the entire range of warfare possible in the 18th century. Commanding what was effectively his own legion after 1778, he led his men on horseback against the "Cowboys," Loyalists, and British regulars in mounted engagements throughout the "no-man's-land" of Westchester County. He also became a master of amphibious assaults. His raids across Long Island Sound, leading his men across miles of British-occupied territory and destroying British fortifications and storage centers, portended the modern techniques of Marine Raiders and Recon Units, Army Rangers, and Navy Seals. He also planned and oversaw sea engagements, such as those which led to the capture of the *Three Sisters* late in the war. And he did all of this while simultaneously running a key intelligence network in Manhattan and Long Island.

Tallmadge was not invariably victorious in his battles, but he was pugnacious, crafty, and relentless, a combination that made him more successful than not. He exemplified the kind of leadership and zeal which the Revolutionary cause needed to endure and triumph. A master of many types of warfare and a man of many talents, he was indeed General Washington's Commando.

Chapter Notes

Chapter 1

1. For example, in 1777, a Tory detachment under Colonel Richard Hewlett partially destroyed the Setauket Presbyterian Church. In 1782, another Loyalist officer, Benjamin Thompson, totally destroyed Huntington's First Presbyterian Church. Following a four-day encampment in Smithtown, Banastre Tarleton's British Legion hauled off 6,396 feet of boards ripped from the Smithtown Presbyterian Church. They also left the village's rum supply 40 gallons short. Jim Scovill, "A Turbulent Occupation," in "Long Island the Way It Was" supplement, *Newsday*, June 13, 1776, 22.

2. Benjamin Tallmadge, *Memoir of Colonel Benjamin Tallmadge*, Publications of the Society of Sons of the American Revolution in the State of New York, Vol. I, edited by Henry Phelps Johnson (New York: Gillis Press, 1904), 5.

3. Charles Swain Hall, *Benjamin Tallmadge, Revolutionary Soldier and American Businessman* (New York: Columbia University Press, 1943), 9.

4. Ibid., 10–11.

5. Benjamin Tallmadge to Nathan Hale, May 9, 1775. Cited in Hall, 12.

6. Tallmadge, *Memoir*, 6.

7. Ibid., 7.

8. BT to William Lockwood, May 31, 1776, American Revolution Collection, Connecticut Historical Society, Hartford, CT.

9. Ibid.

Chapter 2

1. Tallmadge, *Memoir*, 7.

2. Ibid., 113.

3. J. Watson Webb, comp., *Reminiscences of Gen'l Samuel B. Webb of the Revolutionary Army* (New York: Grove Stationery and Printing, 1882), 43.

4. Tallmadge, *Memoir*, 9–10.

5. Letter, George Washington to Laud Washington, September 22, 1776, in Barnet Schecter, *The Battle for New York* (New York: Walker, 2002), 207–208. When a major fire burned a substantial part of British-controlled Manhattan on September 21, 1776, Washington pronounced: "Providence—or some good honored fellow—has done more for us than we were disposed to do for ourselves." Nevertheless, he conceded that "enough of it remains for their [British] purposes." Ibid. Ferling muses that Washington engineered the burning of the city "by expressing hope [that] some enterprising officials would do it." William Ferhling, *Almost a Miracle: The American Victory in the War of Independence* (New York: Oxford University Press, 2007), 142.

6. Ibid., 153

7. Tallmadge, *Memoir*, 12.

8. Ibid., 13.

9. Ibid., 14.

10. Ibid.

11. Ibid., 15.

12. Late in life, when discussing his relationship with Major John André, Tallmadge revealed something about how Hale's fate affected him. See Chapter 8.

13. Tallmadge, *Memoir*, 16.
14. Lawrence R. McGrath, "The Massachusetts Militia under Maj. Gen. Benjamin Lincoln, September–November 1776," *Military Collector & Historian*, Vol. 63, No. 3 (Fall 2011): 169.
15. Tallmadge, *Memoir*, 18.
16. McGrath, 169.
17. Captain Johann Ewald, *Diary of the American War: A Hessian Journal*, translated and edited by Joseph P. Tuston (New Haven: Yale University Press, 1979): 27.
18. McGrath, 171.
19. Burt Garfield Loescher, *Washington's Eyes: The Continental Light Dragoons* (Fort Collins, CO: Old Army Press, 1977), 25.
20. Ibid., 29.
21. Tallmadge, *Memoir*, 123–124.
22. Hall, 23.
23. Captain's Commission, Benjamin Tallmadge, December 14, 1776. Fraunces Tavern Museum, Sons of the Revolution Collection.
24. Tallmadge letter to Washington, March 16, 1777, Constitutional Sources Project, http://www.consource.org/index.asp?bid=582&fid=600&documentid=542 3.
25. Tallmadge, *Memoir*, 24.
26. Loescher, 25.
27. Ibid.
28. Ibid., 26.
29. Ibid.
30. Though the term inoculation was used at the time, the process was actually variolation. This entailed infecting a person with some pus from an active smallpox infection. The recipient would come down with the pox but in a much less severe form, resulting in a 1 percent mortality rate rather than 30 percent, which was the ordinary result in infections contracted "normally." Those who received this form of inoculation/variolation would need 30 days of quarantine from uninfected persons, which made the non-campaigning season the best time

to carry out the procedure. See Elizabeth Fenn, *Pox Americana: The Great Smallpox Epidemic of 1775–1782* (New York: Hill & Wang, 2001).

Chapter 3

1. Tallmadge, *Memoir*, 25. Washington originally ordered only black geldings, no mares, stallions, whites, or grays for his cavalrymen, but soon realized he could not afford to be so particular. In any event, the appearance of Tallmadge's unit satisfied him; see Loescher, *Washington's Eyes*, 26.
2. Loescher, 20.
3. Letter, BT to JW, July 9, 1777, Jeremiah Wadsworth Papers, Connecticut Historical Society.
4. "Battle of Short Hills," Wikipedia, http://wikipedia.org/wiki/Battle_of_Short_Hills.
5. BT to JW, July 9, 1777, JWP, CHS.
6. Ibid.
7. Ibid.
8. Ibid.
9. Ibid.
10. The battle was not fought in what is today Short Hills, New Jersey; it actually took place in present-day Edison and Scotch Plains. "Battle of Short Hills," Wikipedia.
11. Letter BT to JW, July 9, 1777, JWP, CHS.
12. Ibid.
13. Letter, BT to Mrs. Maria J. Cushman (Tallmadge), March 20, 1824, in "Personal Reminiscences of Major Benjamin Tallmadge of Scenes in the Revolutionary War in which he took a prominent part. Written out by himself on the request of his daughter Mrs. J. P. Cushman, and copied verbatim from the original manuscript in possession of his granddaughter, Mrs. George L. Balch," 187, Manuscripts and Archives Division, New York Public Library, Astor, Lenox, and Tilden Foundations. This handwritten account varies from the printed edi-

tion of Tallmadge's *Memoir*, containing additional notations and some personal correspondence and material relating to the André affair. This source will be denoted as "Reminiscences" to distinguish it from the published *Memoir*.

14. J. Watson Webb, comp., *Reminiscences of Gen'l Samuel B. Webb*, 293.

15. Tallmadge, *Memoir*, 36.

16. Ibid., 37.

17. Loescher, 33.

18. Letter, BT to Jeremiah Wadsworth, December 16, 1777, in Hall, 30.

19. Letter, BT to JW, December 30, 1776, JWP, CHS.

20. Ibid.

21. Ibid.

22. Ibid.

23. Ibid.

24. Trumbull was subsequently appointed to the Board of War, but resigned from that in April 1778, due to failing health; he died three months later.

25. Letter, BT to JW, December 30, 1777, JWP, CHS.

26. Ibid.

27. Tallmadge, *Memoir*, 37.

28. Pulaski spoke indifferent English and treated American officers with disdain. Moreover, his concept of cavalry usage was better suited to the North German and Polish plains than the broken terrain of eastern North America. During his brief tenure as cavalry commander, Tallmadge declared, "The Regulations of the Cavalry at present are most despicable, and unless we change our present commander I fear we shall not be respectable [i.e., effective]." In March 1779, Washington secured Pulaski's resignation as cavalry commander and approved his efforts to recruit a legion (in Hall, 31). Letter, Benjamin Tallmadge to George Washington, Chatham, NJ, February 9, 1778, Benjamin Tallmadge Collection,1933-19-0, Litchfield Historical Society, Helga J. Ingraham Memorial Library, Litchfield, CT, I, 2.

29. Ibid.

30. Letter, BT to GW, March 6, 1778, BTC, LHS, I, 3.

31. Letter, BT to GW, May 3, 1778, BTC, LHS, I, 6.

32. Hall, 33.

33. Letter, BT to GW, May 3, 1778, BTC, LHS, I, 6.

34. Letter, BT to Jeremiah Wadsworth, May 15, 1778, JWP, CHS.

35. Letter, BT to Barnabas Deane, July 6, 1778, in Hall, 37.

36. Hall, 38.

37. Loescher, 39.

Chapter 4

1. Ferling argues he preferred those who served him uncritically, if not sycophantically.

.2. Benjamin Tallmadge, *Memoir*, 42.

3. Letter, Benjamin Tallmadge to George Washington, Fairfield, CT, April 20, 1779, BTC, LHS, II, T4&5, LHS.

4. Letter, BT to GW, Bedford, NY, November 19, 1778, BTC, LHS, T4&5P8.

5. Letter, SC to Charles Scott, October 31, 1778, George Washington Papers, Library of Congress.

6. Letter SC to BT, August 27, 1779, GWP, LOC.

7. At the time, Washington was particularly anxious that the British remain in the dark about the "stain" as he had received word that the British governor of New York had a similar substance which might have led to the ink's detection if it were known to be in use. Letter, GW to BT, July 25, 1779, Westchester County Archives.

8. Letter, BT to GW, Bedford, NY, November 19, 1778, BTC, LHS, II, T4&T5, P8.

9. Indeed, Washington urged Tallmadge to advise Townsend to frequent Rivington's coffee house and mix with the British officers and Tory refugees as a method of obtaining information. Letter, GW to BT, October 17, 1779, Benjamin Tallmadge Collection, Manuscripts Di-

vision, Department of Rare Books and Special Collections, Princeton University Library.

10. Letter, GW to BT, September 24, 1779, Electronic Text Center, University of Virginia Library.

11. Ibid.

12. Ibid., October 6, 1779.

13. Culper Correspondence, Penny-packer Papers, East Hampton Public Library.

14. Letter, SC to BT, August 12, 1779, GWP, LOC.

15. Letter, George Washington to Benjamin Tallmadge, September 16, 1780, Private Collection, http://www.christies.com/LotFinder_details.aspx?intObject ID=5176343.

16. One hundred guineas (each guinea valued at a pound and a schilling) was a huge amount of money in the 18th century. That Woodhull was able to offer it, albeit with guaranteed reimbursement, testifies to his success as a farmer-merchant. Letter, BT to GW, Newport, RI, April 25, 1781, Tallmadge Correspondence, LHS, I, 14.

17. Letter, SC to BT, August 27, 1780, GWP, LOC.

18. Indeed, in January 1779, Woodhull told Tallmadge that "continental money will not serve me [for intelligence outlays]. It is much lower now than it was some time ago." Letter, SC to BT, January 22, 1779, GWP, LOC.

19. Letter, GW to BT, June 27, 1779, Spy Letters of the American Revolution, http://www.si.umich.edu/Spies/letter-1779june27.html. The Collections of the Clements Library, University of Michigan.

20. Letter, GW to BT, February 5, 1780, http://www.christies.com/LotFin der/lot_details.aspx?intObjectID= 5176343.

21. Letter, SC to BT, June 10, 1780, GWP, LOC.

22. Letter, GW to BT, Morristown, NJ, January 1, 1780, BTC, RBSC, PUL.

23. Letter, BT to GW, Wethersfield, CT, August 10, 1780, BTC, RBSC, PUL.

24. *Rivington Gazette*, May 16, 1778, in Onderdonck, *Revolutionary Incidents in Kings and Suffolk County* (Reprint: Port Washington, NY: Kennikat Press), 73.

25. Letter, BT to GW, Fairfield, CT, April 20, 1779, BTC, LHS, T4&5, P9.

26. John T. Hays, *Connecticut's Revolutionary Cavalry: Sheldon's Horse* (Chester, CT: Pequot Press, 1975), 25.

27. Ibid., 22.

28. Ibid., 25.

Chapter 5

1. "Address by William Brewster Minuse, President, Three Village Historical Society and Member, Brookhaven Town Bicentennial Commission at the Grave of Captain Caleb Brewster Fairfield, CT, August 9, 1976," Typescript, Fairfield Historical Center and Museum, 3.

2. Ibid.

3. Robert Sobel, "When Whaleboats Were Warships," *Newsday*, December 21, 1975, 12.

4. Ibid.

5. Letter, SC to BT, January 22, 1779, GWP, LOC.

6. Frederic G. Mather, *Refugees of 1776 from Long Island to Connecticut* (Albany: J. B. Lyon, 1913), 205.

7. Ibid., 202.

8. Ibid., 207.

9. Ibid., 208.

10. Ibid.

11. Susan Page, "He Dared to Sign," in "Long Island the Way It Was" supplement, *Newsday*, June 13, 1976, 7.

12. Letter, BT to GW, December 11, 1778, BTC, C0243, RBSC, PUL.

13. Mather, 227.

14. Ibid., 228.

15. Ibid., 230.

16. Letter, BT to GW, November 1, 1779, BTC, LHS, I, 9.

17. Ibid.

18. Ibid.

19. Letter, SC to BT, June 20, 1779, GWP, LOC.

20. Tallmadge, *Memoir*, 43.

21. For example, see letter, SC to BT, November 28, 1778, and February 27, 1780, GWP, LOC.

22. The British continued to carry out foraging expeditions on the east end of the island, however. In 1780, for example, Clinton himself led such an operation from Moriches to East Hampton; see Scovill, "A Turbulent Occupation," *Newsday*, June 13, 1976, 22.

23. William Kelby, ed., *The Orderly Book of the Three Battalions of Loyalists Commanded by Brigadier-General Oliver DeLancey, 1776–1778* (Reprint: Baltimore: Genealogical Publishing, 1972), 72.

24. Tallmadge, *Memoir*, 47.

25. Letter, BT to Mrs. Maria J. Cushman (Tallmadge), March 20, 1824, in "Personal Reminiscences," 187.

26. Letter, BT to General Howe, Canaan, CT, September 6, 1779, BTC, LHS, T4&5, T4, P14.

27. Letter, SC to BT, June 20, 1779, GWP, LOC.

28. Letter, BT to General Howe, September 6, 1779.

29. Ibid.

30. Ibid.

31. Ibid.

32. Ibid.

33. Ferling, 327.

34. Hays, 36.

35. Letter, BT to GW, October 25, 1779, BTC, LHS.

36. Letter, BT to JW, May 20, 1780, JWP, CHS.

37. Letter, BT to Thomas Mumford, June 24, 1780, American Revolution Collection, CHS.

38. Charles Royster, *A Revolutionary People at War: The Continental Army and American Character, 1775–1783* (Chapel Hill: University of North Carolina Press, 1979), 294.

39. Ibid.

40. Letter, BT to GW, Wethersfield, CT, March 6, 1780, BTC, LHS, I, 10.

41. Letter, BT to GW, Wethersfield, CT, May 6, 1780, BTC, LHS, I, 10.

42. Letter, BT to Colonel Samuel B. Webb, Crampond, July 6, 1780, in Webb, 296.

43. Hall, 44.

44. Tallmadge, *Memoir*, 48.

45. Letter, SC to BT, November 28, 1778, GWP, LOC.

46. Letter, SC to BT, June 5, 1779, GWP, LOC.

47. Ibid.

48. Ibid.

49. Letter, SC to BT, November 5, 1779, GWP, LOC.

50. Letter, SC to BT, December 12, 1779, GWP, LOC.

51. Letter, SC to BT, October 29, 1779, GWP, LOC.

52. Letter, SC to BT, November 13, 1779, GWP, LOC.

53. Letter, SC to BT, December 12, 1779, GWP, LOC.

54. Letter, SC to BT, March 11, 1780, GWP, LOC.

55. Ibid.

56. Letter, BT to GW, Wethersfield, CT, August 10, 1780, BTC, RBSC, PUL.

57. Ibid.

58. Tallmadge, *Memoir*, 49.

59. Ibid.

60. Hays, 46–47.

61. The special arrangement Washington provided for Tallmadge anticipated a general restructuring of the entire Continental Army, which was authorized by Congress in October 1780. The new organization, prompted by the imminent conclusion of the three-year enlistments from 1777, called for a reduced number of larger regiments. All dragoon regiments were converted into legions as a result of these measures, which took effect on January 1, 1781.

62. Map, SC to BT, August 7, 1780, GWP, LOC.

63. Tallmadge, *Memoir*, 51.

Chapter 6

1. Loescher, 41.
2. Hays, 26.
3. Gregory J. W. Urwin, "The Continental Light Dragoons, 1776–1783," in *Cavalry of the American Revolution*, ed. Jim Piecuch (Yardley, PA: Westholme, 2012), 15.
4. Hays, 27.
5. Hall, 38–39.
6. Hays, 35.
7. Loescher, 41.
8. John Milton Hutchins, "Cavalry Action at Pound Ridge, New York: Bloody Ban's Education," in Piecuch, 62.
9. McDonald Papers, Testimony of Ezra Lockwood and Mrs. Hunt, Westchester Historical Society. (The McDonald Papers contain an oral history of the evolution in Westchester County, taken from survivors of the Revolutionary generation.)
10. Ibid.
11. Ibid.
12. Ibid.
13. Ibid.
14. Tallmadge, *Memoir*, 32.
15. McDonald Papers.
16. Ibid.
17. Ibid.
18. Susan Cochran Swanson, *Between the Lines: Stories of Westchester County, New York, During the Revolution* (Pelham, NY: Junior League of Pelham, 1975), 36.
19. Hays, 30.
20. This was not the Second Dragoons' only colors. Another is preserved in the Connecticut state capital. Additionally, Tallmadge had a standard for his own troop, which is now housed in the Smithsonian Institution.
21. Letter, George Washington to Benjamin Tallmadge, June 27, 1779, Spy Letters of the American Revolution from the Collections of the Clements Library, University of Michigan, http://www.si.umich.edu/SPIES/letter-1779june27.html.
22. Ibid.

23. Ibid.
24. Loescher, 42.
25. Hays, 39.
26. Tallmadge, *Memoir*, 46.
27. Letter, BT to JW, Cortland Manor on Croton, July 14, 1780, JWP, CHS.
28. Ibid.
29. Ibid.
30. Ibid.
31. Ibid.
32. BT to JW, Middle Patent, August 26, 1780, JWP, CHS.
33. Ibid.
34. Kelby, ed., x.
35. Ibid., 24. Keeping his men in order and preventing their pillaging (and occasionally raping) was a constant concern of Oliver Delancey. He also enjoined the civilians, who lived where his men were quartered, from selling them rum. He insisted, too, that local residents sound the alarm "in case any Rebells shou'd advance near the Town [Huntington] and [if] the Inhabitants not give the speediest Notice such behavior will be resent with the utmost severity."
36. Swanson, 37.
37. Letter, BT to JW, September 4, 1780, cited in Hall, 43.
38. On the other hand, half-hanging was widely used by the Revolutionaries as a method to deal with Tories in the South. Neither side had a clean record in the matter. Scott A. Miskimon, "Anthony Walton Wright: A Revolutionary Dragoon," in Piecuch, 239.
39. Letter, BT to JW, September 4, 1780.
40. Cited in Richard Borkow, *George Washington's Westchester Gamble* (Charleston, SC: History Press, 2011), 124.
41. Letter, BT to GW, Bedford, NY, October 18, 1782, BTC, C0243, RBSC, PUL.
42. Ibid.
43. Hays, 38.
44. Letter, BT to GW, September 12, 1780, BTC, RBSC, PUL.

45. Borkow, 65.

46. Charles Royster, *A Revolutionary People at War: The Continental Army and American Character, 1775-1783* (Chapel Hill: University of North Carolina Press, 1979), 295.

47. Letter, Eben Huntington to Samuel B. Webb, August 30, 1780, in Webb, *Reminiscences*, 209–210.

48. Letter, BT to JW, Cortland Manor on Croton, July 14, 1780, JWP, CHS.

Chapter 7

1. Malcolm Decker, *Ten Days of Infamy: An Illustrated Memoir of the Arnold-André Conspiracy* (New York: Arno Press, 1969), 36.

2. Ibid., 37.

3. Letter, BT to Jared Sparks, February 17, 1833, in "Arnold the Traitor and André the Sufferer: Correspondence between Josiah Quincy, Jared Sparks and Benjamin Tallmadge," Communicated by Mary E. Norwood, from the Tallmadge Ms., *The Magazine of American History with Notes and Queries, Vol. 3* (New York: A. S. Barnes, 1879), http://google.com/books.

4. Ibid.

5. Ibid. Sparks was preparing an edition of Washington's papers for publication and contacted Tallmadge for firsthand information about the Arnold plot. Tallmadge wrote him at least twice, often elaborating on the account subsequently issued in his *Memoir*. These letters appeared in *The Magazine of American History with Notes and Queries, Vol. 3*, http://google.com/books.

6. Hays, 44.

7. Washington was so grateful for Paulding, Williams, and Van Wart's capture of André that he awarded the first military decoration bestowed by the United States, a silver medallion emblazoned with the word "Fidelity." They were later given an annual pension of two hundred dollars by the United States

government, and tracts of land by the state of New York.

8. Jamieson had also been instructed by Arnold to allow Anderson to pass to West Point. However, he was expected to be coming from New York City, not returning to it. Additionally, the plans of West Point's fortifications and the deployments of the troops there should have caused greater vigilance and caution. See Decker, 37.

9. Tallmadge, *Memoir*, 52.

10. On her website, "The Culper Spy Ring and Benedict Arnold," Andrea Myer argues that American intelligence agents were tracking Arnold's actions since the end of August. If so, Tallmadge would have already been alerted to his possible treason. This begs the question of why Arnold was not watched more closely, and why he was allowed to weaken the garrison at West Point. A more serious problem with the argument lies in the accidental nature of André's capture.

11. Tallmadge, *Memoir*, 52.

12. Tallmadge's reasons for concealing the exact nature of his proposals are unclear. In his February 17, 1833, letter to Sparks, he wrote: "My first proposal [to Jamieson] was to give me leave of absence for official object which I fully explained to Col Jamieson & which for special reasons I have not disclosed, as no public benefit could result from it." "Reminiscences," 63, *Magazine of American History, Vol. 3*, 753, Google.

13. Letter, BT to George Clinton, September 30, 1780, Jared Sparks Collection, Houghton Library, Harvard University.

14. Ibid.

15. Ibid.

16. Tallmadge, *Memoir*, 63–64.

17. Letter, BT to Jared Sparks, November 6, 1833, JSC, Ms. Sparks 49.1 (28) JSC, HL, HU.

18. Letter, BT to Jared Sparks, February 17, 1833, *Magazine of American History*, 753.

19. Ibid.

20. Smith's role in the affair was ambiguous and, to many, suspicious. As the brother of William Smith, the former chief justice of New York who defected to the British in 1778, Hett Smith was under a cloud. He persistently maintained that he had been deceived by Arnold, who told him that André's visit was part of an attempt to secure a new intelligence line in New York. This was also the turncoat's cover story with Sheldon and Tallmadge. Smith was acquitted of complicity in treason by a court-martial, but later fled to British lines, further complicating his story. Many Continental officers mistrusted him and refused to believe he could have been so innocent and gullible in visiting a British sloop of war and conveying André, in full uniform, to Arnold. Nevertheless, no evidence was ever produced that he assisted Arnold "because of British sympathy or malicious intent against the United States." See Richard J. Koke, *Accomplice in Treason: Joshua Hett Smith and the Arnold Conspiracy* (New York: New York Historical Society, 1973), 64.

21. John Evangelist Walsh, *The Execution of Major André* (New York: Palgrave, 2001), 112–114.

22. Letter, BT to Samuel Webb, Tappan, NY, September 30, 1780, *Reminiscences of General Samuel B. Webb*, 207.

23. Koke, 150.

24. Ibid., 151.

25. Ibid.

26. Letter, BT to Jeremiah Wadsworth, October 4, 1780, HL, HU.

27. Letter, BT to Jared Sparks, February 6, 1833, *Magazine of American History*, 753.

28. Tallmadge, *Memoir*, 57.

29. The Continental officers were probably affected by the 18th-century fashion for "sensibility," which encouraged feelings of sympathy among those of the same class. See Sarah Knott, *Sensibility and the American Revolution*

(Chapel Hill: University of North Carolina Press, 2009).

30. Judith L. Van Buskirk, *Generous Enemies: Patriots and Loyalists in Revolutionary New York* (Philadelphia: University of Pennsylvania Press, 2002), 101.

31. Tallmadge, *Memoir*, 131–132.

32. Letter, BT to Jared Sparks, February 17, 1833, *Magazine of American History*, 754.

33. Walsh, 207.

34. Ibid.

35. Royster, 207.

36. Michael Stephenson, *Patriot Battles: How the War of Independence Was Fought* (New York: Harper Perennial, 2007), 75.

37. Quoted in Royster, 210.

38. Tallmadge, *Memoir*, 104.

39. Ibid., 57.

40. Letter, BT to Jared Sparks, February 17, 1833, *Magazine of American History*, 754.

41. Letter, SC to BT, September 1, 1780, and October 14, 1780. Woodhull warned that Howell "is now on your shore and positively is an agent for the enemy." GWP, LOC.

42. Letter, BT to GW, Pines Bridge, NY, October 17, 1780, BTC, RBSC, PUL.

43. Ibid.

44. Letter, GW to BT, Passaic, NJ, October 20, 1780, Raab Collection.

45. Loescher, 47.

46. Tallmadge told Samuel Webb that, before his execution, André had written to Clinton complimenting his captors on their treatment of him, and disabusing his commander of the notion, which Arnold may have planted in his mind, that André was dressed in his uniform when captured. "I think his letter to Clinton will effectively ruin Arnold with the enemy," he concluded. Indeed it did. André was highly popular with the British officer corps, and they blamed Arnold for his death. Arnold was never fully trusted or liked by the British Army or government, and died, a controversial

alien, in London, in 1801. André's body was exhumed from its burial site in Tappan, New York, in 1821, and reinterred in Westminster Abbey. Letter, BT to Samuel Webb, September 30, 1780, *Reminiscences of Gen'l Samuel B. Webb*, 297.

47. Letter, BT to Jared Sparks, February 17, 1833, *Magazine of American History*, 754.

Chapter 8

1. Letter, BT to GW, Bedford, NY, July 18, 1780, B TC, LHS, T4&5, T4, 23.

2. Ibid.

3. Ibid.

4. Letter, SC to BT, November 5, 1780, GWP, LOC.

5. Letter, SC to BT, October 2, 1780, GWP, LOC. (Woodhull must have obtained word of the Mastic fort from his contacts near the position.)

6. Alvin R. L. Smith, *The Capture of Ft. St. George at Mastic, NY, and the Burning of the Forage At Coram, N.Y., November 23, 1780* (Brookhaven Town Historical Advisory Committee, 1980), 2.

7. Letter, BT to GW, Fairfield, CT, November 25, 1780, BTC, LHS, T4&5 T4, 26–27.

8. Letter, BT to Mrs. Maria J. Cushman (Tallmadge), March 24, 1824, in "Reminiscences," 187.

9. He may well have met with Woodhull, whom he visited at various times during the war, but he clearly had other friendly persons aiding him. On November 5, Woodhull wrote Tallmadge that the fort "can be taken at any time. The woods are so near that you may cover yourselves and watch a whole day [unobserved]." But by the time Tallmadge received this letter, he had firsthand knowledge of the fort and its surroundings. Letter, SC to BT, GWP, LOC.

10. Cited in Benjamin Thompson, *History of Long Island*, 1843 (Reprint: New York: Robert H. Dodd, 1918), Vol. 4, 159.

11. Tallmadge, *Memoir*, 59.

12. Letter, BT to GW, November 25, 1780.

13. Tallmadge, *Memoir*, 60.

14. Ibid.

15. Ibid., 61.

16. Letter, BT to GW, November 25, 1780.

17. *Rivington's Gazette*, December 2, 1780, in Onderdonck (see below).

18. Letter, BT to GW, November 25, 1780.

19. Tallmadge, *Memoir*, 63.

20. "Return of Prisoners Taken at Fort St. George on the Morning of the 23rd of November 1780," Fraunces Tavern Museum, Sons of the Revolution Collection.

21. Letter, GW to BT, November 28, 1780, in Smith, 5.

22. Ibid.

23. Letter, BT to GW, December 5, 1780, BTC, RBSC, PUL.

24. Despite the effusive praise for Tallmadge and his men, Congress did not order a commemorative medal struck for the raid as it did for Light Horse Harry Lee's equally daring, but possibly less dangerous, assault on Paulus Hook. Congress did approve a ceremonial sword for Tallmadge, as they had for Meigs following his Sag Harbor raid. The sword was never procured, however, and Tallmadge seems to have been unaware of it until Josian Quincy informed him of the Congressional resolution in 1833.

25. *Rivington's Gazette*, December 2, 1780, in Henry Onderdonck, Jr., *Revolutionary Incidents in Suffolk and Kings Counties*, 1849 (Reprint: Port Washington: Kennikat Press, 1970), 99.

26. Ibid.

27. Testimony of Joshua Davis of Fairfield, April 13, 1786, Caleb Brewster Papers, Fairfield (CT) Museum and History Center.

28. Ibid.

29. Robert Sobel, "When Whaleboats Were Warships," *Newsday*, December 21, 1975, 12.

30. Tallmadge, *Memoir*, 64.

31. Hays, 53.

32. Ibid., 54

33. Ibid.

34. Ibid., 57.

35. As usual, Washington also reiterated his need for fresh intelligence from the Culpers, particularly the number and name of detachments being sent south. Letter, GW to BT, April 8, 1781, http://www.familytales.org/dbDisplay.php?id=ltr_gwa4450.

36. Ibid.

37. Letter, BT to GW, April 20, 1781, BTC, LHS.

38. The bastion had been garrisoned by DeLancey's men early in the war, and later by Ludlow's Tories. In June 1781, the Associated Loyalists, commanded by Lt. Col. Joshua Upham, took over defense of the fort. The Associated Loyalists, headed by William Franklin, were formed the previous year as an auxiliary military force intended to carry out operations in rebel-held territory. They were disbanded in 1782.

39. Tallmadge, *Memoir*, 65.

40. Letter, Lt. Col. Joshua Upham to William Franklin, July 13, 1781, *New York Gazette & the Weekly Mercury*, The Online Institute for Loyalist Studies, http://www.royalprovincial.com/history/battles/aslrep4.shtml.

41. Ibid.

42. Hall, 70.

43. Letter, BT to GW, Wethersfield, CT, May 2, 1781, BTC, LHS.

44. Letter, BT to GW, Newtown, CT, August 18, 1782, BTC, LHS.

45. Ibid.

Chapter 9

1. Cited in Borkow, 115.

2. Ibid., 114.

3. Loescher, 53–54.

4. Ibid., 139.

5. Tallmadge, *Memoir*, 66.

6. Ibid.

7. Burke Davis, *George Washington and the American Revolution* (New York: Random House, 1975), 389.

8. British intelligence efforts improved markedly after 1779, and especially after 1780 when Captain Charles Beckwith and Oliver DeLancey began to control them. In August, Clinton received several reports from British spies that the Franco-American forces were moving south. Nevertheless, he remained unconvinced until September 6 when any possibility of reinforcing Cornwallis in a significant fashion had passed. David Kaplan, "The Hidden War: British Intelligence Operations during the American Revolution," *The William and Mary Quarterly*, Third Series, Vol. 47, No. 1 (January 1990): 134–136.

9. Tallmadge, *Memoir*, 67–68.

10. Letter, BT to Barnabas Deane, October 28, 1781, American Revolution Papers, CHS.

11. Ibid.

12. Tallmadge, *Memoir*, 68.

13. Ft. Slongo was apparently named for George Slongo, a Philadelphia contractor who constructed the fortification for the British. During the 19th century, the name mutated into Ft. Salonga, and is used today to denote the area straddling the Huntington–Smithtown town line.

14. Letter, BT to GW, Comps Point, October 3, 1781, GWP, LOC.

15. Letter, BT to Mrs. Maria J. Cushman (Tallmadge), March 20, 1824, in "Reminiscences," 188.

16. Letter, BT to Lemuel Trescott, Norwalk, CT, September 25, 1781, GWP, LOC, 1741–1799, Series 4, 1697–1799.

17. Letter, BT to GW, October 3, 1781.

18. Roberts, 254.

19. Letter, BT to GW, October 3, 1781.

20. Trescott, "Return of Prisoners and Ordnance," October 1, 1781, GWP, LOC.

21. *New Haven Gazette*, October 11, 1781, in Onderdonck, 105.

22. Ibid.

23. Trescott, "Return…" October 3, 1781, GWP, LOC.

24. Letter, BT to GW, October 3, 1781.

25. Letter, BT to GW, Veal's Ford, September 1, 1782, BTC, LHS.

26. Hall, 72.

27. Though still glowing with satisfaction from the victory in the Virginia, Washington took the opportunity to note that he was "much pleased with the success of the Enterprise against the Refugee Post on Long Island." Letter, GW to General Heath, October 27, 1781. GWP, LOC, Series 4, 1697–1799.

28. Letter, BT to Heath, November 12, 1781, cited in Hall, 72.

29. Ibid.

30. Letter, Samuel Culper to BT, July 5, 1782, GWP, LOC.

31. Ibid.

32. Ibid.

33. Order, Captain Conkling to Huntington Town Militia, November 26, 1782, Huntington Town Archives.

34. Letter, GW to BT, October 15, 1782, BTC, RBSC, PUL.

35. Ibid.

36. Letter, BT to GW, North Castle, NY, October 22, 1782, BTC, RBSC, PUL.

37. Letter, BT to GW, Norwich, CT, November 18, 1782, BTC, PUL.

38. Charles R. Street, *Huntington Town Records, 1776–1873.* Vol. III 1889 (Reprint: New York: Guide-Kelkoff-Bernt, 1958), 83–84.

39. Ibid. After the war, Huntington officials, according to the town's records, calculated their losses from Thompson's occupation, which included destroyed gravestones, fruit trees, rails, wood from the "Fresh Pond Meeting House," and loss of barns at £99, 16 shillings, and 0 pence. Thompson's redoubt itself was dismantled and its materials sold at auction, from which the town earned £17, 18 shillings.

40. Letter, BT to GW, Stamford, CT, November 25, 1782, BTC, PUL.

41. Letter, GW to BT, December 3, 1782, BTC, RBSC, PUL.

42. Letter, BT to Maria Tallmadge, March 20, 1824, in "Reminiscences," 189.

43. Tallmadge, *Memoir*, 48.

44. Letter, BT to Maria Tallmadge, March 20, 1824, in "Reminiscences."

45. Ibid.

46. Tallmadge, *Memoir*, 74.

47. Ibid.

48. Letter, BT to GW, December 8, 1782, BTC, LHS, I, 18.

49. Letter, GW to BT, December 10, 1782, The Writings of George Washington, http://books.google.com.

50. Ibid.

Chapter 10

1. Carleton replaced Clinton on March 8, 1782. Shelburne had instructed him to make preparations for removing all troops, supplies, and equipment from Savannah, Charleston, and New York to Halifax, and even surrender rather than engaging in "an obstinate defense." Clinton had issued an order suspending hostile action after Yorktown, though Washington conspicuously refused to reciprocate. William M. Fowler, Jr., *American Crisis: George Washington and the Dangerous Two Years after Yorktown, 1781–1783* (New York: Walker, 2011), 69.

2. Mather, 214.

3. Royster, 272.

4. Letter, BT to GW, Greenfield, CT, January 4, 1783, BTC, LHS, I, 9.

5. This event occurred on February 23, 1783. Hays, 76.

6. Tallmadge, *Memoir*, 76.

7. The entire incident is recounted in Tallmadge's *Memoir*, 75–77, which differs slightly from his immediate report to Washington.

8. www.lordshiphistory.com/Lord shipatWar.html.

9. Letter, BT to GW, Greenfield, CT, February 21, 1783, BTC, LHS, T4, 46.

10. Tallmadge, *Memoir*, 79.

11. Letter, BT to GW, February 21, 1783.

12. Letter, GW to BT, February 26, 1783, GWP, LOC.

13. Michael Stephenson, *Patriot Battles. How the War of Independence Was Fought* (New York: Harper Perennial, 2007), 77.

14. In this missive, Washington asked Tallmadge to return the short-weighted gold coins he had sent, and he would replace them. The general explained that he lacked a means of weighing them accurately. Letter, GW to BT, Passaic Falls, NJ, October 20, 1780, Raab Collections.

15. Letter, BT to Samuel B. Webb, March 6, 1780, in Webb, *Reminiscences*, 295.

16. Letter, BT to JW, Middle Patent, NY, August 26, 1780, JWP, CHS.

17. Ibid., May 26, 1781, JWP, CHS.

18. Letter, BT to JW, February 1778, in Hall, 82.

19. Ibid.

20. Charter, May 3, 1778, BTC, LHS.

21. Letter, BT to JW, March 20, 1779, in Hall, 83.

22. Letter, BT to Peter Colt, Dobbs Ferry, NY, August 18, 1781, Manuscript Division, Library of Congress. In 1777, Congress appointed Colt deputy commissary general of purchases for the Eastern Department encompassing New England and eastern New York State. He was an assistant to Wadsworth in providing supplies to the French, and served as treasurer of Connecticut between 1789 and 1793.

23. Hall, 84.

24. Legal agreement, October 16, 1782, BTC, LHS.

25. Royster, 342.

26. Hall, 86.

27. Royster, 298.

28. Tallmadge, *Memoir*, 79.

29. Fowler, 87.

30. Letter, BT to GW, Croton, Ward's House, Above Pine Bridge, September 17, 1782, BTC, RBSC, PUL.

31. Ibid.

32. Ibid.

33. Ibid.

34. A draft of a provisional treaty was signed by John Jay and Franklin on November 30, and George III declared his former colonies "free and independent states" on December 5. However, no official word to that effect would reach Congress for some time.

35. Letter, BT to GW, March 31, 1783, BTC, LHS, I, 21.

36. Fowler, 90, 204.

37. Letter, Abram Woodhull to BT, Brookhaven, New York, July 5, 1783. Woodhull had sent a statement of accounts on September 18, 1780, when he listed £42 as due him. GWP, LOC.

38. Ibid.

39. Ibid.

40. Letter, BT to GW, Litchfield, CT, August 16, 1783, BTC, LHS, T4, 51.

41. Ibid.

Chapter 11

1. Letter, BT to GW, Litchfield, CT, August 16, 1783, BTC, LHS, T4, 51.

2. Letter, GW to BT, September 11, 1783, GWP, LOC.

3. Bushkirk, 180.

4. Ibid.

5. Hays, 76.

6. Letter, BT to GW, March 31, 1783, BTC, LHS, I, 2.

7. Tallmadge, *Memoir*, 94.

8. Ibid.

9. Ibid.

10. Ibid., 95–96.

11. Schecter, 378.

12. Tallmadge, *Memoir*, 96.

13. Ibid. 97.

14. Ibid.

15. Ibid., 100.

16. Letter, BT to JW, July 9, 1777, JWP, CHS.

17. Letter, BT to Barnabas Deane, May 13, 1783, cited in Hall, 87.

18. Bushkirk, 177.

19. Susan Page, "He Dared to Sign," in "Long Island the Way It Was" supplement, *Newsday*, June 13, 1976, 7.

20. Ibid., 8.

21. Tallmadge, *Memoir*, 103.

22. Letter, MT to Mrs. Maria J. Cushman (Tallmadge), March 20, 1817, in "Reminiscences," 190.

Chapter 12

1. Letter, BT to Asa Spaulding, December 12, 1788, CHS. In this particular missive, Tallmadge explains that he is willing to exercise some forbearance in collecting a mortgage, but that he will foreclose on the property if necessary.

2. www.richfieldohiohistoricalsociety.

3. Letter, BT to John Cushman, Litchfield, CT, August 23, 1821, BTC, LHS.

4. Ibid., May 14, 1821.

5. Ibid., December 27, 1820.

6. EH Net, Economic History Association, Currency Calculator.

7. Gordon S. Wood, *Empire of Liberty: A History of the Early Republic, 1789–1815* (New York: Oxford University Press, 2009), 263.

8. Ibid. See also GW to James McHenry, July 4, 1798, GWP, LOC.

9. Letter, GW to John Adams, July 13, 1798, GWP, LOC.

10. GW to JMcH, July 5, 1798, GWP, LOC.

11. GW to Alexander Hamilton, July 14, 1798, GWP, LOC.

12. Washington concluded his list by stating: "There may be among the foregoing some of bad political principles, and others whose true characters I have been mistaken, and the whole of them requiring to be investigated." The list was sent to the secretary of war. "Proposed Arrangement of General and other Officers," July 14, 1798, GWP, LOC.

13. Ibid.

14. Letter, GW to JMcH, July 22, 1798, GWP, LOC.

15. Letter, GW to JMcH, August 13, 1798, GWP, LOC.

16. "Quotas of Troops from Southern States," October 15, 1798, GWP, LOC.

17. Letter, BT to Manasseh Cutler, January 11, 1800, in *Memoir*, 144–145.

18. Ibid.

19. For a thorough discussion of the rise of the partisan press and the role of immigrants, see Gordon S. Wood, *Empire of Liberty: A History of the Early American Republic, 1789–1815* (New York: Oxford University Press, 2009), 250–256.

20. "Speech of the Hon. Benjamin Tallmadge in the House of Representatives, January 7, 1813," in *Connecticut Herald* (New Haven), February 23, 1813, Vol. X, Issue 19:1, www.GeneaologyBank.com.

21. Ibid.

22. Ibid.

23. Ibid.

24. The two servants, a married couple from the Netherlands or Germany, agreed to an extension of their indenture for six months for each child born while they were bound to Tallmadge. Kathy A. Ritter, *Apprentices of Connecticut, 1637–1900* (Ancestry Publishing, 1986), 94.

25. Letter, BT to JC, Litchfield, CT, February 25, 1819, BTC, LHS.

26. *Connecticut Courant*, June 27, 1836, Vol. LXXII, no. 3727, 3, www.GeneaologyBank.com.

27. *Washington Federalist* (Georgetown), August 30, 1808, 2, www.GeneaologyBank.com.

28. Letter, BT to editor of the *New Hampshire Sentinel*, Litchfield, CT, May 1, 1829, vol. XXXI, 18, 2, www.GeneaologyBank.com.

29. Ibid.

30. Ibid.

31. Ibid.

32. "Speech of the Hon. Benjamin Tallmadge in the House of Representatives, January 7, 1813," in *Connecticut Herald* (New Haven), X, 19, 2, www.GeneaologyBank.com.

33. Ibid.
34. Ibid.
35. Ibid.
36. Ibid.
37. Ibid.
38. Ibid.
39. Ibid.
40. Ibid.
41. Ibid.
42. Notice, *New-York Herald*, July 24, 1816, 2, www.GeneaologyBank.com.
43. Letter, BT to John Taylor, January 1, 1818, BTC, LHS.

Chapter 13

1. Letter, BT to John Cushman, Litchfield, CT, February 19, 1818, BTC, LHS.
2. Letter, BT to Ebenezer Huntington, May 23, 1828, CHS.
3. "Vindication of Van Wart, Paulding and Williams, the three virtuous and patriotic American yeomen, who arrested Major André." March 20, 1817, *Canton* (Ohio) *Repository*, 2, wwwGeneaologyBank.com.
4. Ibid.
5. Letter, Timothy Pickering to BT, September 9, 1822, in *Memoir*, SOR, 135.
6. Letter, BT to Timothy Pickering, September 17, 1822, in *Memoir*, SOR, 135.
7. Ibid.
8. Ibid.
9. Letter, BT to JC, Litchfield, CT, August 24, 1824, BTC, LHS.
10. *Connecticut Herald* (New Haven), May 23, 1826, XXIII, 34, 3.

11. Letter, BT to JC, Litchfield, CT, December 10, 1818, BTC, LHS.
12. Letter, BT to JC, Litchfield, CT, January 3, 1819, BTC, LHS.
13. Letter, BT to Jabez Huntington, February 11, 1831, CHS.
14. Letter, BT to JC, Litchfield, CT, November 12, 1817.
15. Letter, BT to RC, Litchfield, CT, January 1819, BTC, LHS.
16. Letter, BT to Maria Tallmadge, Litchfield, CT, April 9, 1822, BTC, LHS.
17. Ibid.
18. Ibid.
19. Letter, BT to JC, Litchfield, CT, March 8, 1822, BTC, LHS.
20. Letter, BT to JC, Litchfield, CT, June 2, 1824, BTC, LHS.
21. *Independent American*, Ballston Spa, NY, July 28, 1815.
22. Ibid.
23. Ibid., Litchfield, CT, August 9, 1824, BTC, LHS.
24. Letter, BT to Mary Tallmadge, Litchfield, CT, February 5, 1829, BTC, LHS.
25. Ibid.
26. All quotes, ibid.
27. Ibid. Litchfield, CT, February 11, 1831, BTC, LHS.

Chapter 14

1. For a concise account of the transformation of society in the early republic, see Gordon S. Wood's concluding chapter in *Empire of Liberty*.

Bibliography

Primary Sources

Benjamin Tallmadge Collection. Litchfield Historical Society.

Benjamin Tallmadge Collection. Department of Rare Books and Special Collections, Princeton University Library.

"Benjamin Tallmadge, Personal Reminiscences of Major Benjamin Tallmadge of Scenes in the Revolutionary War in which he took a prominent part, written out by himself at the request of his daughter, Mrs. J. P. Cushman." Manuscript and Archives Division, Astor Lenox and Tilden Foundations. New York Public Library.

Culper Correspondence. Pennypacker Papers, Long Island Collection. East Hampton Public Library.

George Washington Papers. American Memory. Library of Congress.

Huntington Town Records. Revolutionary War. Huntington Town Clerk's Office.

Jared Sparks Collection. Houghton Library, Harvard University.

Kelby, William, ed. *Orderly Book of the Three Battalions of Loyalists Commanded by Brigadier General Oliver Delancey, 1776–1778.* Baltimore: Genealogical Publishing, 1972. (Originally published in 1917.)

Norwood, Mary E., ed. "Arnold the Traitor, and André the Sufferer: Correspondence between Josiah Quincy, Jared Sparks, and Benjamin Tallmadge." *Magazine of American History,* 3 (December 1879): 747–759.

Sons of the Revolution Collection. Fraunces Tavern Museum.

Spy Letters of the American Revolution. Collections of the Clements Library. University of Michigan.

Tallmadge, Benjamin. *The Memoir of Colonel Benjamin Tallmadge.* Publications of the Sons of the Revolution in the State of New York. Vol. I. Edited by Henry Phelps Johnston. New York: Gilliss Press, 1904.

Webb, J. Watson, ed. *Reminiscences of Gen'l Samuel B. Webb of the Revolutionary Army.* New York: Globe Stationery and Printing, 1882.

Writings of George Washington. http://books.google.com.

Secondary Sources

Barkow, Richard. *George Washington's Westchester Gamble: The Encampment on the Hudson & the Trapping of Cornwallis.* Charleston, SC: History Press, 2011.

Clement, Justin. *Philadelphia, 1777.* New York: Osprey, 2007.

Davis, Burke. *George Washington and the American Revolution.* New York: Random House, 1975.

Decker, Malcolm. *Ten Days of Infamy: An Illustrated Memoir of the Arnold-André Conspiracy.* New York: Arno Press, 1969.

Ferhling, William. *Almost a Miracle.* New York: Oxford University Press, 2009.

Fowler, William M., Jr. *American Crisis:*

George Washington and the Dangerous Two Years after Yorktown, 1781–1783. New York: Walker, 2011.

Hall, Charles Swain. *Benjamin Tallmadge, Revolutionary Soldier and American Businessman.* New York: Columbia University Press, 1943.

Hays, John T. *Connecticut's Revolutionary Cavalry: Sheldon's Horse.* Chester, CT: Pequot Press, 1975.

Kaplan, Roger. "The Hidden War: British Intelligence Operations during the Revolution." *The William and Mary Quarterly,* Third Series, Vol. 47, No. 1 (January 1990): 115–138.

Koke, Richard J. *Accomplice to Treason: Joshua Hett Smith and the Arnold Conspiracy.* New York: New York Historical Society, 1973.

Loescher, Burt Garfield. *Washington's Eyes: The Continental Light Dragoons.* Fort Collins, CO: Old Army Press, 1977.

Mather, Frederick Gregory. The *Refugees of 1776 from Long Island to Connecticut.* Albany, NY: J. B. Lyon, 1913.

Minuse, William. "Address at the Grave of Captain Caleb Brewster, Fairfield, Connecticut, August 9, 1976." Fairfield Historical Center and Museum.

Myer, Andrea. "The Culper Spy Ring and Benedict Arnold." http://aphdigital.org/projects/culperspying/about.

Onderdonck, Henry, Jr. *Revolutionary Incidents in Kings and Suffolk County.* Reprint, Port Washington, NY: Kennikat Press, 1970.

The Online Institute for Loyalist Studies. http://www.royalprovincial.com.

Page, Susan. "He Dared to Sign." In "The Way We Were," bicentennial supplement, *Newsday,* June 13, 1976.

Rose, Alexander. *Washington's Spies: The Story of America's First Spy Ring.* New York: Bantam, 2006.

Royster, Charles. *A Revolutionary People at War: The Continental Army and American Character, 1775–1783.* Chapel Hill: University of North Carolina Press, 1979.

Schecter, Barnet. *The Battle for New York.* New York: Walker, 2002.

Scovill, Jim. "A Turbulent Occupation." In "The Way We Were," bicentennial supplement, *Newsday,* June 13, 1976.

Smith, Alvin R. L. *The Capture of Ft. St. George and the Burning of the Forage at Coram N.Y.* Brookhaven Town Advisory Commission, 1980.

Sobel, Robert. "When Whaleboats Were Warships." *Newsday,* December 21, 1975.

Stephenson, Michael. *Patriot Battles: How the War of Independence Was Fought.* New York: Harper Perennial, 2007.

Thompson, Benjamin. *History of Long Island* (four volumes, originally published in 1843). New York: Robert H. Dodd, 1918.

Tiedemann, Joseph S., and Eugene R. Fingerhut, eds. *The Other New York: The American Revolution beyond New York City.* Albany: State University of New York Press, 2005.

Van Buskirk, Judith L. *Generous Enemies: Patriots and Loyalists in Revolutionary New York.* Philadelphia: University of Pennsylvania Press, 2002.

Walsh, John Evangelist. *The Execution of Major André.* New York: Palgrave, 2001.

Wood, Gordon S. *The Empire of Liberty.* New York: Oxford University Press, 2002.

Index

Page numbers in **bold italics** indicate pages with illustrations.

Index

Hancock, John 19
Hartford, Connecticut 7
Hawkins, Josiah 37
Hewlitt, Col. Richard 50
Howe, Admiral Sir Richard 17, 32
Howe, Gen. Robert 53
Howe, Gen. Sir William 13–15; and Philadelphia campaign 24–26; at Short Hills 23–24; at White Plains 18
Hoyt, Capt. 120–121
Hubbel, Capt. Amos 121–122
Huntington, Long Island: British occupation 52, 90, 113; Tallmadge targets 113–117

Indian Removal Act 164
inoculation, smallpox 21

Jackson, Andrew 156, 163–164
Jameson, Lt. Col. John 79–80, 85–86, 159–160; Andre-Arnold plot 79
Jefferson, Thomas 148
Johnstone, Capt. 121–122

Knox, Henry 10, 146

Lafayette, Marquis de 161–162
Leavenworth, Maj. Eli 68
Lee, Gen. Charles 18, 32
Leslie, Gen. Alexander 88
Litchfield, Connecticut 125–126, 138, 166, 170
Lloyd's Neck, Long Island 90; British positions 53; Tallmadge raids 54–55; see also Fort Franklin
Lockwood, Maj. Ebenezer 66–67
London Trade 60, 114, 119–122, 127
Long Island, New York 52, 53, 60, 138; British foraging on 58–59
Long Island, Battle of 10, 14
Long Island Sound 46, 116
Loyalist Refugee Corps 73–74
Loyalists see Tories

Madison, James 150, 153
Mastic, Long Island 138
McHenry, Gen. James 146
Meigs, Lt. Col. Return Jonathan 50
Memoirs 168–169
Middle Patent, Westchester County, New York 70–73
Monmouth, New Jersey, Battle of 32
Monroe, James 163
Morgan, Gen. Daniel 18, 23, 27
Moylan, Col. Stephen 23, 31, 67, 70
Muirson, Heathcoat 97
Mulligan, Hercules 134–135

Ohio, Western Reserve 142

Parsons, Gen. Samuel 50, 61
Paulding, John 79, 158–159
Pennypacker, Morton 171–172
Pickering, Timothy 159
plundering, on Long Island 48, 49, 51; by Continentals 76, 98
Presbyterians 5, 35
Privateers 124–125
Prize money 55, 120, 121, 122
Pulaski, Gen. Casmir 30

Queens County, Long Island, New York 37

Rawdon, Gen. Lord 27
Raynham Hall, Oyster Bay, Long Island 38
Real estate 142
Reeve, Judge Tapping 142
Rivington, James 40, 135
Rivington's Gazette 40, 44; on Mastic raid 97
Rochambeau, Comte de 75, 100, 103–104

Saratoga, Battle of 127
Scott, Capt. Charles 36
Scudder, Henry 108
Second Continental Dragoons 19, 70, 104; deficiencies 45, 55; discharged 133; dispersal of 25; and Franco-American communications 75; at Morristown, New Jersey 22; pay 20; reorganization 61, 63; reviewed by George Washington 22; Tallmadge purchases securities from 126
Second Great Awakening 165–168
Sheldon, Col. Elisha 19, 20, 45, 146; at Pound Ridge 67
Short Hills, New Jersey, Battle of 22–24
Simcoe, Lt. Col. John Graves 33; burns Bedford 68; occupies Oyster Bay 37, 53, 54, 58; at Pound Ridge 67
Slavery 150
Smith, Joshua Hett 79
Smith, Judge William 91
Society of Cincinnati 132, 140, 168
Sparks, Jared 84, 161, 168
Strong, Anna 37
Strong, Benjamin 53
Suffolk County, Long Island, New York 5, 59, 90
Sullivan, Gen. John 11, 26
Supplies and provisions 28–29, 31, 55, 75, 99
"Sympathetic stain"/invisible ink 39–40

Tallmadge, Benjamin *91, 141, 165*; see also specific entries
Tallmadge, Rev. Benjamin 6, 10, 46, 136, 138

192

Index

Tallmadge, Benjamin, Jr. 140, 166
Tallmadge, Frederick Augustus 140, 169
Tallmadge, George Washington 140
Tallmadge, Harriet Wadsworth 140
Tallmadge, Henry Floyd 140, *143*
Tallmadge, John 125
Tallmadge, Maria 140, 142
Tallmadge, Mary Floyd *143*
Tallmadge, William 10
Tallmadge, William Smith 140, 166
Tallmadge, Ohio 142
Tarleton, Lt. Col. Banastre 66–68, 107
Third Continental Dragoons at Old Tappan 65
Thompson, Benjamin 112–113
Three Sisters 121–122
Tories 37, 43, 53, 54, 56, 72, 74, 112, 128, 132, 133, 136, 137; at Ft. St. George 95, 98; in Huntington 114; property confiscated 56
Townsend, Robert 37, *38*; Arnold and 89; and British deployments 41; motives 41; and George Washington 43
Trescott, Maj. Lemuel: at Ft. Slongo 108–109
Trumbull, Gov. John 8, 48
Trumbull, Joseph 29
Tryon, Gen. William: raids Danbury 50; raids Norwalk 70

Upham, Lt. Col. Joshua 102, 184*n*38

Valley Forge, Pennsylvania 27
VanWart, Isaac 79, 158–159
Veterans, Revolutionary War 157
Von Steuben, Gen. Baron 32

Wadsworth, Gen. James 9, 14
Wadsworth, Jeremiah 7, 28, 29, 57, 152; commissary 29, 76, 77; and Tallmadge investments 123–124, 125
Washington, Gen. George 9, 21, 90, 162; and Arnold 86; Battle of Long Island 10–12; Brandywine 25; demobilizes army 129; Fabian strategy 63; farewell to officers 135–136; Germantown 26; grand reconnaissance (Westchester) 104–105; intelligence operations 34–35, 41; intelligence routes 43; monetary concerns 129–130; returns to New York 134; on Robert Townsend rewards 42; and Tallmadge 17, 31, 36, 60, 92, 97, 105, 113–118, 127, 128, 129, 132, 146–147, 148; war preparations 1798 145–146
Wayne, Gen. Anthony 65
Webb, Lt. Col. Samuel 45, 51; at Setauket 50
West Point, New York 78
Wethersfield, Connecticut 64, 70, 72, 74
Whaleboat warfare 35, 46, *49*
Whig(s) 5, 8, 35, 47, 155, 163–164
White Plains, New York, Battle of 16–17, *18*; Tallmadge raids 71
Williams, David 79, 158–159
Woodhull, Abraham 36, 42, 47, 52, 88, 91, 101–102, 129; captured 49; desperation of patriots 59; fear of Simcoe 58; on French alliance 57; money 42; motives 36; recruits Townsend 38

Yale College 6, 33